"As Christianity is being de-formed by ideological intersections of nationalism, capitalism, and white supremacy, Johnson and Wymer present a provocative volume addressing problematic religious histories that helped give rise to current spiritual and political locations of Free Churches. Through the lenses of worship and liturgy, *Worship and Power* invites readers to explore how congregational practices can inform, impact, and re-form churches, communities, and a flailing society that desperately need a church who knows where her true power lies."

—LISA M. ALLEN-MCLAURIN
Professor of church music and worship, The Interdenominational Theological Center

"*Worship and Power* is a multifaceted and nuanced scholarly conversation about how power is constructed in worship, and how it can challenge and re-envision other kinds of power. Important but understudied practices from various Free Church traditions are examined using critical theory and an uncompromising ethical commitment to the most vulnerable. This conversation is important not only for Free Church scholars, but for all who do work with liturgy, ritual, or political theology."

—KIMBERLY BELCHER
Associate professor of theology, University of Notre Dame

"In Free Church traditions, the ways worship shapes us can appear confusing to some, like theological signatures written in invisible ink, only discernible to those with the means of revealing hidden text and meaning. *Worship and Power* is a bold, winsome, and insightful collection of essays that changes the ink so a wider, ecumenical community can consider the swirling flow and pathways of the Holy Spirit's power when Christians gather in numbers small and large, in spaces closed and open."

—MALINDA ELIZABETH BERRY
Associate professor of theology and ethics, Anabaptist Mennonite Biblical Seminary

"A breakthrough work by a new generation of liturgical scholars examining the heretofore neglected Free Church traditions of worship, asking the right questions for these times and then addressing them with cutting edge scholarship, critical skill, and pastoral concern. This admirably collaborative project should prove both encouraging and challenging for the churches, as well as informative to the wider liturgical academy."
—BRUCE T. MORRILL, SJ
Chair of Roman Catholic studies, Vanderbilt University

"Embedded in worship is power: the contrast of God's power with the 'powers and principalities' of this one; the power of presiders and laity; the power of worship to empower and transform worshippers. The contributors take up these negotiations of the power of worship with accountability, clarity, and faithfulness. This volume amplifies voices from the Free Church traditions in the field of Liturgical Studies, and it is a needed and revelatory series of reflections."
—STEPHANIE PERDEW (CHEROKEE NATION)
Professor of history, Garrett-Evangelical Theological Seminary

"'Free Churches'—an umbrella term for congregations in the Anabaptist, Baptist, Congregationalist, Evangelical, and Pentecostal traditions—are a notoriously difficult group to pin down. This beautifully curated collection of essays opens a window into the fascinating world of their worship, illuminating commonalities, exposing tensions, and setting new agendas for future research. Essential reading for all who study, shape, and practice Christian worship."
—MELANIE ROSS
Associate professor of liturgical studies, Yale Divinity School

Worship and Power

WORSHIP AND WITNESS

The Worship and Witness series seeks to foster a rich, interdisciplinary conversation on the theology and practice of public worship, a conversation that will be integrative and expansive. Integrative, in that scholars and practitioners from a wide range of disciplines and ecclesial contexts will contribute studies that engage church and academy. Expansive, in that the series will engage voices from the global church and foreground crucial areas of inquiry for the vitality of public worship in the twenty-first century.

The Worship and Witness series demonstrates and cultivates the interaction of topics in worship studies with a range of crucial questions, topics, and insights drawn from other fields. These include the traditional disciplines of theology, history, and pastoral ministry—as well as cultural studies, political theology, spirituality, and music and the arts. The series focus will thus bridge church worship practices and the vital witness these practices nourish.

We are pleased that you have chosen to join us in this conversation, and we look forward to sharing this learning journey with you.

Series Editors:
John D. Witvliet
Noel Snyder
Maria Cornou

Worship and Power

Liturgical Authority in Free Church Traditions

Edited by
SARAH KATHLEEN JOHNSON
and ANDREW WYMER

Foreword by Lisa M. Weaver

Afterword by John D. Witvliet

CASCADE *Books* · Eugene, Oregon

WORSHIP AND POWER
Liturgical Authority in Free Church Traditions

Worship and Witness

Copyright © 2023 Wipf and Stock Publishers. All rights reserved. Except for brief quotations in critical publications or reviews, no part of this book may be reproduced in any manner without prior written permission from the publisher. Write: Permissions, Wipf and Stock Publishers, 199 W. 8th Ave., Suite 3, Eugene, OR 97401.

Cascade Books
An Imprint of Wipf and Stock Publishers
199 W. 8th Ave., Suite 3
Eugene, OR 97401

www.wipfandstock.com

PAPERBACK ISBN: 978-1-6667-3293-1
HARDCOVER ISBN: 978-1-6667-2714-2
EBOOK ISBN: 978-1-6667-2715-9

Cataloguing-in-Publication data:

Names: Johnson, Sarah Kathleen, editor. | Wymer, Andrew, 1982–, editor. | Weaver, Lisa M., foreword. | Witvliet, John D., afterword.

Title: Worship and power : liturgical authority in free church traditions / edited by Sarah Kathleen Johnson and Andrew Wymer ; foreword by Lisa M. Weaver ; afterword by John D. Witvliet.

Description: Eugene, OR: Cascade Books, 2023 | Series: Worship and Witness. | Includes bibliographical references and index.

Identifiers: ISBN 978-1-6667-3293-1 (paperback) | ISBN 978-1-6667-2714-2 (hardcover) | ISBN 978-1-6667-2715-9 (ebook)

Subjects: LCSH: Free churches—Liturgy—History. | Free churches—Liturgy—Theology.

Classification: BX4817 .W67 2023 (paperback) | BX4817 .W67 (ebook)

VERSION NUMBER 030623

With gratitude for the scholars and practitioners of worship in Free Church traditions who have gone before us.

Contents

List of Contributors

Ronald J. Allen, professor emeritus of preaching and gospels and letters at Christian Theological Seminary, Indianapolis.

Emily Snider Andrews, executive director of the Center for Worship and the Arts and assistant professor of music and worship at Samford University, Birmingham.

Andrew Davies, professor of public religion at University of Birmingham, Birmingham.

Sarah Kathleen Johnson, assistant professor of liturgy and pastoral theology, Saint Paul University, Ottawa.

Jaewoong Jung, assistant professor of homiletics at Seoul Theological University, Bucheon.

Dorothy Mendez, lecturer and tutor at Hillsong College, Sydney.

Jonathan Ottaway, doctor of theology candidate at Duke Divinity School, Durham.

Tanya Riches, senior lecturer at Hillsong College, Sydney.

Casey T. Sigmon, assistant professor in preaching and worship and director of contextual education and Seminary Chapel, Saint Paul School of Theology, Leawood.

Isaac Samuel Villegas, ordained minister in Mennonite Church USA and a doctor of philosophy student in religion at Duke University, Durham.

Lisa M. Weaver, assistant professor of worship at Columbia Theological Seminary, Decatur.

John D. Witvliet, director of the Calvin Institute of Christian Worship and professor of worship, theology, and congregational and ministry studies at Calvin University and Calvin Theological Seminary, Grand Rapids.

Andrew Wymer, assistant professor of liturgical studies at Garrett-Evangelical Theological Seminary, Evanston.

Chelsea Brooke Yarborough, assistant professor of African American preaching, sacred rhetoric, and Black practical theology at Phillips Theological Seminary, Tulsa.

Foreword

Lisa M. Weaver

For most people, a conversation about worship would not contain two words that are in the title of this volume: *power* and *authority*. Some people understand the communal, public enterprise of a local assembly gathered to ascribe glory, honor, and praise to God, intercede for others, and listen for and to God as worship. Others understand worship as a category of personal, usually private, devotional practices in which an individual is in communion with God, ascribing glory, honor, and praise to God, interceding for others, and listening for and to God while understanding the communal, public enterprise in which these activities are done as liturgy. Whatever language one employs to characterize the communal, public enterprise (worship or liturgy), it is often felt to be inappropriate, *gauche*, or simply wrong to speak of public worship (or liturgy) in terms of, with respect to, or as a medium of power and authority. People are simply communing with God, praying to God, interceding before God, and giving God glory and praise. There are no issues of power or authority regarding these activities in liturgical (worship) spaces, right?

Sometimes the reticence to speak about worship (or liturgy) in terms of power and authority is because the individuals who have been invested with power and authority experience queries regarding those structures around the central act of the Christian church (worship) as a criticism or an indictment of them, the church, the church's theology, and/or their leadership, *or* as not-so-innocuous attempts to enter into and encroach upon *their* very boundaried domain of liturgical influence, responsibility, power, and authority. Those who raise questions, experienced sometimes as potential interlopers, are often punished in myriad ways, including but not limited to being reprimanded, marginalized, silenced, given ministry placements in geographically remote places, or in even more punitive instances experiencing delay or denial of the investiture of clerical responsibility through the ecclesiastical process known as ordination. Questioning authority is always a dangerous endeavor. Questioning liturgical authority and practice does not necessarily lead to one gaining greater education, understanding, insight, and participation in the liturgy; rather, questions come at an unintended price to the one who asks by the very ones who have been invested with power and authority. The very dynamics of power and authority have their expression in the context of human relationships that we know as politics.

The word "politics" often brings to mind government and political parties. However, one definition of politics is "the total complex of relations between people living in a society."[1] Early Greeks would situate the context of these relations in a *polis*. Thus, wherever you have humans, you have politics. And, wherever you have politics, the dynamics of power and *authority* are at work, including the Christian church. These dynamics are not new phenomena in the church, nor should they be judged as bad or good (although the effects of the stewardship of power and authority should always be evaluated). These phenomena are as ancient as the church itself. When Jesus called the disciples and began to send them out, he gave them "*power and authority* over all demons and to cure diseases."[2] Religious leaders asked Jesus "by what *authority*" he performed miracles[3] (emphases mine). The apostles set aside (authorized, ordained), through prayer and the laying on of hands, seven men "filled with the Holy Ghost and wisdom"[4] to serve as the church's first deacons. Constantine made Christianity the religion of the empire in the fourth century. In later centuries, protesters called for reforms of the church's practices, with those protests coming to a culmination in the Protestant Reformation, with the Counter-Reformation of the Catholic Church as a response. The Protestant Reformation did not, however, end challenges and calls for liturgical reform *within* Protestant traditions.

That is why this volume, *Worship and Power: Liturgical Authority in Free Church Traditions*, is vitally important and timely. One of the things that I have been saying almost since the beginning of the COVID pandemic is that the health protocols recommended by the World Health Organization (WHO) and, in the United States, the Centers for Disease Control (CDC) (and implemented in many church settings) to prevent the spread of the virus and keep individuals safe, have also forced churches to reexamine their liturgical theology and practices, specifically as they relate to issues of

---

1. *Merriam-Webster*, s.v. "politics." https://www.merriam-webster.com/dictionary/politics.

2. Luke 9:1b.

3. Matt 21.23; Mark 11:28; Luke 20:2.

4. Acts 6:3b.

power and authority. There are many examples of the ways in which church leaders have had to theologically think through their liturgical practices in the pivot from in-person to online worship. One such liturgical practice is Eucharist. Hands that were previously only recipients of the body and blood of Christ were now preparing their own elements. Lips that had only spoken responses and received the elements were now speaking consecratory words over gifts of bread and wine (or juice). By virtue of what I have learned to describe as "pastoral circumstance," the laity in many Free Church traditions have become ritual participants in ways that were heretofore the exclusive purview of the ordained. What happens when we return to in-person worship? Does the ministry exercised by the royal priesthood of the laity in their domestic contexts cease and complete consecratory authority return to the ordained priesthood? This is just one example of the myriad questions of liturgical power and authority that the church and its people (not just its leaders) have faced as a result of the pandemic. Yet, questions of liturgical power and authority have existed long before 11 March 2020 (the date WHO declared Coronavirus a global pandemic).

The contributors to this volume are representative of some of the major Free Church traditions: Christian Church (Disciples of Christ), Cooperative Baptist Fellowship, American Baptist Churches USA, National Baptist Convention USA, Assemblies of God, Hillsong Church, Mennonite Church Canada, Mennonite Church USA, and the Korean Evangelical Holiness Church. Coupled with the ethnic and gender diversity of the contributors, this volume provides a great breadth and diversity of fresh insights, raises probing questions, and challenges the readers to revisit, reconsider, and reimagine the structures of liturgical power, authority, and praxis in their contexts. The critical interrogation of traditions and texts accomplished by these contributors illustrates for the reader that everyone and everything in Free Church traditions are not and have not always been liturgically free and that people and inanimate elements (like space) are sources and sites of power dynamics, power struggles, and power plays. With scholarly rigor, pastoral insight, and personal experience, these contributors examine relations within the church and between the church and empire.

Explicitly and implicitly, there are many invitations extended to the reader to think critically and compassionately about the liturgical power, authority, and practices in which individuals participate, in whatever way(s) they do so. These are only a few. Readers are invited:

- to consider what it means to be faithful in worship;
- to hold in tension divine power and human power and the implications of those tensions for human relationships in liturgical contexts;

- to reflect on the authority of sacred Scripture in shaping liturgical practice and what precisely "biblical worship" means;
- to consider the sources of preachers' power;
- to consider the ways in which people own and exercise liturgical power not formally invested in them;
- to reconsider the relationship between liturgical power and the power of the state;
- to consider who gets to speak, when and where;
- to consider who is the minister;
- to consider what and where liturgical space is;
- to consider who and what are the liturgical authorities inside and outside the church;
- to reflect on the tension between outside governing bodies and local liturgical practices and customs.

In all these readings, the reader is reminded (or informed) that Free Church traditions are still evolving so that *free* is not just an adjective reflective of the historical reality and distinctions that have them so named, but that *free* is part of the ethos that informs how these communities can live and participate in worship. As a whole, this volume recognizes that power is a reality in the context of human relationships that can neither be denied nor ignored, and that in the context of the church, *all* participants in the liturgical enterprise are invited to consider how power and authority are invested, shared, and exercised by all in the worshiping community.

This volume is a rich resource for scholars, seminarians, and pastors. The bibliographies provide rich resources for deeper reading on the respective chapter topics as well as resources for exploration of related topics. It is scholarly yet scrutable, pastoral yet probing, indicting yet inviting. It is a significant contribution to scholarship on Free Church traditions. Rev. Dr. Sarah Kathleen Johnson and Rev. Dr. Andrew Wymer are to be commended for their vision and work on this important volume.

May the insights and wisdom of this volume help worshiping communities to revisit, reconsider, and reimagine liturgical power and authority in ways that enable all who participate in worship to do so fully and *freely*.

Introduction

Liturgical Authority in Free Church Traditions

Sarah Kathleen Johnson and Andrew Wymer

Liturgy is power-laden, and this is manifested in distinct ways in Free Church traditions that invite ecumenical dialogue. There are three important dimensions of this thesis. First, *liturgy is power-laden.* That is, Christian worship emerges from and speaks back into human relationships that are necessarily shaped by power and authority. The intersections of worship and power have material and spiritual implications for individuals and communities, including churches and societies. Second, the power-laden nature of liturgy is *manifested in distinct ways in Free Church traditions.* Free Churches structure and negotiate power in relation to worship in ways that reflect the decentralization, local diversity, and personal agency that characterize many aspects of Free Church theology and practice. Third, these distinctives *invite ecumenical dialogue.* Dialogue among scholars and practitioners of Free Church worship, as well as dialogue with the wider church, can be mutually enriching within and beyond Free Church settings. The language of "liturgical authority" provides an entry point for understanding the ways in which the structuring and negotiation of power in Free Church liturgy converges with and diverges from other Christian traditions.

Power is present in all human relationships, including those formed when assembling for Christian worship. Individuals have power as participants and leaders. Communities have collective power, as do groups within communities. Social power has the potential to shape and also emerge from worship practices. Scripture, tradition, and other authorities that are invoked during worship and in decisions about worship are shaped by individual, communal, and social power in the past that still exerts influence today. Furthermore, Christians claim that worship exerts power beyond the assembly, shaping the unfolding of the social realities faced by individuals and communities. Ultimately, Christians acknowledge the power of God within and beyond communities of faith gathered for worship. This array of dynamics raises crucial questions about liturgical authority. Who has the power to determine worship practices, and what types of power do they exert? What authorities are invoked in shaping worship practices? What power do worship practices have to influence individuals, communities, and society? This volume explores the ways worship and power are necessarily entangled and the implications for how Christian communities and traditions understand themselves, negotiate internal power, and determine their relationships to the world, including civic powers.

This volume explores the power-laden nature of liturgy with attention to three distinct areas: (1) contesting power in society; (2) negotiating power in ecclesial institutions; and (3) claiming power through practices. These three areas of focus reflect existing discourse and therefore facilitate ecumenical dialogue, while at the same time speaking to the power-laden nature of liturgy within the heterogeneous and decentralized context of Free Church traditions.[1]

Tracing Porous Boundaries

Each of the key elements in this volume—liturgy and worship, power and authority, and Free Church traditions—are contested categories. As an edited collection, contributors engage these categories in a range of ways. At the outset, it is valuable to trace the ways these concepts are used, while recognizing these boundaries are porous.

Worship and Liturgy

This is a book about worship. The word "worship" is widely used in at least three ways, especially in Free Church settings.[2]

Worship refers to *the act of attributing worth to God*—expressions of honor, praise, and gratitude that may be offered at any time and in many

---

1. As an example, these key themes are manifested in a recent Roman Catholic volume as "liturgy and power," "liturgy in the world," and "liturgy and power in lived religion." See Flanagan and Vento, *Liturgy + Power*.

2. John Witvliet and Greg Scheer develop frameworks for how the word "worship" is used in these overlapping ways. Witvliet, "On Three Meanings," 46–47; Sheer, *Essential Worship*, 26–27.

ways. Worship in this sense also includes worship offered to God through a life of loving service to other people and in care of all creation. In this volume, this expansive sense of worship is explored most fully by Allen in his study of worship in the book of Revelation, and by Mendez, Riches, and Davies in their exploration of everyday spirituality of Latina Pentecostal women.

Worship refers to *the activity of a Christian community gathered for worship*—a worship service. In this sense, the term "worship" refers to all aspects of gathering: proclaiming God's word, gathering at Christ's table, expressing praise and lament, offering prayer, singing and silence, experiencing architecture and art, rituals of healing, and more. This is the main sense in which the word "worship" is employed throughout this volume. Chapters by Wymer, Johnson, Jung, and Sigmon address specific aspects of the activity of communities gathered for corporate worship and the processes through which these practices are shaped. One contribution of this volume is expanding the conception of what constitutes gathering for worship, especially in Yarborough's emphasis on testimony and Villegas's work with public vigils.

Worship refers to *worship through music during a specific portion of a worship service*, especially in the context of contemporary or charismatic worship. This use of the term "worship" is so pervasive in evangelical and Pentecostal contexts that some practitioners encountering this book may assume worship through music is the focus. While this is not the case, there are two chapters that engage worship in this sense: Ottaway's discussion of the tradition that informs praise and worship in Pentecostal communities, and Snider Andrews's examination of Southern Baptist worship.

As a book about worship, this is also a book about *liturgy*. Liturgy is treated as synonymous with worship in the second sense outlined above: liturgy refers to the entirety of the activity of a Christian community gathered for worship. This use of the term may contrast with how the word "liturgy" is used informally in some Free Church settings to refer to certain forms of worship (such as those associated with Roman Catholic and Anglican traditions) or with certain components of worship (such as scripted texts). However, in the context of this volume, Pentecostal and Baptist worship are no less liturgical than Anglican and Roman Catholic worship, and all aspects of worship, structured and spontaneous, are liturgy. Hillsong and historic creeds, communion and charismatic healing, personal testimony and public protest, among many other expressions of Free Church worship, are explored here. Liturgy is what religious communities do when they gather for worship, and this includes negotiating questions of power and authority.

Power and Authority

Power and authority are complex concepts that are used in various ways, within and beyond this volume.

At the most basic level, *power* refers simply to *the capacity to act or to influence*. Power is pervasive—it is always present in human relationships and ever-changing. Power may be employed in ways that are positive or negative. In the context of this book, the terminology of power is not intended to have a negative connotation. Instead, power is simply a reality that can be named and actively addressed, rather than ignored or denied. At the same time, the use of power may or may not be authorized.

Authority refers to *power that is considered to be legitimate by a specific community*. The rightful use of power—legitimate action and influence—may be recognized in official or unofficial ways. There may be formally recognized authorities that do not have power (or that have less power) in terms of being able to take action or exert influence. Authority may be contested within communities. Observers from outside communities may also interrogate who or what is considered authoritative.

Power and authority may be vested in a variety of entities, especially when considering worship. *Individuals*, including participants and leaders, may be the focus, as exemplified by Jung and Mendez, Riches, and Davies in their examination of how individual leaders are authorized. The founders of movements may be seen as especially authoritative individuals, as is evident in Sigmon's engagement with significant historical figures in the Christian Church (Disciples of Christ) tradition. *Groups* may also exercise power and authority, including local congregations, committees, denominations, and parachurch organizations, as many authors discuss. At times, groups that negotiate matters of power may be demographic rather than institutional, as in the chapters that engage gender and race (discussed in more detail below).

Liturgical power and authority are not limited to human beings. There are *sources* that have more or less authority to influence worship, including Scripture and tradition, as Ottaway and Snider Andrews discuss and as Allen models in his exegetical work, although the power these sources exercise is rarely straightforward. Powerful *concepts* like "biblical" and "anarchy" are also at play, as Snider Andrews and Wymer demonstrate. *Ritual* itself exercises power, potentially reinterpreting established sources as Villegas explores, or authorizing individuals as Jung demonstrates. In addition, ritual can form individual worldviews as Allan describes, shape corporate identity as Johnson discusses, and even transform our social imaginations of what is possible as Wymer argues. Furthermore, *social contexts* can exert significant power through structures such as policies, practices, and norms. These structural dynamics are present in each chapter, with Wymer considering the power of the nation-state, Jung examining inculturation in Korean traditional religion, and Mendez, Riches, and Davies critiquing Latinx machismo, to name only a few examples. Finally, from a Christian theological perspective, *God* is the ultimate authority and exercises limitless power.

Individuals, groups, sources, concepts, rituals, and social contexts influence worship and act through worship toward various ends. Power may be employed to oppress or liberate, to resist or embolden. In this sense, liturgy is necessarily *political*: it emerges from and shapes power-laden human relationships with material and spiritual implications for society, ecclesial institutions, and communities of faith, as well as the individuals who comprise them.

The contributors to this volume come from a range of academic, ecclesial, and cultural contexts and draw on a diversity of theoretical material. We did not agree to read or engage common sources at the outset of this project, but rather to draw deeply on our distinctive locations. At the same time, underlying influences are evident. Informed explicitly or implicitly by the work of Michel Foucault, authors approach power as pervasive, relational, dynamic, and productive rather than assuming it is a form of coercive domination.[3] Informed by the ritual theory of Catherine Bell, authors tend to assume that power is negotiated through ritual; as Bell describes, "ritualization is first and foremost a strategy for the construction of certain types of power relationships effective within particular social organizations."[4] Finally, an impulse to employ power, and especially the power of ritualization, toward the end of liberation, underlies much of this work.

Worship and Power

Liturgy is always subject to power—it is under the influence of many entities past and present. Liturgy is also always subject to authority—certain influences are recognized as legitimate by a specific community, whereas others are not. What is authoritative in relation to liturgy is usually contested, meaning multiple powers compete for influence and, potentially, for recognition. Liturgy itself also has the power to influence what and who is considered authoritative more broadly within a community. Liturgy may even exercise power beyond its immediate context. The relationship

3. Foucault, *Power/Knowledge*; Foucault, *Discipline and Punish*.
4. Bell, *Ritual Theory, Ritual Practice*, 197.

between worship and power is dynamic and dialectical, operating at societal, institutional, and individual levels.

Free Church

Indeed, the Free Churches were born amidst the contestations of liturgical power and authority comprising the Protestant Reformation, and that negotiation of liturgical power and authority has continued to unfold as the Free Churches navigate theological and liturgical heterogeneity.

In this volume, we approach the Free Churches with attention to three key characteristics: 1) separation from civic intervention; 2) local autonomy; and 3) voluntarism. *Separation from civic intervention* represents the classic Free Church insistence that the state should not be able to formally legislate, authorize, or in any way govern what constitutes faithful liturgical practice. We offer this with an emphasis on the term "formal" with awareness of what Wymer's chapter illustrates as informal authorizations that are potentially at play and what Johnson's chapter points to as the operation of power in the "background." By *local autonomy* we identify the long tradition of congregational polity in many Free Church traditions that rejects intervention in the worship of the local community by centralized ecclesial bodies, but we also note that there are a variety of possibilities for the configuration of local autonomy. Finally, in naming *voluntarism* as a key characteristic of the Free Churches, we emphasize the many ways in which Free Church polity and practice have been shaped to avoid coercion and to emphasize the willing participation of its adherents.[5] At the same time, several chapters in this volume complicate this notion of voluntarism and freedom from coercion, highlighting the acknowledged or unacknowledged use of coercive power even in traditions informed by a commitment to freedom from coercion.[6]

It is important to note that the term "Free Church" has been accompanied by some ambiguity within liturgical scholarship. Influential Methodist liturgical scholar James White, in his widely read work on the history and practice of Protestant worship, has defined the historical development of the "Free Church" with attention to two key issues, "the freedom to reform worship exclusively on the basis of Scripture" and insistence that "the ordering

---

5. While White does not identify this as a distinguishing characteristic of the Free Churches, he uses the term descriptively in relation to the Anabaptist stream (White, *Protestant Worship*, 81). White also discusses Frontier traditions as preferring believers' baptism (White, *Protestant Worship*, 181).

6. White discusses this independent commitment in the Puritan stream of the Free Churches (White, *Protestant Worship*, 128).

of worship is determined locally by each worshiping community."[7] However, he also observed that as some mainline Free Church traditions developed through the nineteenth century, "biblicism" was "superseded by pragmatism" with only the key feature of commitment to autonomy remaining.[8] The biblicist stream of the Free Churches is evident in the work of Snider Andrews's engagement of the conservative evangelical Free Church worship of Southern Baptists, Ottoway's engagement of the Pentecostal Free Church Latter Rain revival, and Allen's engagement of texts from Revelation as an authoritative source of insight from a Christian Church (Disciples of Christ) perspective. However, these three essays and others in this collection contribute rich examples of the heterogeneity, porousness, and hybridity of the Free Churches, in which the authorities of pragmatism and biblicism are at times interwoven, overlaid, or even unacknowledged.

White's approach to defining the Free Churches shares commonalities with other definitions. For instance, Baptist scholar Christopher Ellis identifies two key characteristics of the Free Churches as (1) a commitment to God's sole authority over the Christian community that is expressed in freedom from civic intervention in worship, and (2) a commitment to congregational autonomy in all matters related to worship.[9] As with White's definition, Ellis names an authoritative source in defining the Free Churches, albeit God rather than the Bible or pragmatism. However, not all definitions of the Free Churches do so, with some popular definitions simply emphasizing English nonconformist and dissenting traditions' insistence on freedom from civic intervention.[10] While a number of definitional variations exist, two consistent themes in definitions of Free Churches are freedom from civic intervention and local autonomy.

White's definition of the Free Churches breaks it into three primary historical streams that are evident in this volume: Anabaptist traditions associated with sixteenth century Radical Reformation in continental Europe and known today in Mennonite, Amish, and Hutterite expressions; Separatist and Puritan traditions emerging in England and known today in Congregationalist, Baptist, and Unitarian Universalist expressions; and Frontier traditions expressed in denominations such as the Churches of Christ (Disciples of Christ) and more broadly across North American Protestantism. For White, Frontier traditions, or more specifically "frontier-revival"

7. White, *Protestant Worship*, 80–81.

8. White, *Protestant Worship*, 172.

9. Ellis, *Gathering*, 26. White also notes this (*Protestant Worship*, 81).

10. As an example, the *Concise Oxford Dictionary of the Christian Church* simply redirects readers from the "Free Churches" entry to the entry for "Nonconformity." Livingstone, *Concise Oxford Dictionary*.

traditions, represent the pragmatic adaptation of theology and practice for primarily unchurched adults in the thinly populated American West that began at the turn of the nineteenth century. However, while White attends to shared origins and possible convergences, he holds Pentecostalism as distinct from the Free Churches.[11] In contrast, this volume contains three chapters that examine Pentecostal contexts as Free Church expressions. We intentionally deploy a broader definition of the Free Churches to account for the emergence and increasing influence of Pentecostal churches in the Free Church tradition. This approach allows us to nonpreferentially engage evangelical, Pentecostal, and mainline Protestant expressions of the Free Churches in ways that emphasize shared characteristics. While White's biblicist and pragmatic traditions can still be identified today, this collection complicates any attempt to tidily characterize evangelicals as biblicist or mainline Protestants as pragmatic, revealing that biblicism and pragmatism, among many other sources of liturgical authority, are inextricably interwoven.

We envision the three defining characteristics of the Free Churches—separation from civic intervention, local autonomy, and voluntarism—as forming a trilateral, the points of which can be engaged on spectrums (Diagram 1.A). Any congregation or denomination can be interpreted as emphasizing each characteristic to a varying degree, with the center of the diagram representing more constrained approaches and the arrows pointing toward greater degrees of freedom. For example (Diagram 1.B), the small dotted circle could represent a state church with an episcopal structure in which membership is assumed at birth. In contrast, the wide, dashed circle could represent a congregational tradition that practices believer's baptism and prides itself on its strong separation from worldly intervention. Not all points need be equidistant from the center; the gray circle, for example, could represent a religious minority that has a strong centralized structure and ethnocultural identity, yet has a clear separation from, or even oppression by, civic authorities. There are likely to be multiple perspectives on how a tradition or community is mapped. This trilateral is not intended to be deployed in a manner that is exclusionary or that imposes a particular stance on a congregation. Rather, this trilateral provides points of reference to consider what makes each congregation or denomination distinct within the continued unfolding and demarcation of the boundaries of what constitutes the Free Churches. As such, this trilateral is also intended to function ecumenically as a reminder of the interconnectedness between those who work and worship in Free Church traditions and other Christian siblings

---

11. White, *Protestant Worship*, 188–94.

who do not identify as Free Church traditions, but who, in valuing any of these three characteristics, can be located in relationship with Free Church theology and practice.

Diagram 1: Defining Characteristics of Free Church Traditions

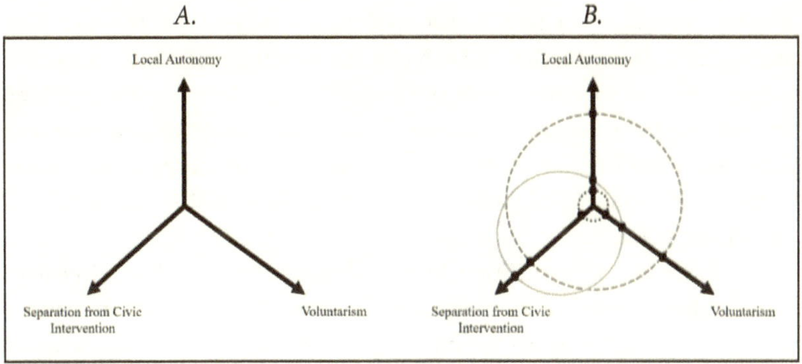

The Free Churches are approached within this volume with attention to diversity. Chapters relate to Mennonite (Mennonite Church USA and Mennonite Church Canada), Baptist (American Baptist Churches, Southern Baptist Convention, and National Baptist Convention), Christian Church (Disciples of Christ), and Pentecostal (Latter Rain, Korean Evangelical Holiness Church, and Hillsong) contexts. This volume also moves beyond the USA-dominant framework employed by White to incorporate global perspectives, with multiple authors from Canada and authors from Australia, Great Britain, and Korea, as well as authors based in the United States who transgress approaches that center the USA in varied ways. As an example, Jung's chapter engages a manifestation of the global expansion of the Free Church that has been profoundly shaped by the expansion and aggression of Western imperialism.

While characterized by diversity, this work is simultaneously limited. Only a handful of the many denominations that can be categorized as Free Churches are represented. This is shaped in part by the limited—but increasing—engagement of Free Church scholars in the North American Academy of Liturgy (NAAL), the ecumenical and interreligious guild of liturgical scholars out of which this volume emerges. While this volume expands geographic boundaries, this remains a collection with a majority of scholars working in the context of the USA. As such, this volume takes an expansive approach to Free Church liturgical scholarship that represents the formative beginning of a conversation as opposed to an all-encompassing summation.

Free Worship

Engagement with what constitutes Free Churches has been accompanied at times by limited discourse examining the worship of the Free Churches, or "free worship." White declares that "Free Church worship is basically liturgical congregationalism."[12] Here, Ellis is also helpful, stating that Free Church worship is characterized by "freedom of local congregations to order their own gatherings for worship."[13] Each of these definitions is rather focused in scope. Within the framework of the Free Church trilateral, we understand free worship to be liturgical practices that are unbeholden to civic intervention, determined autonomously by congregations apart from centralized control, and engaged in by consensual participation that is as free as possible from coercion.

As we noted with the Free Church trilateral, this definition of free worship can be interpreted on spectrums. Congregations and denominations with free worship may, to varying degrees, transgress the boundaries of churches identifying as Free Church or that are located within the previously identified historical and contemporary streams of the Free Churches. As such, this volume engages free worship with an awareness of inclusive possibility. Most authors in this collection work from within the unfolding stream of contemporary Free Church traditions with an eye toward porousness and ecumenism.

This work also reflects an expansive view of what might constitute Free Church worship. While most chapters examine worship within congregations, several chapters explore practices that occur outside of the boundaries of an explicit "church." This is particularly evocative as Western nations move away from formal religious participation in Christian denominations, and it invites continued consideration of the boundaries of what might constitute the Free "Church."

Overview of the Volume

The volume is structured in three major sections that interrogate the power-laden nature of liturgy in ways that reflect the three defining traits of Free Church traditions: (1) the ways free worship can contest power in society; (2) the negotiation of power in ecclesial institutions characterized by congregational polity; and (3) the potential for individuals to claim power through practices.

12. White, *Protestant Worship*, 81.

13. Ellis, *Gathering*, 27.

Part 1: Contesting Power in Society

The first part of the volume examines how Christian worship *contests power in the society* beyond the church. Separation from civic intervention is a central value in Free Church traditions. At the same time, Free Church worship practices speak directly and indirectly to broader social realities.

Ron Allen establishes a scriptural framework for understanding the worship of God in opposition to the worship of empire. Drawing on the book of Revelation, he articulates criteria for evaluating faithful worship as fostering authentic, mutually supportive community and unfaithful worship as lifting up practices that lead to self-serving violence.

Employing related principles, Andrew Wymer reappropriates the concept of "liturgical anarchy" to describe "differently ordered" worship that has the power to reorder society. Drawing on the sweeping historical case of dissenting Baptists in the United States, Wymer argues that decentralized liturgical authority contests the centralized violent power of the nation-state by presenting an alternative political vision.

In contrast to these biblical and historical narratives, Isaac Villegas anchors his analysis of ritual resistance to violence in a close reading of a particular practice—vigils remembering by name those who died crossing the border from Mexico into the United States. This practice reframes Mennonite narratives of martyrdom as a call to solidarity with victims of violence today.

Each of these chapters enriches our knowledge of how the worship of the church challenges the powers of the world through a separation from the state that can still speak powerfully into public matters of social justice.

Part 2: Negotiating Power in Ecclesial Institutions

The second part of the volume explores the *negotiation of power within ecclesial institutions* in relation to worship practices. Local autonomy, often manifested in congregational polity that focuses decision-making in local communities, is a distinctive characteristic of Free Church traditions. At the same time, this decision-making is influenced by denominations and parachurch organizations, powerful leaders and authoritative sources (notably Scripture), as well as dynamics associated with gender, class, race, and culture.

Sarah Kathleen Johnson examines the power of a new Mennonite denominational hymnal to transform the corporate identity of Mennonites in the United States and Canada. However, the hymnal itself is a product of complex explicit and implicit power dynamics which Johnson analyzes, drawing on Michel Foucault, Hannah Arendt, and Judith Butler as synthesized by Amy Allen, modeling a method that could be employed in other contexts.

In contrast to corporate identity, Jaewoong Jung examines how worship practices authorize individual leaders. Employing theory from Pierre Bourdieu and Catherine Bell, Jung examines how Pentecostal liturgical practices and Korean indigenous culture intersect to attribute divine power to revivalist preachers in ways that congregations tacitly consent to on an ongoing basis. This consent also presents the opportunity to disrupt these patterns.

Also investigating the emergence and influence of Pentecostal practices, Jonathan Ottaway explores how tradition exerts power over the liturgical practice of praise and worship. While theologies of praise and worship rooted in the tabernacle of David are explicitly anchored in Scripture as a sole authority, Pentecostal tradition manifested in particular hermeneutics and metanarratives directs, governs, and contextualizes this approach.

Emily Snider Andrews turns her attention to the authorizing power of Scripture in interrogating the Southern Baptist Convention's claim to practice "biblical worship." Snider Andrews examines how the Gospel-Centered Movement has influenced how "biblical worship" is understood as "gospel centered, musically relevant, and pastorally focused." Approaching "biblical worship" in this way opens space for the historically insular Southern Baptist Convention to engage in dialogue with other conservative Protestants and more broadly.

Each of these contributions, and the connections among them, provides a nuanced understanding of what authorizes the worship practices of local communities in Free Church traditions, as well as who and what these practices in turn authorize.

Part 3: Claiming Power through Practices

The third part of the volume considers how individuals and groups exercise their agency to *claim power through practices*. Free Church worship is marked by diverse and distinct practices. These practices, whether they exist within or beyond established rites, have the potential to become sites where historically marginalized groups, including Black and Latinx women and lay leaders, challenge established authorities (notably male-dominated pulpits) and claim alternative modes of empowerment.

Chelsea Brooke Yarborough investigates the subversive authority claimed by Black women who testify in the context of Baptist worship. Resisting exclusion from the pulpit, testimony becomes a space for truth-telling, collective care, and bearing witness to the movement of God.

Dorothy Mendez, Tanya Riches, and Andrew Davies likewise explore how women claim authority in alternative spiritual spaces, in this case Latina Pentecostal women exercising spiritual authority in the midst of everyday life. This alternative sphere of spiritual authority emerged as male authority predominated in cultural and liturgical spaces, and can create an opening for women to exercise liturgical authority as well.

Finally, Casey Sigmon examines the centrality of weekly communion in the Disciples of Christ tradition, and the importance of lay leadership at the communion table, rooted in the founders of the movement and frontier pragmatism. This orthopractic claim to shared sacramental leadership authorizes a distinct understanding of church leadership and a responsiveness to new situations, such as a smooth transition to online communion during the COVID-19 pandemic.

These three papers and the dialogue among them enhance our understanding of how individuals and groups claim power through liturgical practices in ways that unsettle established ecclesial authorities and challenge unequal social structures.

Contributions of the Volume

The broader themes and specific case studies explored in this volume are intended to engage an audience of scholars and practitioners who desire to better understand Free Church worship as well as those who are committed to interrogating questions of liturgical authority across Christian traditions. This includes liturgists, theologians, and church leaders from beyond as well as within Free Church settings. An additional audience is those invested in the prominent secondary themes of gender and race.

Contributions beyond Free Church Traditions

Critical reflection on power and worship in Free Church settings is essential for the ecumenical Christian community today for at least five reasons.

First, *the presence and power of Free Church traditions is growing worldwide.* One way this is visible is in the worldwide growth of Pentecostal and evangelical Christianity which, in the context of this volume, are considered Free Church traditions. As a 2006 Pew Research Center study observes:

Pentecostalism, and its related "renewalist" or "spirit-filled"
movements, was one of the most influential developments in
global Christianity in the 20th century, and it is poised to have
an even greater influence in the 21st century. Nowhere is this
more evident than in the "global South," where pentecostalism is
reshaping the social, political and economic landscape of many
countries in Latin America, Africa and Asia.[14]

While the explosion of Free Church traditions is most evident outside
Europe and North America, it is also present in the religious landscape
in the United States, particularly in terms of the share of Protestants who
self-identify as "born-again or evangelical" Christians remaining steady or
increasing while the overall number of self-identified Protestants declines.[15]
Furthermore, the number of congregations with no denominational affiliation has been steadily rising over the past two decades which also points to
the presence and growth of Free Churches.[16] While not all the denominations represented in this volume are characterized by this type of growth,
they reflect many of the same patterns in relation to worship and power.
Taking contemporary religious realities seriously requires paying attention
to the enduring and expanding presence of Free Churches.

Second, *episcopal and state churches increasingly function in ways
that echo Free Churches* in contemporary social contexts characterized by
increasing religious diversity, declining religious authority, and formal
separation of church and state. Individuals freely choose which congregations they attend rather than relying on parish boundaries. Congregations
often develop specific expressions of worship aligned with certain liturgical
subcultures. Religion has decreasing institutional influence in public life. As
historically established churches begin to function more like Free Churches
in many contexts, it is helpful to turn to Free Churches to explore how to
navigate these realities, which are connected to questions of power and
authority.

Third, *worship practices associated with Free Church traditions are increasingly embraced across Christian traditions*. Data from the fourth wave
of the American Congregations Study suggests that Catholic and mainline
congregations are increasingly adopting more informal and expressive
forms of worship and embracing the use of technology during worship.
These are patterns that Swee Hong Lim and Lester Ruth associate with

14. "Spirit and Power," para. 2.

15. "In U.S., Decline of Christianity Continues."

16. Chaves and Anderson, "Changing American Congregations," 676–86.

contemporary worship practices emerging in Free Church settings.[17] The adoption of worship practices emerging from Free Churches is also present in the widespread embrace of contemporary worship music across Christian traditions.[18] While Free Church worship is not defined by these practices, they are examples of the ecumenical influence of liturgical patterns emerging in Free Church settings.

Fourth, *a commitment to attend to voices that have been historically marginalized demands engagement with Free Church traditions.* Free Church traditions have often existed on the social margins, particularly in settings with established state churches. More specifically, Free Churches have long been on the margins of mainstream academic theology, including the discipline of liturgical studies. As discussed below, this is one of very few scholarly volumes focused on Free Church worship intended for an ecumenical audience.

Fifth, *a focus on worship and power offers a new avenue for ecumenical engagement.* A focus on power invites increased awareness of shared connections across traditional fault lines among Free Church traditions, and between Free Churches and the broader Christian tradition in relation to liturgy. Questions of authority create space for conversation that is both foundational and adjacent to issues that have traditionally divided churches such as baptism, Eucharist, and ministry.

Free Church scholars studying Free Church traditions are making important contributions to understanding questions of worship and power with implications that reach across the Christian tradition.

Contributions within Free Church Traditions

In addition to these broader implications, this volume has particular implications for scholars and church leaders who study and work within Free Church traditions. It is a starting point for greater *self-understanding* through robust engagement with questions of worship and power in a diversity of Free Church contexts in relation to a range of liturgical practices. It approaches these themes from within Free Church traditions and aims to understand these communities and practices on their own terms in ways that are both sympathetic and critical. In addition, this volume can contribute to *dialogue among Free Church traditions.* The congregational nature of Free Churches has often fostered division. Ecumenical conversation

17. Roso et al., "Changing Worship Practices in American Congregations," 675–84; Lim and Ruth, *Lovin' on Jesus.*

18. Johnson and Loepp Thiessen, "Contemporary Worship Music."

between diverse Free Church traditions is necessary, and questions of worship and power both point to common ground and highlight distinctions in ways that invite dialogue. Furthermore, this volume can *promote liturgical scholarship* in Free Church traditions, which is still in the early stages of development. Finally, there are *practical implications* for worship that emerge from the case studies presented here.

Contributions to Liturgical Scholarship

This volume makes specific contributions to ongoing liturgical discourse in its (1) focus on liturgical authority and power from a diversity of perspectives, and (2) sustained analysis of worship in a variety of Free Church contexts from within Free Church traditions.

The first contribution of this work to the discipline of liturgical studies is a focus on liturgical authority and power from a diversity of perspectives. Treatments of liturgical authority and power in monographs or edited volumes is limited; however, in 2017, a collection of essays, *Liturgy + Power*, drawn from the 2016 annual meeting of the College Theology Society, was published.[19] This work, which is primarily comprised of Roman Catholic perspectives, examines the intersection of liturgy with ecclesial political structures, engagements of the church with the broader politics of the world, and theological reflection on God's power. We believe the *Liturgy + Power* volume, as well as our work here in *Worship and Power*, reflect an emerging area of interest in liturgical authority and power, and this volume distinctively contributes to this discourse by introducing a diversity of perspectives from Free Church traditions.

The second contribution of this book is a sustained analysis of worship in a variety of Free Church worship contexts from within Free Church liturgical traditions. There are four existing bodies of work on Free Church worship that are significant for situating this volume. The first body of work is scholarship engaging Free Church worship by non-Free Church scholars connected to the NAAL. James White's *Protestant Worship: Traditions in Transition* is an early example.[20] A more recent example is Swee Hong Lim and Lester Ruth's work on the history of contemporary worship.[21] Second, there is a body of work done by Free Church scholars connected to

19. Flanagan and Vento, *Liturgy + Power*. Of additional note is a pamphlet published in 1979, Stevenson, *Authority and Freedom in Liturgy*.

20. White, *Protestant Worship*.

21. Lim and Ruth, *Lovin' on Jesus*; Ruth and Lim, *History of Contemporary Praise & Worship*.

the NAAL, including both established and emerging scholars such as Melanie Ross, Todd Johnson, John Rempel, Khalia Williams, Rebecca Spurrier, Heidi Miller, and additional works by contributors to this volume. Third, there is also a body of work done in Free Church settings by Free Church scholars who are not affiliated with the NAAL. An early example of this is Robert Webber's *Worship Old and New*.[22] A recent example of this is Simon Chan's *Liturgical Theology: The Church as Worshiping Community*.[23] Fourth, there is work done on topics related to Free Church worship that is situated in other disciplines such as Pentecostal studies and musicology. One example of this is Monique Ingalls's work on music in Evangelical worship.[24] However, within dominant discourse in liturgical studies, the Free Churches continue to be underrepresented. This book is distinguished by the diversity of the contributors—most of whom are formally trained as liturgical scholars—bringing together varied Free Church perspectives from a broad swath of social locations and utilizing a wide range of methodologies. Scholarly monographs or edited collections of scholarly essays dedicated to the study of worship in Free Church traditions are rare, and this collection is noteworthy in its curation of numerous diverse Free Church perspectives.

Significant Secondary Themes

In curating this collection on worship and power, we note the emergence of critical approaches to gender and race as important secondary themes across a number of the chapters, which is significant for two reasons. First, this collection reflects the diversity of Free Church engagements of power, with some chapters centering critical theories, some chapters attending to critical theories in secondary ways, and other chapters not attending to critical theories in a significant way. Second, these secondary themes reflect the commitment of a number of the contributors to situate liturgical power in ecclesial and social contexts in which power is contested along lines of gender, race, and other social hierarchies.

The relationship between *gender*, power and authority, and worship in Free Church settings is an important secondary theme. While various Free Church traditions have welcomed women in liturgical leadership in the early years of their development, this practice often declines over time as traditions become more structured (although with congregational polity

---

22. Webber, *Worship Old and New*.

23. Chan, *Liturgical Theology*.

24. Ingalls, *Singing the Congregation*.

there is always variation in practice).[25] Nevertheless, women continue to exercise power and lay claims to authority, as contributors to this volume demonstrate. Gender is at the center of Yarborough's and Mendez, Riches, and Davies's studies of the ways Black and Latina women exert power and are seen as authoritative in Black Baptist and Latinx Pentecostal contexts, although they are often formally excluded from the pulpit. Johnson draws on the feminist critical theory of Amy Allen in her analysis of power in the process of shaping centralized worship resources in the Mennonite tradition, which includes attention to gender. Although secondary to their broader arguments, Snider Andrews and Sigmon name the ways that women have been excluded from liturgical leadership. Snider Andrews describes how the terminology of "biblical worship" is used to limit the role of women in Southern Baptist settings. Sigmon observes how broader cultural dynamics have overwhelmed the radical equality at the communion table that is central in the Christian Church (Disciples of Christ). It is particularly noteworthy that all of the female contributors to this volume comment on the relationship between gender and power in worship, although they explore a range of themes, practices, and traditions. Wymer's naming of heteropatriarchy and Allen's use of intentionally expansive language for the Realm of God also reflect attention to gender and power. In various ways, this volume contributes to broader questions about gender and authority within and beyond Christian worship.

An additional secondary theme within this volume is the contestation of *race* within the Free Churches. Free Church traditions—particularly the Anabaptist and English Separatist streams identified by White—originated in the Protestant Reformation in Europe amidst a milieu of anti-Semitic and anti-Islamic antecedents of contemporary racial hierarchies that later emerged in the Americas in the seventeenth century. As an expanding constellation of traditions emerging alongside the expansion of Western colonial aggression, the Free Churches eventually expanded overseas to European colonies in the Americas. Within this context, the Free Churches have an ambiguous legacy. Race is an explicit theme within the essays by Wymer and Yarborough, who examine the impact of racial hierarchies on human communities and grapple with resistance to heteropatriarchal white supremacy in liturgical communities and liturgical practices. Race is also an implicit theme in essays by Jung, Villegas, and Mendez, Davies, and Riches. In their work, we can trace the continued unfolding of racial hierarchies that also intersect with expressions of patriarchy. In particular,

---

25. A focus on women and power is not intended to reinforce binary conceptions of gender but rather reflects the specific case studies that are included in this volume.

these authors illustrate the global dimensions of the Free Churches that are themselves caught up in the still-unfolding drama of Western colonialism. In other essays, such as Snider Andrews's and Ottaway's work examining white-dominant worship, the role of race in shaping theories and practices remains unexamined. The theme of race in this collection contributes to ongoing examination of what it means to actually be the Free Churches or to engage in free worship when racism and its intersecting expressions of domination still stifle freedom in the Free Churches and beyond.

Future Questions

Like all published works, this volume captures a vignette of a conversation unfolding over many years, and we anticipate rich discourse in the future. The questions engaged in this collection have, as good questions so often do, opened additional avenues of inquiry.

Some of the questions we carry forward relate to the challenge of *ecumenical dialogue.* In the NAAL, which has been historically focused on liturgical scholarship and worship practices apart from Free Church traditions, we are aware that we represent underrepresented traditions whose liturgical theology and practice have long been characterized by some as "non-liturgical."[26] While this characterization—that is in itself inherently power-laden—may be decreasing, vestiges of this paradigm remain, and a sensitivity to such dynamics underlies our work and engagement in ecumenical discourse. This volume invites further consideration of how we can engage with these historically centered fields in ways that both bridge divides and allow us to maintain and even celebrate Free Church particularity.

Even as we are committed to maintaining our particularity as Free Church scholars, ecumenical engagement provides opportunities to identify remarkable points of connection. One such example is the power of *tradition,* which is a thread that is woven throughout these essays in implicit and explicit ways. White writes of the role of tradition in Frontier worship, "In a sense, it is a tradition of no tradition, but that attitude soon became a tradition in its own right."[27] We observe that appeals to tradition in these essays are made in acknowledged and unacknowledged ways. What is the authority of history and tradition in Free Church worship? Awareness of the tensions that exist between tradition and the pragmatic bent of the Free Churches calls us to interrogate the power we implicitly or explicitly give to tradition as well as what we consider to be "tradition." Identifying and

---

26. An example of discourse contesting this is Ross, *Evangelical versus Liturgical?*

27. White, *Protestant Worship,* 172.

critically engaging these traditions is essential not only to more fully understand our own particularity and our place in relationship to other Christian traditions, but it is integral to pursuing matters of justice and liberation.

As the great Civil Rights leader Fannie Lou Hamer declared, "Until I am free, you are not free either."[28] The previously identified secondary themes in this volume of gender and race underlie important tasks for Free Church and ecumenical liturgical scholarship. These themes were not directly curated by the editors of this volume; rather, to the degree that these and other themes of *injustice* and *inequality* are repeated through this volume, they reveal a shared conviction that we must continue to collectively work toward worship that is aligned with God's vision for liberation in our world. Perhaps in Hamer's words, Free Church worship—and *all* Christian worship—will never be truly free until all of our siblings—Christian and non-Christian alike—are treated with justice and respect. Here we note that we have so much further to go. Many important topics at the intersection of worship and power are not directly addressed in this volume, including but not limited to indigenous justice; full participation of LGBTQ+ persons; and just relationships with nonhuman creatures and the earth. This volume provides limited but poignant evidence of the ways Free Church worship is enmeshed in oppressive economic structures, and it is crucial that we continue to work to unravel these systems and our own places within them.

In this world of shifting religious and social landscapes, it is necessary to approach our work with awareness of the ebb and flow of power, who has it, and how it operates. This volume attends to particular contexts and realities unique to particular spaces and times, yet power is fluid and changes over time. It is necessary for liturgical scholars and practitioners to attend to this *evolution of power*. This includes both the fluid adaptation of power in our society and our evolving understandings of how this power is at play in our ecclesial contexts and liturgical practices. This is necessary as we identify oppression and aim to resist it. These are not matters we can address once and for all; instead, work on worship and power is part of an ongoing struggle.

Free Church Traditions Meeting at the North American Academy of Liturgy

These essays emerge from the activities of the Free Church Traditions meeting at the annual meeting of the NAAL. Emerging as part of the liturgical renewal efforts ensuing from the Second Vatican Council, the academy has

28. Hamer, "Until I Am Free."

expanded in denominational and religious diversity since the mid-twentieth century. The launch of the Free Church traditions meeting in 2017 is just one manifestation of this trajectory of increasing diversity, reflecting the increasing participation of Free Church liturgical scholars representing an expanding number of traditions. Initially launched as the Baptist premeeting, the group was refocused in 2018 as the Free Church traditions meeting in order to make space for scholars from a number of underrepresented denominations. At the 2019 meeting, we intentionally selected the topic of liturgical authority for further discussion, and this culminated in a decision to develop the conversation more fully by sharing papers on the topic at our 2020 meeting. This work continued at the 2021 annual meeting with the remaining papers being presented for review and discussion. As such, this work represents the efforts of an increasing array of Free Church scholars involved in the North American Academy of Liturgy to contribute to ecumenical discourse on liturgy while attending to Free Church particularity.

Gratitude

Finally, a word of thanks to the editorial and production team at Cascade who have diligently shepherded this volume toward publication. The support of the Calvin Institute of Christian Worship, especially Noel Snyder, John Witvliet, and Maria Cornou as editors of the Worship and Witness series, has been invaluable. Lisa Weaver and John Witvliet generously authored a foreword and afterword, and we are grateful for their thoughtful framing of this work. Above all, we are grateful to our colleagues—both those who have contributed chapters to this volume and those whose contributions have remained less visible—in the Free Church Traditions meeting at the NAAL who laid the groundwork and shaped the development of this book over the past six years. Both the authors of chapters in this volume and the participants who reviewed and discussed these chapters have contributed immensely to this conversation about liturgical authority and will carry it forward in their own work and worship.

Bibliography

Bell, Catherine. *Ritual Theory, Ritual Practice.* Oxford: Oxford University Press, 1992.
Chan, Simon. *Liturgical Theology: The Church as Worshiping Community.* Westmont, IL: IVP Academic, 2006.

Chaves, Mark, and Shawna L. Anderson. "Changing American Congregations: Findings from the Third Wave of the National Congregations Study." *Journal for the Scientific Study of Religion* 53.4 (2014) 676–86.

Ellis, Christopher. *Gathering: A Spirituality and Theology of Worship in Free Church Tradition*. London: SCM, 2004.

Flanagan, Brian, and Johann Vento, eds. *Liturgy + Power*. College Theological Society 62. Maryknoll, NY: Orbis, 2017.

Foucault, Michel. *Discipline and Punish: The Birth of Prison*. New York: Vintage, 1995.

———. *Power/Knowledge: Selected Interviews and Other Writings, 1972–1977*. New York: Pantheon, 1980.

Hamer, Fannie Lou. "Until I Am Free, You Are Not Free Either." In *The Speeches of Fannie Lou Hamer: To Tell It Like It Is*, edited by Maegen Parker Brooks and Davis Houck, 121–30. Jackson: University Press of Mississippi, 2014.

Ingalls, Monique. *Singing the Congregation: How Contemporary Worship Music Forms Evangelical Community*. New York: Oxford University Press, 2018.

Johnson, Sarah Kathleen, and Anneli Loepp Thiessen. "Contemporary Worship Music as an Ecumenical Liturgical Movement." Worship, forthcoming.

Lim, Swee Hong, and Lester Ruth. *Lovin' on Jesus: A Concise History of Contemporary Worship*. Nashville: Abingdon, 2017.

Livingstone, Elizabeth, ed. *The Concise Oxford Dictionary of the Christian Church*. 3rd ed. New York: Oxford University Press, 2013.

Pew Research Center. "In U.S., Decline of Christianity Continues at Rapid Pace." October 17, 2019. https://www.pewforum.org/2019/10/17/in-u-s-decline-of-christianity-continues-at-rapid-pace/.

———. "Spirit and Power—A 10-Country Survey of Pentecostals." October 5, 2006. https://www.pewforum.org/2006/10/05/spirit-and-power/.

Roso, Joseph, et al. "Changing Worship Practices in American Congregations." *Journal for the Scientific Study of Religion* 59.4 (2020) 675–84.

Ross, Melanie. *Evangelical versus Liturgical?: Defying a Dichotomy*. Grand Rapids: Eerdmans, 2014.

Ruth, Lester, and Swee Hong Lim. *A History of Contemporary Praise & Worship: Understanding the Ideas That Reshaped the Protestant Church*. Grand Rapids: Baker Academic, 2021.

Sheer, Greg. *Essential Worship*. Grand Rapids: Baker, 2016.

Stevenson, Kenneth, ed. *Authority and Freedom in Liturgy: Patristic, Free Church, Pentecostal, Ecumenical*. Grove Liturgical Studies 17. Bramcote, UK: Grove, 1979.

Webber, Robert. *Worship Old and New*. Grand Rapids: Zondervan, 1994.

White, James. *Protestant Worship: Traditions in Transition*. Louisville: Westminster John Knox, 1989.

Witvliet, John. "On Three Meanings of the Term Worship." *Reformed Worship* 56 (June 2000) 46–47.

PART 1

Contesting Power in Society

1

The Power to Resist Empire

You Are What You Worship: Worship, Identity, Power, and Mission in the Book of Revelation

Ronald J. Allen

A POPULAR ADAGE HAS it, "You are what you eat," meaning that the kinds of food we eat play a significant role in the conditions of our bodies and minds. Eating nutritious food enhances our capacity for life, whereas eating foods with low nutritional value works against good health, and they diminish our capacity to live fully.

Similarly, "We are what we worship," meaning that we become like the God or gods whom we serve. As Alfred North Whitehead epigrammatically says, "The power of God is the worship [God] inspires."[1] Likewise the power of the gods is the worship they inspire. I think here of worship as both a broad recognition of the gods or God around whom we organize our lives as well as worship as specific liturgical enactments that represent and shape these recognitions as well as the values and practices associated with them.[2]

---

1. Whitehead, *Science and the Modern World*, 192.

2. The relationship between the gods/God and liturgy is reciprocal. Just as we shape our worlds to coincide with the nature and purposes of the gods or God, so we shape our visions of the gods and God in light of the values and practices of our worlds. James K. A. Smith deals with these and related issues in his Cultural Liturgies series. See: Smith, *Desiring the Kingdom*; Smith, *Imagining the Kingdom*; and Smith, *Awaiting the King*.

Liturgy in the Christian assembly empowers values and practices that shape our individual lives, households, and communities by legitimating and symbolizing such attitudes and behaviors in the name of the gods or God.

In a broad sense, politics has to do with activity intended to support the common good more than with partisan affiliation. In this broad sense, worship, both as life orientation and as liturgical action, is political in that it implies attitudes and actions that affect the common good. We choose what we worship and then live under its authority.[3] Sometimes we choose consciously and critically. Sometimes we choose consciously but on the basis of theological misperception. Sometimes we choose almost subconsciously. Sometimes it is imposed. As a result of such choices, we can worship God and live faithfully, or we can worship lesser deities and live lesser lives. Such choices are inevitably political in the broad sense. One of the church's important responsibilities in the early twenty-first century is to reflect critically on the degree to which its choices are appropriate or inappropriate, that is, the degree to which worship serves the purposes of God or the purposes of the god as life orientation, in the Christian assembly, and in everyday life actions.

The book of Revelation offers a model of how to do this very thing.[4] John, the writer, contrasts two patterns of worship and their consequences: (1) the worship of the living God, which reveals the true nature of present existence and offers the community the path to a new heaven and a new earth and (2) the worship of Satan (the dragon), embodied through the

---

3. In this essay I distinguish slightly between "authority" and "power." "Authority" refers to indicating what a community takes to be right. "Power" refers directly to the ability to cause things to happen. Authority establishes the nature and purposes for which power is used. In the Christian community, God is the ultimate authority and sets the purposes for which God and communities should use power. The empire system creates its own authorities in order to justify its uses of power to further its own self-serving, self-destructive ends.

4. In my approach to process theology, Scripture is a primary authority in the church but does not stand alone. In this theological configuration, authority derives from conversation and negotiation between Scripture and experience. Scripture suggests how the community might shape its experience, and the experience of the community suggests the degree to which the possibilities set out in Scripture seem to be trustworthy. In my view, experience across history verifies the trustworthiness of the attitudes towards the two empires set out in the book of Revelation. In short, trust in empires like Rome eventually leads to destruction, whereas trust in the values and practices of the Realm (Empire) of God leads to conditions moving in the direction of the new heaven and new earth of Revelation 21–22. I am aware of the dangers involved here, particularly of using experience to remake authority in the church in my own image, bypassing points at which Scripture could and should challenge experience. This is why interpretation should be critical and should take place in community. See Williamson and Allen, *Adventures of the Spirit*, 117–26.

Roman Empire (the beast), which deceives the community, invokes judgment, and ends in eternal punishment.

After background on John's theological and literary approaches, this chapter uses two key passages as lenses that bring the themes of worship and authority into focus: worship of the true and worthy God (Rev 4:1—5:14) and worship of the deceptive and unworthy Satan, represented by the beast and Roman civil religion (Rev 13:1–18). I include brief consideration of other passages in the book which resonate with these themes. Along the way I compare the two understandings of worship and their effects. The chapter concludes by reflecting on how this material can help the church reflect critically on worship today.

As a biblical scholar who has been involved in developing resources to support the worship of the Christian Church (Disciples of Christ), I seek to respect the otherness of the book of Revelation and other biblical texts while recognizing the difficulties of identifying and dealing critically with the biases that so easily come from my social location. Moreover, I benefit from my status in the empirelike conditions of North American culture even as I hope for transformation of these conditions in the direction of the values and practices of the Realm of God.[5]

A Little Background on John's Theological and Literary Approaches

The John associated with the book of Revelation was a prophet in the Jesus movement who prophesied in a circuit that included the seven churches of Revelation 2:1—3:22.[6] John does not claim to have written the book as a creative act but, like other prophets, claims to have received the book as a revelation from God, giving a theological interpretation of present circumstances and pointing toward future developments (Rev 1:1, 10).

---

5. I render the Greek *basileia* as "realm" rather than the older "kingdom." When referring to the Realm of God I capitalize the word. Throughout I provide inclusive alternatives to the male language of authority such as "lord," "king." The rationale is that the language we use evokes patterns of social relationship. For example, even when not intended, the use of "king" reinforces patriarchy. By contrast, inclusive language subtly suggests more inclusive and equitable social relationships and distribution of social power. See Williamson and Allen, *Adventures of the Spirit,* as well as the classic work by Watkins, *Faithful and Fair.*

6. I develop these historical and literary perspectives more fully in Allen, *I Will Tell You the Mystery,* esp. xix–xxxi. Exegeses of specific passages in the book of Revelation in this chapter rely on *I Will Tell You the Mystery* except as noted. On John as prophet, note especially Boring, *Revelation,* 29.

Like other apocalyptic theologians, John sees history divided into two great ages—the present broken era and a coming new world, sometimes known as the Realm of God, the new Jerusalem, or the new heaven and the new earth. In the prophetic eschatology of the Torah, Prophets, and Writings, the present world is significantly broken, but it can be repaired. In apocalyptic eschatology, the present world is so broken that it cannot be repaired. God must replace the current evil age with a world so transformed that the seer calls it "a new heaven and a new earth."

Satan, the archenemy of God, is presently seeking to claim the world for Satan's self-serving purposes. Satan operates by deception—offering people destructive things as if those things are promising. Satan (represented as a dragon) has given his power to the Roman Empire (the beast) (Rev 12:18; 13:2). The empire thus embodies the values and practices of Satan. Satan, through the empire, imitates God in many ways. The worship of the empire centers in idolatry not only of the Roman gods but increasingly of Caesar, whereas the worship of the churches is in dialogue with the one who created all things (e.g., Rev 4:11c).

According to the book of Revelation, God is already beginning the process of transformation in the present. The current era is a conflict zone between the domains of God and Satan. God is thereby already initiating the process of judgment that will result in the eternal punishment of Satan and the empire (Rev 20:7–14). John follows a contemporaneous Jewish theology of judgment that envisions people being punished by the very means by which they sin (e.g., Wis 11:15–20, esp. 16). The prophet sees condemnation beginning not by God coming in a singular way from the heavenly world but by idolatry, injustice, and violence inside the empire creating a self-destroying culture that leads to the violent destruction of the empire. John is clear: this outcome results from false worship (Rev 13:4, 8, 12, 15; 14:9, 11; 16:2; 19:20).

From John's point of view, God will guide history towards an apocalyptic cataclysm that will result in the destruction of the current world so that its evil impulses can never misshape life again. Beyond the apocalypse lies the new heaven and the new earth. Those who worship God need to endure the struggle of the period of transition. Those who do so will be part of the new world (e.g., Rev 7:15; 11:1; 14:7; 19:10; 22:3, 9). The apocalypse includes a cosmic battle eventuating in the eternal punishment of the dragon and the beast (e.g., Rev 1:7; 19:11–21; 20:1–14) and the realization of the new heaven and new earth (21:9—22:5).[7]

---

7. These things being said, we must also say that while the prophet believes in a future consummation, John does not posit a simple chronological timeline by which these things will take place. Biblical scholars vary widely in interpreting what might

Like other apocalyptic writers, John communicates much of his message in elaborate word pictures. While I do not want to press this idea too far, the visions function much like a code in which each element signals a meaning.[8] The elements spark listeners to recall associations from the Torah, Prophets, and Writings, or from the wider world of the first century. The first beast of Revelation 13:1–10, for example, is the Roman Empire. The second beast of Revelation 13:11–22 is Roman imperial worship.

While the book of Revelation puts forward a series of seven visions, the visions are not a wooden chronology of events moving from one to another. For John, the movement of history is more like a spiral in which similar things happen repeatedly, albeit each succeeding vision has a more intense level. John essentially says, "The things I am narrating in these visions are already happening, and they will continue to happen in more extreme ways until the present is destroyed and the new emerges." John does not set dates by which these things will happen but assures listeners that since God is behind these events, they can endure the increasing struggles of the present toward an end that will come at an indeterminate but assured time.

It is significant that John claims to have received the vision that is the book of Revelation "in the spirit on the Lord's Day," i.e., in worship (Rev 1:10). The first thing God gives John is a vision of the victorious, cosmic Christ who is ruler over all rulers (Rev 1:13–16). While the elements of the vision of Christ echo material in the first thirty-nine books, the elements are also reminiscent of Caesar. John's message is clear: Caesar, with his imperial dress and other pretensions, is a pretending imitator. In worship, the congregation should learn to recognize the Ruler of rulers and to distinguish this Ruler from imitators. The congregation should further receive the power of the victorious, conquering Christ who gives the people the power to stand together faithfully as a community of witness against imperial pretension and threat of violence.

Worship in Heaven: Revelation 4:1—5:14

In apocalyptic literature, events that take place in heaven often have effects on things which are happening, or will soon happen, on earth. The heavenly world is a kind of prototype of things as they are and as they will be. Listeners can count on the reality of what John describes in the vision.

---

or might not happen at the consummation. For an excellent table summarizing leading views, see Reddish, *Revelation*. Barbara Rossing offers a penetrating theological critique of popular premillennialism in Rossing, *Rapture Exposed*.

8. On "decoding Revelation," see Murphy, *Fallen Is Babylon*, 31–33.

These things are particularly true of Revelation 4:1—5:14. These chapters articulate a vision of worship taking place in heaven; the purpose of the vision is to assure John's congregations that they can count on the realities associated with worship in heaven even as the congregations continue to live and witness in the present. Moreover, as the congregations engage in worship in the present, they experience in miniature the realities depicted in the vision.

When the service of worship ends, the communities can count on the theological content represented in this vision as the authority for their life and witness. For the heavenly scene reveals to them who is in control of the universe and how to respond. John communicates this message by painting a word picture in which each element in the heavenly vision symbolizes particular theological associations. While not explicit, John implies a contrast between the throne room of heaven and the court of Caesar. For the sake of brevity, I focus on representative elements of the vision and their power to shape the listeners' perceptions and behavior in the present.

The throne, of course, is a traditional representation of the seat of power. Since this is the throne room of heaven, it is the seat of power for all things that exist. John does not describe the one who sits on the throne but compares this being to the luminescence of precious stones of jasper. The visual effect is dazzling and in stark contrast to the lifeless idols of the Romans as well as feeble Caesar sitting on his throne.

Twenty-four additional thrones surround the main throne; on these thrones sit twenty-four elders wearing white robes and crowns. The twenty-four represent the fullness of the community of God by recalling the twelve tribes of Israel and the twelve apostles. They sit on thrones and wear crowns, indicating that the people who represent God have real power; they can make things happen. The question is: How will they use their power? John poses an answer in Revelation 4:10: they cast their crowns before the one seated on the throne. That is, they use their power to serve the purposes of God. In summary, those purposes are to end the exploitive practices of the old age and to reestablish human community on the model of the new heaven and the new earth. To worship is to join these elders in using one's power for the new heaven and the new earth.

A "sea of glass, like crystal" lies before the throne. In the Bible the sea often represents chaos (e.g., Gen 1:1-2). According to one tradition, God must defeat chaos to establish the world (e.g., Job 9:8; Ps 74:13-17; 89:9-12). For the revelator, the process of the destruction of the old and the birth of the new is a struggle fraught with suffering (like God's defeat of chaos), but the congregations can endure the struggle because in worship they see that beyond the struggle lies a world "like crystal."

Four living creatures (lion, ox, human being, bird) surround the throne and sing of God as holy. To be holy is to be set apart. While the holiness of God has multiple dimensions, in the book of Revelation the accent is on power. God's power is set apart from other powers because it is not derived, and because God uses it to establish and reestablish authentic community. As the title "Lord God *Almighty*" indicates, God's power supersedes all other powers.

The creatures in Revelation 4:8 echo 1:8: God "was and is and is to come." In Greek and Roman circles, such affirmations typically took forms closer to "who was, and is, and ever shall be," in which the emphasis is on the continuing existence of the deities in a static way. Such deities preserve the status quo. By contrast, God has come and is still coming, entering into the world to reconstruct it.

The first part of the vision climaxes with the hymn of verse 11, which declares that God has created all things. There are four elements here. The first is that God is creator, not the Roman gods, and certainly not Caesar. The second is that God as creator intends for the world to be a community of mutual support in which all things work together in the manner depicted in Genesis 1. The qualities of life in the old age undermine that purpose. The third is that since God is creator, God has authority over all things. God has decided to replace the old world with the new. Because God has the authority for such a transformation, the fourth implication is that the worshiping community can trust that it will happen. They can continue to trust even when they encounter resistance and experience the pain of the transformation.

In the second part of the heavenly scene, the focus shifts. The one seated on the throne holds a sealed scroll. The scroll reveals the meaning of what is happening in the present and points toward the great transformation. Initially, no one is worthy to open it until one of the elders spies the Lion of the tribe of Judah, one who has conquered and is therefore able to open the scroll. The Lion, of course, is so powerful that he has conquered. This sounds like the Lion has simply overpowered the enemies, but listeners soon discover that "conquering" in the book of Revelation refers in the first instance to continuing to make a faithful witness even in the face of opposition.

The revelator then sees "a Lamb standing as if it had been slaughtered" (Rev 5:6). Christians often immediately interpret the Lamb in terms of atonement theology in which the slaughter (death) of the Lamb makes atonement for sin or brings about reconciliation between God and humankind. However, the book of Revelation never implies that the death of the Lamb affects the relationship between humankind and God. Rather, the Roman Empire slaughters the Lamb thinking the empire can thereby end the threat posed by the Lamb to the continuing rule of the empire. The Lamb's death is that of a martyr. John uses the figure of the slaughtered Lamb in the mode of pastoral counsel: worshipers need to know that if they follow Jesus on the journey to the Realm, they will encounter opposition similar to the hostility the Lamb faced. However, resurrection lies beyond.

The Lamb is standing (Rev 5:6). Moreover, the Lamb has seven horns. The horns represent power (cf. Dan 7:8, 20, 24). The awesome power of God is at work in all phases of the ministry of the Lamb. The empire exercised its maximum power when it put the Lamb to death. But the authority of God proved stronger when God raised the Lamb from the dead. Those who follow the Lamb can expect the same (e.g., Rev 7:9–17).[9]

With respect to worship and authority, John's message is plain. God is the fundamental authority of the universe. Those who worship God agree to order their lives under the aegis of this authority. Moreover, God gives them the authority to interpret what is going on in the world and to witness to God's purposes in the present and the future. The authority of God empowers the witnessing community to remain faithful even when opposition does its worst.

Subsequent passages that deal with worship reinforce these motifs. We can mention only representative texts. In Revelation 7:9–14, a great multitude surrounds the throne, waving palm branches, and singing. The make-up of the faithful multitude is a model of inclusivity: "no one could count, from every nation, from all tribes and peoples and languages." However, as we learn from 13:16, the simple fact of diversity does not guarantee its authenticity. The community that follows Satan by participating in the Roman Empire is equally diverse. Diversity must serve the purposes of authentic, mutually supportive community of the kind envisioned in the new heaven and the new earth.

Worshipers have "come out of the great ordeal," that is, they have survived the conflict between God and the empire because they ordered their lives around the values and practices of God. The seer's message is that the worshiping community on the earth that remains faithful can join this multidimensional worship in heaven.

Revelation 11:15–19 contains the famous text, "The [realm] of the world has become the [realm] of our [God] and of [the Messiah]" (Rev 11:15a). God has taken "great power and begun to reign" (Rev 11:16). While God has begun to reign, God has yet to bring the fullness of that reign to

9. Interpreters often discuss the nature and exercise of divine power in the book of Revelation. For particularly insightful treatment, see Farmer, *Revelation*, 65–70.

expression. The worship of the church is a protoeschatological experience of the coming world. Worshiping thus adds to the experiential authority by which the community can endure the intensifying struggle between God and Satan.

According to Revelation 20:4–6, God will bring to life those who were martyred because they do not worship the beast or receive the mark of the beast.

In Revelation 21:9—22:5, John uses the imagery of a city to climax the book of Revelation. As we point out more fully below, the images in these verses symbolize the qualities of life in the new world. The characteristics of mutually supportive life in the new Jerusalem are opposite the exploitative and violent conditions of life in Rome.

While the complete and final manifestation of the new heaven and new earth is the future, the vision of Revelation 21:9—22:5 suggests qualities of life for communities in the present. The vision urges listeners to end the book thinking, "I want to be part of the new heaven and the new earth."

Worship in the Roman Empire: Revelation 12:18—13:18

Revelation 12:18—13:18 falls into two scenes that reveal both the nature of the Roman Empire (Rev 12:18—13:10) and how Roman imperial religion supported the empire by facilitating worship (Rev 13:11–18). The state and its values co-opted religion so that the imperial cult served the state.[10] Roman imperial religion is a classic case of a community creating gods in its own image.

Revelation 12:58—13:2 explicitly interprets the relationship between Satan and the empire. John represents Satan as a dragon. The revelator sees a beast rise out of the sea. The beast represents the Roman Empire. In Revelation 13:2b, the dragon infuses the beast with the dragon's power and gives the beast the dragon's authority and throne. Those who worship the beast (and, hence, worship the dragon) place themselves in the sphere of the authority of the beast and the dragon. Per our remarks on 4:6, the sea calls to mind chaos and thus associates the work of Satan with creating chaos and suggests that the beast is itself a social-political instrument of chaos. To the degree that a people become like the gods they worship, those who worship the beast create a culture of chaos.

The beast is the Roman Empire. The ten horns represent rulers who oppose God (Dan 7:7, 24). The seven horns are reminiscent of the seven

10. Brian K. Blount offers a lucid discussion of imperial worship in Blount, *Revelation*, 8–14.

hills of the city Rome. John amplifies the savagery of the beast by describing the beast in parts from the leopard, the bear, and the lion (Rev 13:2).

The prophet alludes to a Roman myth when describing one of the heads receiving a deathblow which was healed (Rev 13:3). According to a popular story in John's time, Nero had killed himself but came back from the dead. Nero was, in other words, resurrected. John is hyperbolic in saying "the whole earth followed the beast," though many people worship the dragon and the beast, believing that no one could fight against the beast. (13:4–5). With respect to both raising someone from the dead and inspiring worship, Satan imitates God to deceive people into living in an old-age mentality.

Revelation 13:5–8 reveals the character and purpose of the beast acting as agent of Satan. The beast blasphemes the name and dwelling of God which John relates "to those who dwell in heaven," that is, to the communities of the faithful. Moreover, the beast makes war on the saints (the faithful), thereby seeking to eradicate the community that witnesses to the presence and coming of the new heaven and new earth.

Revelation 13:8 reveals yet another point at which Satan and the beast imitate God. The group that worships the beast is comprised of people from "every tribe and people and language and nation." Indeed, in another burst of hyperbole, John claims, "All the inhabitants of the earth" worship the beast. By worshipping the beast, inhabitants of the earth invite upon themselves a share in the final condemnation of the beast. We are what we worship.

In Revelation 13:11–18, the seer reveals a second beast: Roman imperial religion. The seer later calls this beast "the false prophet," but it is a community of false religious practice and not simply a misguided individual (Rev 16:13; 19:20; 20:10). The Romans regarded the empire as a creation of the gods. While impulses toward declaring Caesar as divine had risen and fallen in the empire, by the time of John many people accorded divine honors to Domitian, who ruled from 81 to 96 CE. This is a form of superidolatry since the idol is no mere image but is a living entity (Caesar) through whom the power of Satan works.

John underlines the symbiotic relationship of the empire and the imperial cult by referring to the cult as "another beast." Through word pictures, John calls further attention to the motif of deception as practiced by the false prophet. It looks like a lamb (Rev 13:11; cf. Rev 5:6–10) but it speaks with the voice of the dragon, that is, its religious work serves Satan. Both the empire and its civil religion are beastly.

The purpose of the second beast is to provide the means whereby "the earth and its inhabitants worship the first beast," that is, it provides a religious rationale for people ordering their lives according to the values, expectations, and practices of the empire (13:12). Religion, then, which is supposed to empower community for the good of all, becomes a means for justifying the destruction of real community so that a few can benefit at the expense of the many.

The imperial cultic religion has real power, again in the mode of deceiving. Not only does the second beast exercise "all the authority of the first beast" but it performs "great signs." These include miracles such as Elijah making fire come down from heaven and "giving breath to the image of the beast so that the image of the beast could even speak" (Rev 13:14–15). But, the purpose of this resurrection is so that the voice "would cause those who would not worship the image of the beast to be killed" (Rev 13:15b). God raised Jesus to give life. Satan raised Caesar to destroy and kill.

The prophet then mentions that all who worship the dragon will be marked "on the right hand or on the forehead" (Rev 13:16). This mark will be "the name of the beast or the number of its name," the famous number "six hundred sixty-six." Ancient languages did not have numerals, so they assigned numerical values to letters of the alphabet. In Hebrew, the numerical values assigned to the letters for "Nero Caesar" total 666.

The Roman Empire has left no record of a physical mark applied to those who participated in the imperial cult, but we get a clue to the nature and function of this mark by recollecting that elsewhere John refers to the faithful community moving towards the new Jerusalem while bearing its own mark (3:12; 14:1; 22:24). The mark of the beast and the mark of God are invisible. The "mark" is the characteristic values and practices of the deity who inscribes the mark. Those marked by God live according to the Realm, whereas those marked by the second beast live in the ways of the empire.

Just as the mark of God creates a multicultural community, so does the mark of the beast as it involves all, "both small and great, both rich and poor, both slave and free" (Rev 13:16). Diversity is not an end in and of itself. A diverse community can serve the purposes of God or of Satan.

The consequence of false worship is condemnation. "Those who worship the beast and its image and receive a mark on their foreheads or on their hands, they will also drink the wine of God's wrath, poured unmixed into the cup of [God's] anger, and they will be tormented with fire and sulfur" (Rev 14:10).[11] John has in mind more than the punishment of individuals in the afterworld. As Revelation 18:1–24 makes clear, the Roman Empire is

---

11. For direct connection between worship of the beast and punishment, cf. Revelation 16:2 and 19:20.

condemned as an empire. Judgment has social consequences as it includes the collapse of the empire.

This judgment has both present and future dimensions. The processes of judgment are already underway through the continuing false worship and exploitative and unjust ways of life in the empire. As we noted earlier, a strain of Judaism holds that "one is punished by the very things by which one sins" (Wis 11:16). John explicitly endorses this point of view in Revelation 13:9, "If you kill with the sword, with the sword you must be killed." From this point of view, Caesar's practices of violence within the empire and with other nations set in motion patterns of violence that will result in violence destroying the empire. John goes as far as to imagine that war with the Parthians may be a part of this scenario (Rev 6:2; 9:17–19; 16:12). In the present stage of judgment, God does not intervene from outside of history but allows historical processes themselves to be the means whereby judgment occurs.

Additionally, of course, John imagines God acting directly against the beast (Rome), the false prophet (Roman civil religion), and the dragon. At the conclusion of the destruction of the Roman Empire, God casts the beast and the false prophet into "the lake of fire," the final and ultimate punishment (Rev 19:20). An angel binds the dragon and throws the dragon into a pit for a thousand years (the infamous millennium) (Rev 20:1–3) after which Satan makes one final attempt to deceive the world whereupon God casts the devil into the lake of fire and sulfur where the dragon joins the beast and the false prophet in eternal torment (Rev 20:7–10).

A Lens for Thinking Critically about Worship in Church and World Today

Some Christians today, especially progressives, have significant theological differences with John. For reasons that I have articulated elsewhere, as a process theologian I join these Christians in being troubled by John's apocalyptic worldview and by the idea of everlasting punishment.[12] Nevertheless, John's perspective on worship and its consequences can be a revealing lens through which to think critically about the authority of worship and its outcomes today.[13]

---

12. Allen, *I Will Tell You the Mystery*, xxxi–xxxiv. Cf. Williamson and Allen, *Adventures of the Spirit*.

13. For a thoughtful perspective on worship today in dialogue with the book of Revelation, see Reddish, *Revelation*, 102–5.

Worship leaders continue to struggle with important matters. For example, to what degree should worship balance tradition and innovation, structure and flexibility, or the global and the local? What are the gains and losses of using a lectionary as a basis for tracing the seasons and days of the Christian year and for preaching? How often and in what manner does a congregation partake of the loaf and the cup or celebrate baptism?

Such questions are important, and churches should respond to them from a theological perspective, considering cultural context. Our choices regarding such matters play a role in how congregations are formed theologically. Form and content are always related.

However, the lens that John offers has to do less with matters of form and more with the core purpose of worship. We can look at any form of worship through the question of whether it focuses on the purposes of God or the purposes of lesser deities.

In the book of Revelation, God's fundamental intent is to bring about the qualities of life evoked in the vision of the new heaven and the new earth (Rev 21:9—22:5). As we noted earlier, while the new Jerusalem can fully come about only after the apocalypse, the vision of the city contains elements that point to characteristics of community that God would have now. Keeping the dangers of anachronism in mind, I lift several images that evoke the broad lines of the new community. The high wall represents lasting security (Rev 21:12). The wall is a symbol of safety through community as we can see in its height—144 cubits (Rev 21:17). Twelve is a number representing community; in antiquity to square a number (twelve times twelve) was to intensify the idea that this community is truly a safe place. The wall has three gates on each side, and the gates are always open (Rev 21:13, 25) as if to indicate that real security, real community, comes not from keeping people out but by inviting them in.

God creates the community so the light of the city can illumine the path to blessing for the nations, that is, gentiles (Rev 21:24). Indeed, many in the nations will find its vision so compelling they will repent and will bring their glory and honor to the new heaven and the new earth (Rev 21:26). The river of the water of life, that is, the power of life itself, flows through the community, signaling that the purpose of the community is itself to be life-giving (Rev 22:1). The presence of the tree producing twelve kinds of fruit, one kind each month, redoubles this theme (Rev 22:2). "Fruit" is a traditional Jewish symbol for qualities of life with emphasis on ethics, that is, living for the benefit of the community.

The leaves of the tree are for the healing of the nations (Rev 22:2). Drawing on the idea that people in the ancient world often made medicine by grinding up leaves, John sees the way of life epitomized by the vision of the new heaven and the new earth as medicine for the idolatry, exploitation, and violence of the nations.

When John says, "Nothing accursed will be found any more" (Rev 22:3), the prophet means that the repressive curses of Genesis 3:14–19 will no longer regulate relationships in the world; these curses include such things as the rule of the husband over the spouse (Gen 3:16), enmity between humankind and nature (Gen 3:17–18), and death (Gen 3:19).

We can distill the function of this vision as a criterion for evaluating worship into a single sentence: Worship is faithful when it lifts up the values and practices that lead to mutually supportive community as the purposes of God for the church and, indeed, for all communities. God is the authority behind this criterion. Individuals and communities who worship God in settings animated by these values and practices should manifest the values and practices in their everyday worlds. Worship is trustworthy when it displays the qualities of life in the new heaven and new earth.

Churches across the ecclesial spectrum, from the Orthodox to the Pentecostal, can worship in ways that promote the attitudes and actions of the Realm. Other religions, such as Judaism and Islam, for instance, share many core values with Christian tradition and can join with Christianity in encouraging characteristics of life that Christians associate with the Realm. Communities beyond the immediate pale of religion can also set out visions for reality that are similar to the attitudes and actions that Christians associate with the Realm of God. For instance, peace movements or groups promoting human welfare who articulate their purposes without any religious reference may nevertheless point to qualities of life reminiscent of the Realm.

By contrast, worship is unfaithful and undermines God's purposes when it functions like Roman imperial religion by serving the purposes of the beast and thereby serving the purposes of the dragon. The religion of the empire operates by deception: it offers the community a limited, self-serving vision of life, as if that vision is transcendent, good, and faithful. As we have noted further, the imperial cult imitates the ways of God. Roman civil religion made its gods into the self-serving image of the beast and used the deity to support the status quo of the old age. These attitudes and corresponding social behaviors, as we have noted, include exploitation, exclusivity, rigid social hierarchy, and other things to limit the possibilities of the many so the few can continue in power and luxury. The religion of the beast relies upon violence to maintain power both inside the empire and in the empire's relationships with other nations.

As in the case of the vision of the new heaven and the new earth, we can distill the function of John's presentation of the worship of the beast and the dragon as a criterion for evaluating worship into a single sentence: Worship is unfaithful when it lifts the values and practices that lead to idolatry, self-serving uses of power, and violence as the purposes of the god(s) for social groups, including churches. Religious groups (and others) who worship the god(s) in settings animated by these old-age values and practices manifest and promote those attitudes and actions in their everyday worlds. Worship in this mode reinforces the inequities, prejudices, exploitation, and acceptance of violence found in empire and beyond. Worship is deceptive when it works against authentic community.

Any community can potentially fall for the deception put forward by the beasts and dragon who inhabit individuals and systems in the contemporary world. Churches can promote worship in this vein when they are co-opted to serve the interests of particular groups to the exclusion of others. For example, churches can serve political ideologies, racial and ethnic groups, or particular sexual orientations. Other religions can fall into this trap, and groups beyond the immediate pale of religion can also do so. Such groups develop self-authorizing perspectives to maintain these things.

Of course, given the fact of human finitude, few communities can be altogether faithful in worship. Even individuals and churches who earnestly desire to be trustworthy witnesses can be deceived from time to time. Moreover, from time to time even individuals and communities who have the mark of the beast and worship its image can serve some of the purposes of the new heaven and new earth.

Given such ambiguity, an important work for the church is to think critically about its worship, seeking to optimize manifestation of the true worship that points to the new heaven and the new earth and to minimize worship that serves the beast and authorizes attitudes and behavior that lead to collapse. If we are what we worship, then we want to worship as fully as possible in cooperation with the new heaven and the new earth.

Bibliography

Allen, Ronald J. *I Will Tell You the Mystery: A Commentary for Preaching from the Book of Revelation.* Eugene, OR: Cascade, 2019.

Andrews, Dale, et al. *Preaching God's Transforming Justice: A Lectionary Commentary Featuring 22 New Holy Days for Justice.* Louisville: Westminster John Knox, Year A, 2013; Year B, 2011; Year C, 2012.

Beale, G. K. *The Book of Revelation.* The New International Greek Testament Commentary. Grand Rapids: Eerdmans, 1999.

Blount, Brian K. *Revelation: A Commentary.* New Testament Library. Louisville: Westminster John Knox, 2009.

Boring, M. Eugene. *Revelation: A Bible Commentary for Teaching and Preaching.* Interpretation. Louisville: Westminster John Knox, 1989.

Farmer, Ronald L. *Revelation.* Chalice Commentaries for Today. St. Louis: Chalice, 2005.

Murphy, Frederick J. *Fallen Is Babylon: The Revelation to John.* The New Testament in Context. Harrisburg, PA: Trinity International, 1998.

Reddish, Mitchell G. *Revelation.* Smith & Helwys Bible Commentary. Macon, GA: Smith & Helwys, 2001.

Rossing, Barbara. *The Rapture Exposed: The Message of Hope in the Book of Revelation.* New York: Basic, 2004.

Smith, James K. A. *Awaiting the King: Reforming Public Theology.* Cultural Liturgies 3. Grand Rapids: Baker Academic, 2017.

———. *Desiring the Kingdom: Worship, Worldview, and Cultural Formation.* Cultural Liturgies 1. Grand Rapids: Baker Academic, 2009.

———. *Imagining the Kingdom: How Worship Works.* Cultural Liturgies 2. Grand Rapids: Baker Academic, 2013.

Watkins, Keith. *Faithful and Fair: Transcending Sexist Language in Worship.* Nashville: Abingdon, 1981.

———, ed. *Thankful Praise: A Resource for Christian Worship.* St. Louis: Chalice, 1987.

Whitehead, Alfred North. *Science and the Modern World.* New York: The New American Library, 1948.

Williamson, Clark M., and Ronald J. Allen. *Adventures of the Spirit: A Guide to Worship from the Perspective of Process Theology.* Lanham, MD: University Press of America, 1997.

2

The Power to Reimagine Society

"Liturgical Anarchy": A Liturgipolitic of Differently Ordered Liturgy Ordering the World Differently

Andrew Wymer

IN THE LATE NINETEENTH century, as revolutionary anarchist movements rose to popular awareness across Europe, the term "liturgical anarchy" began to appear in liturgical discourse as a rhetorical protest of decentralized liturgical authority in the church, and declarations of "liturgical anarchy" continued to be deployed in the twentieth century by liturgical scholars in contestation of the decentralization of liturgical authority.[1] In this essay, I will analyze rhetoric of "liturgical anarchy," arguing that: 1) the term frames liturgical authority within the conceptual boundaries of contemporary contestations of the centralized political and cultural authority of the nation-state, briefly defined as a structure of governance joining together power and cultural identity; 2) as the term is brought into conversation with anarchist political theory, it can be used to describe the radical polity and varied

1. As will be stated later in the essay, common themes within anarchist movements and thought are: 1) an emphasis upon individual worth and self-determination; 2) the rejection of the imposition of the remote, centralized political authority of the nation-state, and 3) the formation of decentralized political authority that is negotiated regionally and as free from coercion as possible, i.e., as close to voluntary as possible.

41

antistate commitments of dissenting Baptists' commitment to severely decentralized and autonomous liturgical authority; and 3) to the degree that dissenting Baptist worship parallels anarchist political structures, dissenting Baptist worship and its vision of decentralized and autonomous liturgical authority has the potential to function as a resource for the contestation of the centralized, brutally violent power of the nation-state here in the United States of America and more broadly in Western society.

In order to effectively support these arguments, I will begin by surveying late-nineteenth and twentieth-century liturgical and sacramental discourse on the negotiation of liturgical authority in which scholars utilize the term "liturgical anarchy," drawing a connection between this discourse and the corresponding emergence of anarchist movements and anarchist thought. I will then survey Baptist approaches to the negotiation of liturgical authority, utilizing historical, theological, and liturgical sources. I will argue that dissenting Baptist understandings of liturgical authority have anarchist parallels, and that deeply embedded within dissenting Baptist polity is a heightened suspicion of the nation-state and a potential to undermine its power. Finally, I will further engage anarchist and Baptist sources as I reflect on Baptist worship as a liturgipolitical resource for continued efforts to resist the settler colonial, heteropatriarchal, white supremacist violence of the nation-state of the USA.

This essay approaches "liturgical authority" in an inductive manner that avoids a formal, deductive definition. However, in surveying sources that engage liturgical authority, glimpses will emerge of it as the ambiguous and always contested power to establish and enforce rubrics regarding the leadership, order, content, or practices of Christian worship. A key term in this definition and in relationship to the broader collection is "power." I primarily approach "power" through the lens of practice theory in which power is simultaneously and continually enacted and contested amidst the celebration of human practices—for the sake of this essay, Christian liturgy.[2] Building upon this initial approach, I will attend to "power" with care for anarchist critiques of it as a coercive force structurally deployed as a means of control, but I will also constructively engage the possibility of alternative structures of power—specifically a liturgipolitic—to serve as a resource for imagining, contesting, and restructuring civic and ecclesial configurations.

2. See Bell, *Ritual*, 76–80.

"Liturgical Anarchy"

Deployment of the term "liturgical anarchy" in liturgical discourse emerges in the late-nineteenth century, which chronologically parallels the emergence and increasing notoriety of formal European anarchist movements rejecting, among other issues, the political, social, and economic violence of Western liberalism. In light of this, calls of "liturgical anarchy" must be located in the context of the sociocultural utilization of that term in relationship to anarchist political movements and ideas.

The use of "liturgical anarchy" by liturgical scholars and practitioners to address concerns about the negotiation and implementation of liturgical authority is notable for several reasons. 1) These uses uniformly assume a pejorative interpretation of "anarchy" within the broader sociocultural utilization of that term in relationship to anarchist political movements and ideas. 2) These uses ultimately serve to reinforce the validity and necessity of some degree of centralized liturgical authority, and both of these characteristics parallel the secular priorities and centralized political authority of contemporary nation-states. This suggests that the centralized power of the Western nation-state has interacted with Christian formulations of the validity and necessity of centralized liturgical authority. As such, it is crucial to frame protests of "liturgical anarchy" within the context of broader anarchist movements, the violent interests of nation-states and consequently state churches—or churches historically shaped by associations with nation-states in the past—in quelling such movements, and the longstanding, strategic misconstrual of anarchistic politics as movements promoting dystopian chaos.

Anarchist movements' rejection of hierarchy and centralized power has rendered them diverse, fluid, and ambiguous; however, common themes in self-identifying anarchist thought are: 1) an emphasis upon individual worth and self-determination; 2) the rejection of the imposition of the remote, centralized political authority of the nation-state, and 3) the formation of decentralized political authority that is negotiated regionally and as free from coercion as possible, i.e., as close to voluntary as possible. The association of anarchist movements with an agenda of stateless dystopian chaos is a mischaracterization functioning to constrict the political imagination of society in a way that reinforces the necessity of the nation-state. The nineteenth-century anarchist slogan, "Anarchy is order; government is civil war," encapsulates this contrast.[3] Anarchy is an attempt to find alternative ways of

3. The source of this phrase is contested, with some authors attributing it to Pierre-Joseph Proudhon, (e.g. Kinna, *Anarchism*, 5). However, the earliest document I have found containing this slogan is by Anselme Bellegarrigue. In 1850, he wrote, "Oui,

negotiating power in society that are voluntary, regionally particular, and as free as possible from domination and its corresponding violence.

Anglican Discourse on Nineteenth-Century Liturgical Reforms

An early utilization of the term "liturgical anarchy" in the context of the Church of England is recorded in J. Wickham Legg's *Some Principles and Services of the Prayer-book Historically Considered.*[4] Upset by the consequences of the Act of Uniformity Amendment Act of 1872, Legg critiques what he understands to be the weakness of its liturgical restrictions that allow for "liturgical anarchy."[5] He writes, "There is no permission given by the Act to mutilate the Divine Service on Sundays. It is habitually done. There is no permission given in the Act to mutilate the Order for the Administration of the Lord's Supper. It is habitually done."[6] He goes on to decry other local revisions to the liturgy, rather dramatically proclaiming that the removal of an exhortation at the beginning of the marriage service, "can only be a prelude to the discarding of those solemn words introduced into the Marriage Service at the Reformation: 'Those whom God hath joined together let no man [sic] put asunder.'"[7] The widespread practice of local adaptation is particularly troubling to Legg, and he critiques the newfound liturgical flexibility and local liberty taken by clergy under the act.

David Edwards, in *Leaders of the Church of England, 1828–1978,* observes of the mid-nineteenth century that the archaic liturgical rules of the Church of England forced each bishop "to act as the legal authority in his diocese, with the archbishop of Canterbury playing an appellate role."[8] Edwards negatively characterizes this and other developments, writing, "The later developments of the Oxford Movement had plunged the Church of England into a condition approaching liturgical anarchy."[9] His critique

---

l'anarchie c'est l'ordre; car, le gouvernement c'est la guerre civile" (See Bellegarrigue, "L'Anarchie, c'est l'orde," para. 12).

4. Legg. *Some Principles.*

5. The Act of Uniformity Amendment Act of 1872 made amendments to the Act of Uniformity of 1662. It was also called the Shortened Services Act, because it allowed for some degree of variation from the original Act of 1662. The Act of Uniformity of 1662 impacted Dissenter and Separatist movements by strictly enforcing use of the *Book of Common Prayer* and removing anyone from office who refused to do so.

6. Legg, *Some Principles,* 131.

7. Legg, *Some Principles,* 131.

8. Edwards, *Leaders,* 360.

9. Edwards, *Leaders,* 360.

primarily utilizes this term in reference to a decentralization of liturgical authority to the diocesan level.

Legg and Edwards's perspectives on "liturgical anarchy" reflect the disruption of centralized liturgical authority within the context of the historical role of the nation-state in governing the liturgy of the Church of England. This is particularly evident in Legg's writing. His work is intriguing in that he both critiques the parliamentary Act of 1872 for seemingly unintentionally allowing "anarchy" and also defends the Act of 1872 against what he perceives to be its local subversion in liturgical adaptations. Issues of the liturgical authority of the church as well as the authority of the nation-state are at stake in Legg's writing. He is more or less arguing that liturgical authority and parliamentary authority are being subverted by what could, in his own terminology, be called "liturgical anarchists." In the setting of an established church, with a centralized approach to liturgical authority that mimics and ultimately is controlled by the centralized authority of the nation-state, liturgical authority and the authority of the nation-state are necessarily intertwined. The shifts in the maintenance of a centralized liturgical authority critiqued by Legg were perceived to have direct implications on the vitality of the centralized authority of the nation-state.

Roman Catholic Twentieth-Century Discourse on Liturgical Reforms

Anglicans have not been alone in the utilization of this term. In "The Genius of the Roman Rite," a paper presented in 1899 and later published in *Liturgica Historica: Papers on the Liturgy and Religious Life of the Western Church*, Edmund Bishop deploys the term "liturgical anarchy" to describe what he understands to be the state of the liturgy before the consolidation of the Carolingian Empire when Charlemagne ascended the Frankish throne in AD 769.[10] According to Bishop, the Roman rite had been "enriched . . . according to individual fancy and discretion."[11] He argues that Charlemagne brought an end to this state of liturgical anarchy by introduction of the Gregorianum to which local and diocesan liturgical authorities were expected to conform. The cessation of "liturgical anarchy" described by Bishop is ultimately brought about by the consolidation of liturgical authority that directly parallels the consolidation of the Carolingian Empire. Bishop's usage of "liturgical anarchy" describes a state of chaos during the consolidation

10. Bishop, *Liturgica Historica*, 1–19.
11. Bishop, *Liturgica Historica*, 3.

of the Carolingian Empire due to a lack of centralized liturgical authority imposing liturgical conformity.

Anscar Chupungco critiques and reframes this term's use in discourse on the state of liturgy prior to the consolidation of the Carolingian Empire. While not engaging Bishop directly, Chupungco critiques the usage of this term in the mid-twentieth-century scholarship on the imposition of the Roman rite during and after the rule of Pepin III (751–68) of Cyrille Vogel.[12] In *Handbook for Liturgical Studies: Introduction to the Liturgy*, Chupungco notes the usage of "liturgical anarchy," and he describes it as "quite improperly described."[13] He disagreed with the insinuation of "liturgical chaos," i.e., a complete lack of liturgical authority.

Instead, Chupungco argues that liturgical practice was diverse, because, even more than today's Roman Catholic Church, liturgical authority was then dispersed under the diocesan control of local bishops who in turn shaped their worship in the particularity of their contexts. For Chupungco, this is not an issue of "anarchy" or a breakdown of liturgical authority but one of differently ordered liturgical authority, which allowed for a degree of inculturation particular to various regions. His response reveals the bias of the political imaginations of historians and liturgical scholars such as Bishop.

Chupungco's critique and reframing parallels a longstanding challenge faced by anarchist political groups in achieving widespread awareness and possible acceptance of anarchist politics. Anarchists have not been able to move past the negative definition of "anarchy" to argue for a different ordering of society that is not intended to entail chaos. The potential negative interpretation of "anarchy" as it relates to anarchist movements has been exploited by agents and institutions supporting the power of the state in order to caricaturize anarchisms as chaos movements threatening a dystopian future to which the only antidote is the centralized power of the state.[14]

"Liturgical anarchy" has also appeared in resistance to mid-twentieth-century Roman Catholic liturgical reforms. It was utilized by Higini Anglés in his resistance to the Second Vatican Council and the accompanying

---

12. I have not been able to procure Vogel's essay from which Chupungco cites in order to determine whether or not Vogel utilizes Bishop as a source. I cannot ascertain if Vogel recognizes the term as emerging in Bishop's work or if he utilizes it as what may have become a common term within liturgical discourse on Carolingian liturgical development.

13. In Chupungco, *Handbook for Liturgical Studies*, 142, Chupungco cites from Vogel, "Les motifs de la romanization," 17–20, and Pinell, "La Liturgia gallicana," 62–67.

14. "Anarchisms" is commonly utilized to reference the broad array of local and unique manifestations of anarchist thought and struggle in the past and present.

liturgical renewal movement. He called for adherence to the musical and liturgical standards of the Council of Trent, writing, "*Existit hodie vera anarchia sive in campo liturgico sive in regione musicali.*"[15] Anthony Ruff translates this as, "There exists today true anarchy in the liturgical field and in the musical area. Under the pretext of serving pastoral liturgy, the Roman liturgy is disparaged, along with the Latin language and sacred music endowed with true art."[16] In another article, "*Das Kommende okumenische konzil und die kirchenmusic,*" he writes of a "*anarchistischer Zustand*" or a "state of anarchy."[17] Anglés's critique occurred during the height of the contestation of liturgical reforms as the liturgy shifted at least partially away from Latin.[18]

While Anglés's political commitments are not as explicit here as in some of the works previously surveyed, his utilization of this term is meaning-laden. In the assertion of an *anarchistischer Zustand*, he deploys a term that can either indicate a "condition of anarchy" or a more civic and structural "state of anarchy" in which anarchy is a governing force. While his use of the term may have only spoken to a "condition," at the very least the choice of words reveals the ways in which rhetoric of anarchy is connected to the nation-state and its centralized power.

Shortly after the Second Vatican Council, George Devine utilized "liturgical anarchy" in his book, *Liturgical Renewal: An Agonizing Reappraisal.* In this work, he reflects upon what he understands to be the limitations of the liturgical changes, and he calls for a more pronounced liturgical renewal. He critiques the "abdication of responsibility by so many diocesan liturgical commissions" as the sources of widespread liturgical anarchy in the Roman Catholic Church in the USA.[19] Devine laments liturgical renewal as "haphazard, awkward, erratic, confusing—and which, in all too many cases, has yet to actually begin."[20] While several of the previous scholars engaged have construed as "anarchy" the localization of liturgical authority, Devine uses the term in a different way. He understands anarchy to be a failure of these localized diocesan authorities to act on a degree of centralized liturgical authority. The "liturgical anarchy" he is decrying is one in which liturgical authority ultimately rests in individual priests and congregations.

15. In Ruff, *Sacred Music*, 330–31.

16. Anglés, "Opus liturgico-musicale Concilii Tridentini," 329.

17. Anglés, "Das Kommende okumenische Konzil," 154.

18. Anthony Ruff is fairly critical of Anglés's position, suggesting that it represented an "idealization of Latin High Mass, if not idolization" (Ruff, *Sacred Music*, 253).

19. Devine, *Liturgical Renewal*, 66.

20. Devine, *Liturgical Renewal*, 67.

In *Liturgical Question Box: Answers to Common Questions about the Modern Liturgy*, Peter Elliott responds to statements made by Pope John Paul II to a gathering of French bishops on March 8, 1997, in which he states:

> Whatever directs believers to God, what gathers them and what unites them with one another and with all the other assemblies should be given priority. The Council [*Sacrosanctum Concilium*.11] was clear on this matter: "Pastors of souls must, therefore, realize that when the liturgy is celebrated, something more is required than the laws governing valid and lawful celebration. It is their duty also to ensure that the faithful take part fully aware of what they are doing, actively engaged in the rite, and enriched by it."[21]

Elliott expresses concern that the shifts brought about since the Second Vatican Council have allowed for the emergence of an "anarchist approach to liturgy," writing:

> While there are more options and a more flexible pastoral approach is evident today, this is no excuse for a cavalier attitude toward directives, rubrics, and traditions. The anarchist approach to liturgy has caused great harm among the Catholic people. It cannot provide that "something more" that the Council Fathers called for, going beyond lawfulness and validity, because it has scorned the foundational structure of Christian worship.[22]

Elliott's utilization of this term reflects concern for local and regional liturgical flexibility that does not conform with the centralized liturgical directives, rubrics, and traditions. However, what exactly can constitute the "something more" called for in *Sacrosanctum Concilium* in Elliott's thought is not explicitly clear.

Elliot's work illustrates what is at stake in questions of liturgical authority and claims of "liturgical anarchy." In the negotiation of liturgical authority are embedded theological and political assumptions that will necessarily shape the way in which the liturgy interfaces with particular communities and broader societies. Pope John Paul II here is arguing that uniformity and validity are potentially dangerous to the church and the world if they are separated from grounding in the particularities of each context in which they are celebrated. As radical Protestant traditions which at times violated liturgical authority know all too well, souls, traditions, identities, power, and

21. John Paul II, "Address of His Holiness Pope John Paul II," sec. 4, para. 1.

22. Elliott, *Liturgical Question Box*, 15.

even bodies are at stake—though such traditions have also imposed liturgical authority at later junctures in history in harmful ways.

Baptists, the Nation-State, and Liturgical Anarchy

"Liturgical anarchy" is not just a critique emerging from within established churches or those with Episcopalian structures. It is also a critique that has appeared in Baptist discourse. In an article titled "Thinking among Baptists: The Renewal of Liturgy in a Local Church," Stephen Winward reflects on the maintenance of a necessary tension between liberty, a common Baptist theme, and what he calls "liturgy," a term he uses to denote liturgical order. He writes:

> At the one extreme is the prescribed, inflexible liturgy which leaves little or no room for variation and adaptation, for the 'inspired spontaneity' and freedom of the Holy Spirit. At the other extreme is the disorder and anarchy, the subjectivism and individualism, the confusion and poverty of content which results when the Biblical and traditional forms of worship are jettisoned . . .[23]

Winward's utilization of "liturgical anarchy" denotes what he deems to be liturgical chaos, and he argues that Baptists have generally failed in providing unified order. By implication, he suggests Baptists tend toward liturgical anarchy. While he does not explicitly grapple with liturgical authority, his reflections implicitly grapple with how autonomous Baptists might benefit from a more centralized liturgical authority providing guidance without domination.

Winward's argument parallels previously surveyed usages of the term "liturgical anarchy" in that he is grappling with how to negotiate the decentralization of liturgical authority to each worshiping community. His definition of liturgy has embedded within it a commitment to worship that is structured to, in part, "enable the people to make an adequate response in union with the whole Church," and his desire for a liturgical order that unifies Baptists with the whole church brings him into tension with highly decentralized Baptist liturgical order. Winward maintains a distinctively Baptist sensitivity throughout his argument. His work engages the direct connection between Baptist suspicion of influence by the nation-state on worship and Baptist liturgical tradition emphasizing decentralization and local autonomy. He writes:

23. Winward, "Thinking among Baptists," 27.

> In their laudable resistance to a fixed, excessively stylised, and
> enacted (State enacted) liturgy, many of our forefathers [sic]
> were driven into opposition to liturgy as such. Among Free
> Churchmen [sic] there is still a widespread misunderstanding of
> the true nature of liturgy. It is assumed that liturgy is necessarily
> a form of service in which all the words are written down, pre-
> scribed by ecclesiastical, or even State, authority, and constantly
> repeated.[24]

Here Winward's work explicitly suggests a possible connection between centralized liturgical authority and the power of the nation-state.

Baptist loathing of the influence of the nation-state in worship is well documented. Dissenting Baptists in the seventeenth century developed liturgical practices and polity with anarchist parallels.[25] As I delineated earlier, there are three common themes in self-identifying anarchist thought, and Baptist polity has to varying degrees been characterized by these traits in relationship to the negotiation of liturgical authority. Baptist worship is characterized by: 1) an emphasis upon self-determination encapsulated in concepts such as soul freedom, soul liberty, or soul competency; 2) a staunch rejection of the imposition of remote, centralized liturgical authority; and 3) the formation of decentralized liturgical authority that is negotiated regionally and locally and as free from coercion as possible, i.e., as close to voluntary as possible.[26]

This antistate impulse, at least antistate to the degree that the state controlled Christian worship, in early Baptist worship is evidenced in the work of Roger Williams, a prominent friend and sympathizer of early Baptists in the British colonies, who argued against established religion. He viewed the centralized liturgical authority of the church and its alignment with the interests of the nation-state as a "policy of Satan" and "soul rape."[27][28] His emphasis on individual religious freedom, or what he called "soul freedom," and his rejection of the influence of the nation-state on religion brought him into increasing conflict with the alignment of Puritan religion and British civic power in the Massachusetts Bay Colony. Williams's decentralized approach to religion, emphasizing freedom and autonomy, was thus not

24. Winward, "Thinking among Baptists," 27.

25. I am using the term "parallels" to emphasize that I am not anachronistically suggesting that seventeenth-century Baptist worship emerged out of an anarchist political vision.

26. "Soul liberty" emerged as a term in Roger Williams's works.

27. Williams, "Bloody Tenent," 108.

28. While Williams is staunchly claimed by the Baptists as a foreparent of Baptists in North America, his relationship with Baptists was fairly informal and limited.

only a threat to the religious commitments of the Puritans but also to the British colonial governance of the colony. Byrd provides evidence of this in *The Challenges of Roger Williams: Religious Liberty, Violent Persecution, and the Bible*. He notes that Puritans believed Williams's polity, "would not only corrupt the churches, it would also "dissolve the continuity of the state."[29] Byrd further characterizes the Puritans' perspective, writing, "In the Puritans' view, the dreaded alternative to [their understanding of] godly rule in the state was political anarchy and religious chaos."[30]

While the Puritans may have believed Williams represented religious and civic chaos, Williams was, in effect, disordering religious and civic power. I argue that the source of the threat of Baptist polity to the nation-state lies in the anarchist parallels of Baptist worship; however, these parallels have not always been expansively applied. Early Baptists such as Williams did not explicitly critique the broader validity of the nation-state. They were primarily concerned with keeping the influence and violence of the nation-state out of the church. Williams's quest for religious freedom and the contemporaneous pursuit of civil liberty from the British nation-state were applied with a preferential focus on the white colonist. The profound but limited dissenting Baptist critique of the power of the nation-state and its subsequent violence reflects broader patterns in anarchist political movements, which have also struggled to justly negotiate the dividing lines of race and gender.

The shifting drama of Baptist engagements with enslaved persons in the South provides another helpful viewpoint of how the radical nature of Baptist worship can represent a stark threat to the nation-state and how Baptist worship can restrict that radical nature and align with the power of the nation-state—even in direct persecution of other nondominant Baptists. In *Southern Cross: The Beginnings of the Bible Belt*, Christine Leigh Heyrman shows how Baptists initially experienced persecutions in the South as the horror of chattel slavery in the USA unfolded, because their understanding of liturgical authority was so revolutionary as to represent a stark threat to the power of the Anglican Church and the interests of enslavers.[31] In addition to persecution by landed elites and Anglican clergy, Heyrman argues that Baptists were long held in suspicion by nonclergy and nonelites due to the cultural and social threat they posed to communities and families.

Thomas Kidd and Barry Hankins argue in *Baptists in America: A History* that, while they did not generally speak against slavery, early white

29. Byrd, *Challenges of Roger Williams*, 60.

30. Byrd, *Challenges of Roger Williams*, 59.

31. Heyrman, *Southern Cross*.

Baptists in North America were distinct from most other contemporaneous Christian movements in attempting to limit the brutality of chattel slavery and in emphasizing spiritual egalitarianism between whites and enslaved persons. Kidd and Hankins argue that this was tied to "democratic ecclesiology" emerging out of concepts of individual competency.[32] However, they also note that this democratic ecclesiology and spiritual egalitarianism would be increasingly revoked over time as Baptists in the South aligned themselves with, and eventually became, slaveowners and social elites. Kidd and Hankins write, ". . . over time most white Baptists in the South made peace with the institution, whether they owned slaves or not. This trend accelerated as Baptists helped fashion a new kind of cultural and religious establishment, especially in the southern states of the Atlantic seaboard, and many Baptist elites came to own slaves."[33]

However, while dissenting white Baptist worship was slowly moving toward alignment with the state in relationship to whiteness and chattel slavery, their practices and polity were increasingly adopted by black Christians. Baptist themes of spiritual equality, individual freedom, and local autonomy were attractive to persons held in brutal bondage. As decentralized practices allowed early British Baptists to better avoid detection while illegally worshiping, Baptist polity also helped enslaved persons to illegally worship somewhat more safely. Banks writes, "Often blacks resorted to secret meetings, something that Baptist polity—lack of a central headquarters—enabled them to do. Those who participated in such clandestine services ran the risk of physical abuse as well as excommunication from the white churches."[34] Here, Banks observes that these worship services were interpreted as acts of rebellion against the dominant churches and the broader powers of the nation-state at play in the creation and maintenance of the institution of slavery.[35]

Not only was Baptist worship desirable to some black persons because it emphasized autonomy and local authority, but Baptist worship and the anarchist parallels undergirding it also rendered Baptist worship a fertile location for the growth of black revolutionary movements attempting to free themselves from slavery and ultimately to overthrow the power and

32. Heyrman, *Southern Cross*, 48.

33. Heyrman, *Southern Cross*, 99.

34. Banks, *History of Black Baptists*, 20.

35. However, Banks also notes that this autonomy and decentralization also had a negative dimension in that slaveowners could much more easily control it. He writes, "Congregational church polity well-suited the temper of widespread plantations, for they were little societies within themselves, and easily controlled by whites" (Banks, *History of Black Baptists*, 37).

violence of the nation-state manifested in the institution of slavery. Autonomous worship was frequently seen by landowning elites as a clear and present danger to the dominating social fabric of the South. The potential connection between emphasis upon spiritual egalitarianism and efforts by enslaved persons to achieve fuller, material liberty was widely acknowledged by slaveowners. Kidd and Hankins write:

> Virginia Baptists were particularly defensive about the Turner episode, as critics argued that the radical evangelicals had deluded blacks with "a ranting cant about equality." Some antagonists even proposed banning missionary and educational work among blacks. White Baptists insisted that missionary efforts should continue, but educators and evangelists should discourage any forms of black independence. Turner and his minions were not real Baptists, white Virginia Baptists said. They were deluded, depraved fanatics.[36]

Fear of black religious autonomy and black agency in any form persistently concerned Southern whites, and Kidd and Hankins note that Baptists were frequently blamed for "inspiring slave revolts."[37] The connection of Baptist worship to revolutionary efforts was also visible in Jamaica in the Baptist War of 1831–32, a slave revolt led by Samuel Sharpe, a Baptist pastor. This slave revolt was initially led by Baptists, at least in part, because experiences of autonomy and agency in worship led to heightened social, economic, and political expectations.

Black Baptist worship during the period of chattel slavery is important to consider in relationship to its threat to the state-sponsored agenda of white supremacy, because it reveals Baptist liturgical resistance that moves beyond a fairly narrow antistate critique of established religion. Black Baptist worship was threatening to the state because it did not just threaten the state's liturgical power, which, though differently organized than the state control of established church liturgy, was predominantly manifested in white liturgical complicity in the hegemony of white supremacy. Black Baptist worship threatened the very economic, political, and social agenda of the state, and it implicitly and explicitly called into question the validity and authority of a white-dominant state, while also threatening said state's viability.

Even after the abolition of slavery, Baptist worship was particularly attractive to black persons. In *A History of Black Baptists in the United States*, William Banks argues that the decentralized and local approach to liturgical

36. Kidd and Hankins, *Baptists in America*, 124.

37. Kidd and Hankins, *Baptists in America*, 103.

authority was one of several reasons why black persons were attracted to Baptist practice and polity. He writes that black persons were drawn to Baptist polity and practice because:

> . . . each local Baptist assembly is its own sovereign body. Each church is autonomous or self-ruling. It is easy to understand how such a church government or polity . . . would appeal to an oppressed people. Allowing blacks some modicum of self-determination helped draw blacks to the Baptist denomination. For a people long experienced at being "second class" citizens, it was heady stuff to be able to choose their own pastor, manage their own affairs without "outside" interference.[38]

Paul Harvey argues in *Through the Storm, through the Night: A History of African American Christianity* that Baptist emphasis upon autonomy resulted in Baptists drawing the greatest number of free people in the nineteenth century.[39]

The local and autonomous polity of black Baptist churches was deeply influential in the formation of black communities, organizations, and institutions promoting black welfare and black identity. Kidd and Hankins note that in embracing Baptist autonomy, ". . . they [African Americans] turned their churches into institutions of African American identity within a society dominated by whites. Long after white Baptists became insider elites, especially in the South, black Baptists were still marked by the outsider/dissenter posture of early Baptist history."[40] Baptist worship provided a radical resource utilized by black persons against the dominating brutality of chattel slavery, Reconstruction, and Jim Crow, maintaining a relationship in which black autonomy and black liberty represented distinct threats to the dominant social powers.

Meanwhile, the white-dominant Southern Baptist Convention expanded and became an elite Southern institution. The anarchist parallels of early white Baptist worship were increasingly muted. Churches replicated and created broader patterns of segregation, and, in so doing, they aligned themselves with the centralized power of the nation-state, muting decentralized control through the imposition of legal and theological codifications of white supremacy. In addition, Baptist emphasis on religious liberty and the competency of all believers was slowly reversed. White Baptists could not affirm the liberty and competency of black Baptists, because white Baptists were increasingly resistant to black economic, political, and social equality.

38. Banks, *History of Black Baptists*, 32.

39. Harvey, *Through the Storm*, 72.

40. Kidd and Hankins, *Baptists in America*, 165.

Southern Baptists publicly continued to champion liberty and freedom, but in reality this liberty and freedom were only for white folk, replicating and recreating the racial injustice of the nation-state and falling back on claims of the "separation of church and state" when pressed to extend equality to black persons. Kidd and Hankins write, "One can scarcely imagine a more complete perversion of the Baptist concept of soul competency."[41] They also note that the Baptist theology of individual religious freedom and competency functioned to essentially strengthen white inaction in regard to racism and white supremacy.[42]

In several ways, the dominance of the Southern Baptist Church Convention effectively rendered it an established church through its complicity with state-sponsored white supremacy in the South. What resulted was the sinisterly convenient and fluid inversion of the anarchist parallels of early white- and later black-dissenting Baptist worship. Kidd and Hankins write:

> Even as the denomination's [SBC] leaders position themselves as dissenters, the SBC in some ways still represents the dominant ethos of large portions of the American South and Midwest. Ironically, they often voice their dissent as invited guests in the halls of Congress, on network television programs, or in op-eds in major newspapers and magazines. They drift from the center to the margins and back again, depending on the issue.[43]

It cannot be understated that white Baptist affirmation of autonomy, competency, and liberty are conditional, and for white Baptists, racial loyalty has generally minimized these themes to some degree in order to align with the nation-state's agenda of reinforcing whiteness.

Toward a Radical Liturgipolitical Vision

Though the anarchist parallels of dissenting Baptist worship have only ever been unevenly applied in North America, might a fuller embrace of "liturgical anarchy," or differently ordered worship, function to order our world differently, particularly our structures of government, which are the source of so much violence? Such an embrace would invite us—not just Baptists, but all Christians—into a liturgipolitic in which we frankly name the ways in which worship mimics or resists the power of the nation-state. As was stated previously and bears repeating, dissenting Baptist worship has been

---

41. Kidd and Hankins, *Baptists in America*, 224.
42. Kidd and Hankins, *Baptists in America*, 225.
43. Kidd and Hankins, *Baptists in America*, 246.

characterized by: 1) an emphasis upon self-determination encapsulated in concepts such as "soul freedom," "soul liberty," or "soul competency"; 2) a staunch rejection of the imposition of remote, centralized liturgical authority; and 3) the formation of decentralized liturgical authority that is negotiated regionally and locally and as free from coercion as possible, i.e., as close to voluntary as possible. A fuller embrace of the anarchist parallels of dissenting worship might enliven not just the Baptist tradition of dissent for today but even more broadly a Christian tradition of dissent.

Commitments to soul liberty, local autonomy, regional cooperation, and decentralized authority comprise a radical, revolutionary set of values, structures, and practices that have the potential to run contrary to the centralized power and cultural dominance of the nation-state and its coercive violence. However, as was previously stated and which bears repeating, history shows that once-dissenting Christians have, at points in time, aligned with the dominant, centralized power and culture of the nation-state. When they have done so, the anarchist dimensions of worship have been muted in order to reinforce the centralized power and culture of the nation-state, particularly on the part of white Christians as it relates to complicity in white supremacy.

Dissenting Christians' negotiation and implementation of liturgical authority has, at numerous points in history, deeply threatened the ongoing and contested formation and negotiation of the centralized political authority and cultural dominance of the nation-state. This is because a dissenting perspective on liturgical authority potentially represents the liturgical ordering of a radically different politic, or way of negotiating power in the governance of society, which, due to its anarchist parallels and antistate beginnings, undermines the interests of the nation-state. This is a dissenting *liturgipolitic*.

This term brushes past contestations over whether or not liturgy or any of its particular expressions, such as preaching, are, or even should be, political.[44] At the very foundation of our liturgical structures is embedded an interconnectedness with the political structures of secular governance. The centralized political and cultural power of the nation-state is the sociocultural context in which Christians negotiate and implement liturgical authority, and we must consider how our models of liturgical authority mimic, recreate, or even sponsor the centralized dominance of the nation-state. Whether the reader is a dissenting Baptist, a Baptist whose worship agenda is aligned with the violence of the nation-state, or from another Christian

---

44. Here, I am remembering the numerous times I have heard folk push against a given element of worship that troubles their politics by asserting that worship (or one of its component practices such as preaching, prayer, etc.) should not be political.

sect, all of our negotiations of liturgical authority are situated alongside and amidst the secular workings of the nation-state. The nation-state has engaged (and still does engage consistently) in liturgical interventions, some quite overt and others more subtle, such as in voluntary, white alignment with the political and liturgical agenda of whiteness.

However, this is only half of the equation of liturgipolitics. Liturgipolitics cannot simply be restrained to detailing the ways in which Christian engagements of liturgical authority are influenced by secular governing structures such as the nation-state. Liturgipolitics here also names how Christian worship may provide a radical, revolutionary resource for critique, reform, or even the overturning of the nation-state. There is an urgent need for all of these. Here in the USA, the centralized political authority of the nation-state ensures the continued and violent imposition of settler colonial, heteropatriarchal white supremacy.

Liturgipolitical awareness, particularly as it relates to the radical dissenting negotiation and implementation of liturgical authority done by Baptists actively opposing the interests of the nation-state, raises one possibility of Christian liturgy serving as a resource for political intervention. The anarchist parallels and antistate beginnings of dissenting liturgical practice and polity not only represent a resource for intervening against the violent agenda of the nation-state but also represent an alternative approach to restructuring power through which the political structures of society could be radically reimagined. The liturgical anarchy, or "differently ordered" nature, of dissenting worship presents an alternative structure of negotiating power and authority in a way that could radically reorder the world.

However, at least in the case of Baptists, the greatest challenge toward a vision of liturgical intervention in politics is widespread and outspoken—albeit frequently duplicitous—commitment to the "separation of church and state." In grasping for survival from the nation-state and asserting the separation of church and state, dissenting Christians have potentially limited the degree to which their radical worship practices could inform more just possibilities for the negotiation of power in society.[45]

However, the current arrangement of the separation of church and state in the USA is the result of a Christian willingness to intervene in the power of the nation-state. These interventions might also be understood

---

45. Laws securing the separation of church and state can be vitally important to the welfare of dissenting worshipers. As evidence for this claim, I observe that amidst the anti-immigrant, white supremacist enforcement of immigration laws in the USA, Immigration and Customs Enforcement (ICE) officers generally will not enter into a worship space out of concern that they be seen as undermining the separation of church and state.

as liturgipolitical interventions to the degree that they disrupted the state's control over Christian worship and represented antistate values that were fully expressed in liturgy itself. Such liturgipolitical interventions were certainly done by the earliest champions of the separation of church and state. They secured religious autonomy through much spilled blood and a willingness to commit liturgipolitical interventions that boldly spoke into the very heart of the centralized power and cultural dominance of the nation-state. This essay particularly examined such revolutionary activities on the part of early European, Euro-American, and black Baptists. The assertion of dissenting arguments for the separation of church and state has historically required a calling into account of centralized political authority.

Dissenting negotiation of liturgical authority may be a resource for liturgipolitical critique of the nation-state and its violence as well as a resource for imagining an alternative to the current structure of the nation-state. Early Euro-American Baptists and black Baptists have a long history in negotiating, both successfully and unsuccessfully, autonomous, regionalized structures of liturgical authority that might provide insight into how political authority could be negotiated in an autonomous, regionalized structure, reducing the coercive violence of the nation-state and restructuring power in more just ways.

While many Christians champion "separation of church and state," those words may have little effectual meaning beyond limiting the degree to which the state can directly meddle in liturgical authority and polity.[46] In a truly separate church and state in which the church's interests starkly diverge from the interests of the state, the church would likely find it much less difficult to reimagine alternative possibilities of the structure of the nation-state and to speak into those realities. The degree to which we are unwilling to engage in a liturgipolitical critique of the state and to offer up alternatives to it is a reflection of the *lack* of separation between church and state. What we call separation of church and state may only be a *détente* between the church and state in which the state agrees not to meddle with liturgical authority and polity as long as the church voluntarily agrees to be acquiescent and complicit.

---

46. This also begs the question: Why would the nation-state even need to intervene in or meddle with liturgical authority in white churches that have aligned their theological agendas with the imperial, capitalist, patriarchal, and white supremacist agenda of the nation-state?

Conclusion

Embrace of "liturgical anarchy" and antistate commitments found in the examples of early dissenting Baptists and black Baptists could radically change us as Christians and subsequently could radically change the world. Even though there are shining examples of revolutionary Christian efforts at undermining the violence of the nation-state, Christians *en masse* have never fully lived into the anarchist dimensions of our negotiation and implementation of liturgical authority. I can only imagine a world in which dissenting emphasis upon "soul freedom," "soul competency," and local autonomy allowed for individuals and communities to flourish in an ecologically sustainable, minimally violent, and culturally appropriate manner that released us from our current bondage to the settler colonial, heteropatriarchal white supremacist agenda of the nation-state, with its imposition of violent inequities and injustice. Might dissenting Baptist worship offer up for all Christians both an ecclesial model for individuals and communities to more fully and equally approach and serve God and the world and a liturgipolitical model in which folk, regardless of their race, gender, sexuality, or class, could more fully and equally enjoy access to the sustainable bounty of this earth and the fellowship of its inhabitants?

Bibliography

Anglés, Higini. "Das Kommende okumenische Konzil und die kirchenmusic" *Singende Kirche* 8 (1960) 150–56.

———. "Opus liturgico-musicale Concilii Tridentini maneat exemplum et exemplar novi Concili." In *Sacred Music and Liturgical Reform: Treasures and Transformations*, translated by Anthony Ruff, 329–30. Chicago: Hillenbrand, 2007.

Banks, William. *A History of Black Baptists in the United States*. West Conshohocken, PA: Infinity, 2013.

Bell, Catherine. *Ritual: Perspectives and Dimensions*. New York: Oxford University Press, 1997.

Bellegarrigue, Anselme. "L'Anarchie, c'est l'orde." *L'Anarchie: Alliance ouvrière anarchiste, Journal de l'ordre* 1 (April 1850).

Bishop, Edmund. *Liturgica Historica: Papers on the Liturgy and Religious Life of the Western Church*. Oxford: Oxford University Press, 1918.

Byrd, James. *The Challenges of Roger Williams: Religious Liberty, Violent Persecution, and the Bible*. Macon, GA: Mercer University Press, 2002.

Chupungco, Anscar. *Handbook for Liturgical Studies: Introduction to the Liturgy*. Collegeville, MN: Liturgical, 1997.

Devine, George. *Liturgical Renewal: An Agonizing Reappraisal*. Staten Island, NY: Alba House, 1973.

Edwards, David. *Leaders of the Church of England, 1828–1978*. London: Hodder and Stoughton, 1978.

Elliott, Peter. *Liturgical Question Box: Answers to Common Questions about the Modern Liturgy*. San Francisco: Ignatius, 1998.

Harvey, Paul. *Through the Storm, through the Night: A History of African American Christianity*. New York: Rowman & Littlefield, 2011.

Heyrman, Christine Leigh. *Southern Cross: The Beginnings of the Bible Belt*. Durham: University of North Carolina Press, 1998.

Jaschinksi, Eckhard. *Musica sacra oder Musik im Gottesdienst*. Regensburg, Germany: Pustet, 1990.

John Paul II, Pope. "Address of His Holiness Pope John Paul II to the Bishops of France on Their *Ad Limina Apostolorum* Visit." *Vatican.va*, March 8, 1997. https://w2.vatican.va/content/john-paul-ii/en/speeches/1997/march/documents/hf_jp-ii_spe_19970308_ad-limina-francia.html.

Kidd, Thomas, and Barry Hankins. *Baptists in America: A History*. New York: Oxford University Press, 2015.

Kinna, Ruth. *Anarchism: A Beginner's Guide*. London: Oneworld, 2009.

Legg, J. Wickham. *Some Principles and Services of the Prayer-book Historically Considered*. London: Rivingtons, 1899.

Pinell, Jordi. "La Liturgia gallicana." In Anàmnesis: Introduzione storico-teologica alla Liturgia, vol. 2: la Liturgia, panorama storico generale, edited by Salvatore Marsili et al., 62–67. 7 vols. Torino: Marietti, 1978.

Ruff, Anthony. *Sacred Music and Liturgical Reform: Treasures and Transformations*. Chicago: Liturgy Training, 2007.

Vogel, Cyrille. "Les motifs de la romanization du culte sous Pépin et Charlemagne." *Culto Cristiano: Politica imperial carolingia. Convegni del Centro di Studi sulla Spiritualità Medievale* 18 (1979) 13–41.

Williams, Roger. "Bloody Tenent Yet More Bloody." In *Roger Williams: His Contribution to the American Tradition*, edited by Perry Miller, 108–11. Indianapolis: Bobbs-Merrill, 1953.

Winward, Stephen F. "Thinking among Baptists: The Renewal of Liturgy in a Local Church." Annual meeting notes of the Christian Brethren Research Fellowship, 1967. https://biblicalstudies.org.uk/pdf/cbrfj/vols/15.pdf.

3

The Power to Re-Member

The Power to Re-Member Community: Vigils in the Borderlands

Isaac S. Villegas

Introduction

In the fall of 2018, I participated in a ritual of remembrance in Douglas, Arizona, near a US-Mexico port of entry. Residents in the borderlands have organized and gathered for their Healing Our Borders Vigil, as they've come to name the religious practice, every week for the past twenty years. This chapter begins with a thick description of the vigil, followed by a distilled interview with two organizer-participants whose insights, in conclusion, provoke an interpretation of the worship practice as belonging to the Mennonite tradition remembered in the *Martyrs Mirror*. The spiritual and political work of the Healing Our Borders Vigil involves the power to constitute a community through a liturgical act of remembrance—to re-member a peoplehood that reaches across the divide between the living and the dead as a protest against the lethal violence of the southern border of the United States.

I develop this chapter from my experience as a participant-observer. I recognize that, depending on the vantage point, the vigil signifies different religious and nonreligious meanings to each organizer, participant, and onlooker, according to their personal narrative, relationships, and life situation. In his first chapter of *Interpretation of Cultures*, in his account of "thick descriptions," Clifford Geertz confronts cultural interpreters with the hubris involved in claiming to know the significance of a ritual for the participants, that is, the effect of a social act on the life of the actor. "Cultural analysis is (or should be) guessing at meanings, assessing the guesses, and drawing explanatory conclusions from better guesses," Geertz cautions, "not discovering the Continent of Meaning and mapping out its bodiless landscape." Included in his sober assessment of this type of analytic work is a guiding principle for interpretive explanations. "A good interpretation of anything—a poem, a person, a history, a ritual, an institution, a society— takes us into the heart of that of which it is an interpretation." There is no definitive meaning, no way to distill a religious practice into an authoritative description that leaves behind the people whose lives determine the significance of the activity. Instead, to write about such a communal act broadens the range of the religious event's communicative effects—not to disseminate a final word but as an invitation to consider the meaningfulness of the ritual. As Geertz characterizes the work of this type of writing, "a piece of anthropological interpretation consists in: tracing the curve of a social discourse; fixing it into an inspectable form."[1] This paper traces the liturgical movements of a Healing Our Borders Vigil into a discursive form, which I depict as part of ongoing Christian responses to US immigration policies and border enforcement. I add my perspective to this conversation as a participant in the vigil who still thinks about the crosses and names, the march and prayers—memories that inform my own political and religious sensibilities as a Latino Mennonite.

Vigil—Douglas, Arizona: October 9, 2018

Carol Rose, our Christian Peacemaker Team (CPT) leader, arranges our rendezvous with Jack and Linda Knox, two Mennonite retirees who relocated from Salem Mennonite Church in Oregon to a neighborhood in Douglas, Arizona—a stone's throw from the border wall—to run a hospitality house as a hub for immigration justice work. I'm here as part of a CPT delegation

---

1. Geertz, *Interpretation of Cultures*, 18–20.

of ten people, all of us members of Mennonite congregations in the United States and Canada.[2]

From their house, we get in our cars and follow the Knoxes to a McDonald's parking lot along the Pan American Avenue, a half-mile walk to the Raul Hector Castro port of entry, the border-crossing station with the Mexican city of Agua Prieta on the other side of the iron fence stretching from horizon to horizon. Linda and Jack unload a hundred white crosses from their truck, stacking them in a shopping cart, which they push to where all of us have congregated—our Mennonite cohort interspersed in a crowd of community members who gather every Tuesday to remember people who have died in the desert, their migrant neighbors.

Jack Knox welcomes the crowd, around thirty of us, and tells a brief story of the vigil's origins, locating our gathering in the nearly twenty-year history of this weekly ritual. The first gathering happened on December 10, 2000, he explains, organized as a community response to the growing number of corpses found in remote regions of Sulphur Springs Valley, where the twin cities of Agua Prieta and Douglas are located, a community divided by a massive wall of steel slats. Jack points to the wagon full of crosses, each of them with the name of a person who was found dead in the Sonoran Desert surrounding the cities. The ones with us this evening, he says, are a portion of the 313 crosses that he and Linda keep at their house. When a body is found, another crucifix is nailed together, another name painted. If the coroner's office cannot determine a person's identity, Jack adds, instead of names we mark the crosses with the words "no identificado" or "no identificada."

We begin our procession at dusk. A friar from the local Franciscan community invites us to take several crosses in our hands and follow the seasoned participants. I grab three of them from the wagon and follow the lead of an older woman. I walk behind her, all of us in a single-file line, down the Pan American Avenue's sidewalk with the border ahead of us. I see the first person at the front read out the name written on his cross as he lifts it above his head, and everyone responds in unison, with a shout: "¡Presente!" He bends his body toward the ground to place the base of the crucifix in the street, at the edge of the pavement, leaning it upright against the curb, on display for the passengers of cars on their way to and from Mexico. After this bowed reverence, he steps out of the way and walks slowly to the back of our procession, awaiting his next turn. The second person in line, now at

2. Since the 1980s, representatives from the North American historic peace churches (Mennonites, Church of the Brethren, and Quakers/Friends) have been organizing the work of Christian Peacemaker Teams as a way to organize nonviolent solidarity efforts among communities in various crisis regions of the world.

the front, calls out another name and places one more cross several yards further down the sidewalk. We process like a dirge, our crosses as memorials, the avenue hallowed with our lament.

As my turn approaches, I memorize the names in my hands: Juan Tovar Hernández, Rosalía Ana Lilia Ramos Reyes, and Lucina López de Olmos. As I'm deciding which cross to place along the curb, the woman before me has reached the front of our procession. She stops, so we all wait for her shout. "No identificada," she calls out with a crucifix stretched to the sky. "¡Presente!" we reply. She makes her way to the back, picking up a couple more crosses from the cart that Linda Knox pushes down the sidewalk alongside the procession. I glance over my shoulder at the crosses along the curb behind us, remembrances for the dead in our wake, the named and unnamed people lost to the wilderness, victims of US border enforcement and immigration policy.

We veer from the walkway into a clearing before the kiosks where US officers check identity documents to determine who may pass legally across the border. Our group forms a circle for the closing ritual. Mark Adams, a Presbyterian minister who has helped organize the vigils from the beginning, takes three crosses from the shopping cart. He steps into the center and reads aloud the name from one of them. All of us respond, "¡Presente!" He calls out the next name. We reply, "¡Presente!" The last of the three doesn't have a name, only the words "no identificado." Adams lifts the crucifix and shouts into the night, "Jesucristo!"—four times, facing east then north then west then south, bearing witness to the corners of the earth. And each time we answer, "¡Presente!" Adams joins our circle as we link hands and silence ourselves in honor of the dead. In the middle, on the ground, the three crosses identify the area as another Golgotha, with the militarized border as the crucifer.

After the vigil we wander back along the sidewalk, gathering the crosses—one by one, name after name—and placing them in Linda's cart. The night shrouds our return, except for the cars' piercing headlights which flash across the glossy paint of the crucifixes we've yet to collect. The names flicker to mind the lives of strangers, my last fleeting acknowledgment of the presence of their absence.

Interview—Online via Zoom: December 11, 2020

During the past two years those crosses have appeared in my dreams. On occasion I've retraced the vigil's path in my sleep. The names I heard that day haunt me. "[W]e will have to learn to talk to and listen to ghosts, rather than banish them," Avery F. Gordon counsels in *Ghostly Matters: Haunting and the Sociological Imagination*. "[W]hen ghosts appear to you, the dead or the disappeared or the lost or the invisible are demanding their due. They are, for better or worse, very much alive and present."[3]

In an attempt to give the crosses in my dreams their due, I interview Linda and Jack Knox to learn more about their involvement with the vigil. Zoom connects my computer screen in North Carolina to theirs in Arizona. They tell me about community leaders who organized the first vigil in 2000, twenty years ago this month. The organizers have moved the ritual online since March, in response to the COVID-19 pandemic. This past Tuesday was the 1,040th vigil. The Knoxes have participated since 2012, when Jack retired from the pastorate at Salem Mennonite Church and they moved from Oregon to dedicate themselves to immigration justice efforts on the US-Mexico border.

The weekly vigil is a spiritual discipline, they explain, the religious practice at the center of their work, a ritual of faith that organizes their life commitments.

"When Tuesday evening comes around," Linda tells me, "we head over no matter if the heat is really bad or if it's freezing cold—we're there no matter if it's rainy or if we're tired." She continues, "We just have to be there by five-fifteen to meet up with the others."

The vigil is a discipline, Jack adds, "that focuses us on people, on the lives of people who've died, people our country forgets about too easily." He goes on, "We call out their names because we believe their lives matter, their deaths matter, even if we've never met them, even if we don't know some of their names."

"Once," Linda cuts in with a story, "a man came up to us after the vigil and said he was on his way back to Mexico, but before he walked back across through the border station, he heard someone shout the name of his brother who had died the year before." Her eyes widen as she recounts what happened next. "We let him know that we remembered his brother's name every week, and we showed him the cross with his name. The man asked if he could have the cross, he wanted to give it his mother, to let her know that we kept her son's name alive."

I ask if passersby ever join the vigil.

"That's rare," Jack says, "but people do take notice, which is a big part of why we do it there at the port of entry, because we want to draw attention to the impact of the border wall, to bear witness with a public action aimed at US authorities."

3. Gordon, *Ghostly Matters*, 32, 182.

I wonder about border agents, if law enforcement officers ever bother the march and service. "Does the border patrol ever interrupt the vigil?"

I see Linda and Jack shake their heads on the screen. "They've never bothered us," Linda responds. "But I think they pay attention to what's going on from where they're stationed."

"Yes," Jack agrees, "it looks like officers monitor us, which is good, because we're there to let them know that we want a different world from the one they're working for, we want change at the border."

Linda adds, "Our friends on the other side, in Agua Prieta, see us too—through the wall's metal slats or when they're on their way back home from this side."

The conversation shifts to the convictions and relationships we share as members of an Anabaptist denomination in the United States. The Knoxes became part of the tradition as adults, they explain, first by joining a Mennonite Church USA congregation in Texas, then in Oregon where Jack served as a pastor. Upon relocating to the borderlands in Arizona for retirement, they transferred their membership to the closest MC USA church—a congregation in Tucson, more than a two-hour drive from their home on the border. Now, they not only extend the vigil's hospitality to Mennonite pilgrims from their church, but they also invite participants from throughout our denomination's networks of institutional relationships. Jack mentions a regular flow of visitors from programs operated by Mennonite Mission Network, Mennonite Central Committee, and Christian Peacemaker Teams. I remind them of my visit, two years ago, as part of a Mennonite Church USA and Mennonite Mission Network partnership with Christian Peacemaker Teams to assemble Mennonite pastors and Mennonite Voluntary Service workers for a borderland delegation.

The vigil, Linda explains, fits within the Anabaptist spirituality passed along from one generation of faith to the next in the *Martyrs Mirror*, a seventeenth-century martyrological storybook that traveled with the earliest wave of European Mennonites who migrated to North America.

"We are spiritually connected to the dead," Linda comments. "The people in *The Martyrs Mirror* are part of our story, our church family. We honor them as ancestors of our faith, people who lived in the truth of the gospel to the point of death." To honor the people who have died in the borderlands is an extension of the spirituality of the *Martyrs Mirror*, Linda proposes. "When we say that the dead are *presente* during the vigil, we're including them in our lives, in our story of faith, that they're part of our community." She pauses, then asks, "Isn't this what we mean when we talk about the communion of saints?"

I wonder aloud—to myself, with them—about Christian practices of reverence for the dead, and if the vigil imbues the crosses with the spiritual power of a relic for the participants whose pious devotion opens them to experience their lives as in communion with the saints.

"I don't know about all that," Linda responds, "but I will say that I feel like I've gotten to know them, with the crosses, through their names."

Jack tells me that, before the pandemic, they had kept the crosses at their house. "We've taken care of the crosses," he notes. "We'd transport them to the vigil and bring them back with us."

Their presence invites the hope of mutual belonging.

"Over the years I've memorized their names, after saying them so many times," Linda says. "And now I can't help but imagine their lives, to think about who they were, to make up little stories."

Interpretation—Durham, North Carolina: Spring 2021

In 1660, Thieleman van Braght, a Dutch Mennonite minister, published a compilation of martyr stories as a book titled *The Bloody Theater, or Martyrs Mirror of the Defenseless Christians, also known as The Martyrs Mirror.*[4] This collection of folkloric accounts of torture and death narrates the history of God's people as a martyrological tradition, an ecumenical storyline that begins in the Bible and extends into the early decades of the seventeenth century, culminating with the Anabaptist martyrs of Europe. The narrative positions the Mennonite reader as an heir of this story, as a descendant of these people who were faithful unto death—to read one's self into the drama of faith as a member of the persecuted community, as recipients of the violence alongside, for example, Perpetua and Felicity in the third century and the Waldensians and Albigensians in the twelfth century. Van Braght fashioned the book as a mirror for Mennonite readers to see themselves as people called to suffer for their convictions. "The martyrs would provide inspiration for renewal," Brad Gregory writes, characterizing the purpose of *The Bloody Theater*. "The martyrologist would make spiritually slack Mennonites look at themselves in the martyrs' mirror."[5] The stories were an invitation to belong to "a heroic legacy," to be people worthy of the martyrs.[6]

With van Braght's book of martyrs, subsequent generations of Anabaptist communities passed along this invitation to belong to this "heroic legacy." In his social history of the *Martyrs Mirror*, David Weaver-Zercher

4. Braght, *Bloody Theater*.

5. Gregory, *Salvation at Stake*, 246.

6. Gregory, *Salvation at Stake*, 245.

documents the book's function in linking the Mennonite reader to "a line of faithful witnesses that stretches back to the New Testament."[7] The "teleological thrust" of the narrative invites later Anabaptists to identify their tradition with a "soft triumphalism," Weaver-Zercher explains, in which they are "at the center of God's providential plan" and receive "God's blessing and triumph" in response to the sacrifices of their ancestors in the faith—modest victories of survival, the marginal yet persevering witness of the faithful's sacrifice.[8] Van Braght depicts "a trans-historical picture of what it meant to be authentically Christian"[9] as a summons for Anabaptist readers to locate themselves with the persecuted victors of the story. A trend among contemporary Mennonites (and Amish) of European descent, Weaver-Zercher notes, is to read the *Martyrs Mirror* as their family story—"to claim genealogical connections to people in the book." They are the heirs of the martyrs by virtue of a genetic genealogy, according to heredity. Weaver-Zercher categorizes them as "ancestry-minded Mennonites" who identify themselves with the characters in the stories because "the martyrs' blood courses through their veins"—readers with a "sense of genetic participation."[10]

The Knoxes are not Mennonites according to ancestry. Jack and Linda do not read themselves as among the persecuted in *The Martyrs Mirror*. The book is not a mirror through which to see themselves as doubles of the stories' protagonists. Those Anabaptist figures do not function as models to measure their own faithfulness. Instead, in my interview, Linda Knox indicated another hermeneutic: to read the text as a call to solidarity with peoples who undergo analogous violences now. In her hands the book becomes a source for a Mennonite faith attuned to people whose lives bear a likeness to the stories told in *The Martyrs Mirror*—people today who are outside the fold of Anabaptism yet recognizable as spiritual kin.

While the normative hermeneutic has been to read *The Martyrs Mirror* as the story of Anabaptist ancestors, a genealogy of the faithful for the inheritors of the faith, the Knoxes' reading of the text fits within a marginal interpretive tradition evidenced in the asides of Mennonite writers, the tangents of a line of thought, the digressions within a reflection. For example, when the novelist Rudy Wiebe writes as an heir of Mennonite peoplehood about the sacrificial faithfulness described in *The Martyrs Mirror*, he can't help but turn his gaze to life beyond the genetic pool and outside the confessional fold. His focus is on the brutality of martyrdom

7. Weaver-Zercher, *Martyrs Mirror*, 74.

8. Weaver-Zercher, *Martyrs Mirror*, 229–30.

9. Weaver-Zercher, *Martyrs Mirror*, 66.

10. Weaver-Zercher, *Martyrs Mirror*, 262.

that his people suffered—to remember them, he exhorts in his conclusion, to "not forget those who we know have suffered, and especially who died as martyrs for their faith and convictions." However, he makes an observation in passing about present horrors, about other peoples with analogous experiences: "we all know very well that the violence and the martyrdom goes on."[11] This throwaway line—at the beginning of Wiebe's remarks, a sentiment absent from the rest of the piece—acknowledges an alternative imagination cultivated in readers of the Anabaptist book. The same type of gesture occurs in Julia Spicher Kasdorf's 2013 reflections on *The Martyrs Mirror*.[12] She centers her exploration on "ideologies of sacrifice and self-denial that are grounded in cultural memory and the function of *Martyrs Mirror* in creating that memory"[13]—this memory of "heroic, mythic martyr tales" that "inspire pacifist warriors who pledge allegiance to the Anabaptist example and follow its ethic of nonviolence at any cost."[14] Yet, a third of the way into her piece, in a parenthetical comment, she swerves away from her Anabaptist subjects. Like Wiebe, Kasdorf glances outside her Mennonite frame of reference as she recounts an episode from the *Martyrs Mirror*, a scene memorialized in one of Jan Luyken's sixteenth-century engravings included in those pages. "Enduring a torture similar to waterboarding—not long ago sanctioned by American president George W. Bush—Brother Mattheus always said 'no' as long as he was able to speak."[15] The Bush administration's horrific abuse of detainees in clandestine facilities overseas—in Iraq, Afghanistan, Guantanamo Bay, and God knows where else—flashes into Kasdorf's account of the torture and execution of Mattheus Mair in 1592. Kasdorf sees Abu Ghraib when she looks at Luyken's image of Mair's torment. She shifts—as if a function of the natural reflex of her Mennonite imagination—from Anabaptist martyrology to contemporary atrocities. *Brother* Mattheus—she identifies him as a brother, the two of them sharing in the kinship of Anabaptism. For her to name this martyr as a brother in close proximity to the victims of President Bush's regime of terror invites a reader to recognize other tortured peoples as potential siblings.

The Knoxes display this type of hermeneutic—a minor interpretive reflex within Anabaptist approaches to the text—when they link the *Martyrs Mirror* to the border vigil. Their Mennonite disposition likens the stories of the book to the lives of the people who have died in the desert.

11. Wiebe, "Flowers for Approaching the Fire," 124, 111.

12. Kasdorf, "Mightier than the Sword."

13. Kasdorf, "Mightier than the Sword," 46.

14. Kasdorf, "Mightier than the Sword," 58.

15. Kasdorf, "Mightier than the Sword," 50–51.

This interpretive method resembles what James McClendon calls "a baptist hermeneutic," a "mystical vision" that reads passages from the Bible as descriptions of our contemporary world—the past as present. "'This is that' and 'then is now,'" McClendon writes, "a trope of mystical identity binding the story now to the story then."[16] However, beyond McClendon's scriptural purview, this Anabaptist hermeneutic (which McClendon calls "baptist" with a lowercase "b") displayed in the work of Wiebe and Kasdorf and the Knoxes' religious practice extends to other texts (e.g., *The Martyrs Mirror*) as an ethical orientation, as guidance—to experience our world as within the story of God, to consider the narrative of every tortured life as a plot line into the mysteries of Christ's crucifixion. "This is that"—*this* death in the borderlands is *that* horrific scene on Golgotha. The procession of crosses in Douglas, Arizona marks a route of the *Via Dolorosa*, another station of the cross.[17]

For Linda and Jack, the weekly ritual at the border is an act of faith that invites the remembered lives into their spiritual communion. Deceased migrants, named and unnameable—people sacrificed for the rights and privileges of US citizens[18]—become their siblings through a faith enacted along the Pan American Avenue. In the shadow of the wall's steel slats, metal spires slashing into the sky for as far as the eye can see, miles of monument to US imperial power—there, in a clearing, neighbors and pilgrims form a column of priests, each bearing a crucifix of Christ, as the gathered perform a holy ritual of kinship, a declaration of their belonging to a community of the dead whose lives are remembered and declared, "¡Presente!" Through the power of their liturgy, the assembly announces that their identity includes people whom the government has rendered absent by means of the violence of the state.

16. McClendon, *Doctrine*, 466, 45. McClendon takes as paradigmatic for this hermeneutic Peter's sermon on Pentecost, in which the apostle quotes Joel 2:17, then makes this claim regarding the crowd's experience of the outpouring of the Holy Spirit: "This is that which was spoken by the prophet Joel" (Acts 2:17). See McClendon, *Ethics*, 32.

17. The Jesuit theologian Jon Sobrino makes a similar point: "The cross of Jesus points us to the crosses that exist today.... The crucified peoples of the Third World are today the great theological setting, the *locus*, in which to understand the cross of Jesus" (Sobrino, *Jesus the Liberator*, 195–96, emphasis original).

18. For an account of the collateral damage involved in the establishment of US citizenship, see Villegas, "Then Solomon."

Conclusion

In May, 2021, I returned to Douglas, Arizona to join the vigil again. Pandemic safety protocols had limited the number of people who gathered in person. Four people marched down the sidewalk with the cart of crosses. One person walked at the back with the camera of his iPhone fixed on the procession. He was broadcasting the vigil for the online participants—almost a hundred devices were logged on for the service, a diaspora of people across the continent present via Zoom.

After the vigil, I pushed the cart as a participant picked up the crosses. I asked him why he shows up every week.

"I'm not religious," he told me, "but I do believe we shouldn't let people die in the desert, and Christians are the people around here who keep on organizing against the wall, so I tag along."

For him, the Christianness of the ritual was beside the point. His reasons for being there did not fit within the religious symbology of the service, the distinctiveness of his narrative went unpronounced within the Christocentric discourse. Yet, every Tuesday, he has been there with crosses in his hands, living out the logic of his own mysteries, making his own meaning from the weekly discipline.

To offer a good interpretation of a ritual, Geertz argues, "takes us into the heart of that of which it is an interpretation." The Healing Our Borders vigil has many hearts, as many as the people who gather to perform the service, and as many as the onlookers in their cars—a jumble of faces and crosses flash across their vision. "[A] piece of anthropological interpretation consists in," Geertz continues, "tracing the curve of a social discourse." In this chapter I have traced the significance of the vigil according to the guidance of two participants, Linda and Jack Knox, taking their observations as cues for an interpretation of the religious act. Linda's comment about the Anabaptist spirituality of *The Martyrs Mirror* curved my exploration into that book—an intersection where one route of the Mennonite tradition crosses into a communal ritual of faith, a spirituality that conjures a communion of the living and the dead, a belonging that transgresses national borders.

After that first time I participated in the vigil in 2018, I mentioned my experience in a piece I wrote for *Sojourners Magazine*.[19] A reader from Seattle emailed me her interest in the list of names recited as part of the Healing Our Borders liturgies, because a group in her congregation wanted to host a solidarity vigil. A few months after I had put her in touch with

---

19. Villegas, "When Death," 24–29.

the organizers in Douglas/Agua Prieta, she contacted me again to let me know about the success of the event and that her church group had already begun to plan for another vigil. The Tuesday evening ritual at the border had migrated 1,600 miles north. The shared liturgy broadened the reach of a peoplehood constituted through their remembrance of a communion of migrant saints.[20]

Bibliography

Braght, Thieleman J. van. *The Bloody Theater, or Martyrs Mirror of the Defenseless Christians, also known as The Martyrs Mirror*. Translated by Joseph F. Sohm. Scottdate, PA: Mennonite/Herald, 1938.

Derrida, Jacques. *Specters of Marx: The State of the Debt, the Work of Mourning, and the New International*. Translated by Peggy Kamuf. New York: Routledge, 1994.

Geertz, Clifford. *The Interpretation of Cultures: Selected Essays*. New York: Basic, 1973.

Gordon, Avery F. *Ghostly Matters: Haunting and the Sociological Imagination*. Minneapolis: University of Minnesota Press, 2008.

Gregory, Brad S. *Salvation at Stake: Christian Martyrdom in Early Modern Europe*. Cambridge: Harvard University Press, 1999.

Kasdorf, Julia Spicher. "Mightier than the Sword: Martyrs Mirror in the New World." *Conrad Grebel Review* 31.1 (Winter 2013) 44–70.

McClendon, James Wm., Jr. *Systematic Theology, Volume 1: Ethics*. Second edition. Nashville: Abingdon, 2002.

———. *Systematic Theology, Volume 2: Doctrine*. Nashville: Abingdon, 1994.

Sobrino, Jon. *Jesus the Liberator: A Historical-Theological Reading of Jesus of Nazareth*. Maryknoll, NY: Orbis, 1993.

Villegas, Isaac S. "Then Solomon Took a Census of All the Aliens." *Religions* 10.3 (Spring 2019) 1–15.

———. "When Death in the Desert Is Not an Accident." *Sojourners* (June 2019) 24–29.

Weaver-Zercher, David L. *Martyrs Mirror: A Social History*. Baltimore: Johns Hopkins University Press, 2016.

Wiebe, Rudy. "Flowers for Approaching the Fire: A Meditation on *The Bloody Theatre, or Martyrs Mirror*." *Conrad Grebel Review* 16.2 (Spring 1998) 110–24.

20. I am grateful for Jack and Linda Knox's hospitality and for their permission to recount their stories.

PART 2

Negotiating Power
in Ecclesial Institutions

4

The Power of Naming Power

Domination, Resistance, Solidarity: An Analysis of Power in the Making of a Mennonite Worship Book

Sarah Kathleen Johnson

Liturgical authority in the Mennonite tradition is not a question I considered until, at the age thirty, while a doctoral student at the University of Notre Dame, I became a Mennonite liturgical authority. Between 2016 and 2020, I served as the worship resources editor for a new hymnal and worship book, *Voices Together*,[1] that is intended to serve Mennonite Church USA (MCUSA) and Mennonite Church Canada (MCCanada).[2]

1. *Voices Together* includes both songs and worship resources; about ninety pages of the 1000-page volume are dedicated to nonmusical resources, including readings and prayers, Scripture readings arranged for use in worship, and visual art. More information about *Voices Together* is available at www.voicestogetherhymnal.org.

2. The Mennonite tradition is a Christian tradition that began in sixteenth-century Europe as part of the Anabaptist movement within the Radical Reformation. Through immigration and global mission, Mennonites have become a worldwide community that is culturally and theologically diverse. More than 80 percent of Mennonites affiliated with Mennonite World Conference are African, Asian, or Latin American, and Mennonite congregations affiliated with MCCanada and MCUSA worship in more than twenty-five languages. MCCanada and MCUSA are progressive in terms of being integrated into mainstream society—they do not limit the use of technology

Although I agreed to facilitate a collaborative process, I quickly discovered that little structure or accountability was built into the position and that my role consisted not only of determining what worship resources are required, but also who should be involved in decisions about curating or creating these resources. Furthermore, unlike traditions where church leaders or a general assembly are required to approve liturgical resources, there was limited formal oversight from the denominations. It is therefore reassuring, on some level, that Mennonite worshiping communities are not required to use these resources. Every local congregation makes its own decisions about worship, including whether and how to use a hymnal and worship book. In this decentered structure, the power of centralized resources and those who create them is ambiguous. Who has the power to shape worship in the Mennonite tradition? What is the nature of the power of local congregations and centralized resources? How is power operative in the process of creating centralized resources?

I consider power in Mennonite worship as someone who, in the context of these small denominations and the process of creating a specific set of resources, held significant power. A critique of power from a position of power is a perilous endeavor. It was a privilege to do this work. I am grateful for the opportunity that I had to serve the church, and for the institutions that made *Voices Together* possible. It is therefore with some hesitation that I offer this critique of power in Mennonite worship, and specifically in the process of creating *Voices Together*. My objective in this chapter is to provide an example of how to analyze the multiple ways that power is operative in shaping worship in Free Church traditions, and beyond. The goal of this analysis is to enable leaders and communities to make intentional choices about how to employ power in relation to worship—power is always present; the question is only how we use it.

Power in Free Church Traditions

Mennonites have a hard time talking about power. Historically, culturally, and theologically, certain Mennonite values—the priesthood of all believers, *gelassenheit* as submission to God and the community, humility, and nonviolence and nonresistance—have made Mennonites uneasy with acknowledging power.[3] This is beginning to change with volumes like *Power,*

---

or wear distinctive dress, for example. However, they are theologically diverse, with congregations that would be more theologically conservative and those that are more progressive.

3. Ainlay, "Mennonite Culture Wars," 137.

Authority, and the Anabaptist Tradition[4] and *I've Got the Power!*[5] that name the problematic uses and positive potential of power in Mennonite contexts. As Dorothy Yoder Nyce and Lynda Nyce state, "Power, which is inherent in all social relationships, actively shapes church life, whether church members and leaders own, confront, deny, or ignore the extent of its influence within ecclesial settings."[6]

Theological claims regarding divine power are an additional barrier to acknowledging human power in worship. The foundational claims that Christians worship God through Christ in the power of the Spirit and that worship is a Spirit-led human response to a loving and powerful God can lead to reticence to acknowledge the power of human beings in shaping experiences of worship. We trust that the power of God is at work in worship in local congregations and in the creation of centralized resources, and there are moments when the movement of the Spirit is palpable. However, there are also times when these experiences feel very human: navigating relationships enmeshed in structures of gender, race, and class; struggling to raise the funds necessary to accomplish worthy goals; managing painstaking details; sending thousands of emails; and more. There are also many occasions to recognize the power of Christ that is found in human weakness (1 Cor 12:9). However, acknowledging divine power is not an excuse for ignoring the power of human beings in shaping the worship of Christian communities.

Two classic sociological studies examine power in Free Church traditions: Nancy Ammerman's *Baptist Battles* analyzes conflict in the Southern Baptism Convention in the 1970s and 1980s,[7] and Paul Harrison's *Authority and Power in the Free Church Tradition* assesses the evolution of the American Baptist Convention from its origin through the publication of the volume in 1959.[8] Both Ammerman and Harrison note that, when considering authority—the officially legitimated and voluntarily accepted use of power[9]—the landscape is very different in Free Church traditions than in hierarchical ecclesial structures:

> Leaders in voluntary organizations have very few resources at their disposal, especially compared to leaders in hierarchical or business organizations. They cannot offer rewards or threaten

---

4. Redekop and Redekop, *Power, Authority, and the Anabaptist Tradition*.

5. Castro, *I've Got the Power!*

6. Yoder Nyce and Nyce, "Power and Authority," 155.

7. Ammerman, *Baptist Battles*.

8. Harrison, *Authority and Power*.

9. Harrison, *Authority and Power*, 61.

sanctions, at least not beyond the immediate scope of their or-
ganizational staff. When related to the local units or voluntary
members who make up the bulk of the organization, they must
rely on persuasion, symbolic rewards, and the intangibles of
friendship.[10]

This creates a situation ripe for the exercise of unacknowledged yet very real power by those in bureaucratic leadership positions:

> The Baptist denominational executives are given responsibil-
> ity and limited power, but no legitimate authority. In order to
> overcome the lack of official status, they seek more power, and
> when they are successful in this enterprise, they seek authority.
> Relatively speaking, it has not been difficult for them to acquire
> the power necessary for the achievement of their assigned tasks.
> This has been accomplished by means of an unanticipated for-
> mation of an informal system of interpersonal and inter-group
> relations which bypasses the formal rules of order.[11]

Mennonite denominational worship resourcing is likewise characterized by tremendous responsibility, limited power, and the absence of authority, which leads to development of informal networks of influence both in the creation of resources and their implementation, where power is unacknowledged and unexamined. At the same time, the pre-Foucauldian model of power-as-domination that Harrison employs is inadequate for a nuanced analysis of the complexity of power relations in Mennonite worship.

Amy Allen's Theory of Power

To assess power in Mennonite worship, I draw on the critical theoretical work of Amy Allen.[12] Ingeniously integrating the insights of three influential late-twentieth-century theorists of power—Michel Foucault, Judith Butler, and Hannah Arendt—Allen defines power simply as, "the ability or

---

10. Ammerman, *Baptist Battles*, 176.

11. Harrison, *Authority and Power*, 62. Harrison defines power as "the ability of a person or group of persons to determine the action of others without regard for their needs or desires" and authority as "the right to exercise power" (4).

12. Allen, *Power of Feminist Theory*. Allen's approach to power is motivated by feminist concerns and emerges in dialogue with feminist theory. Although I borrow Allen's theory of power, my approach of power in Mennonite worship does not employ gender as a primary category of analysis. Although a feminist analysis of power in Mennonite worship would be a worthwhile endeavor, it is beyond the scope of this chapter.

capacity of an actor or set of actors to act."[13] She then identifies three senses of power that are "not best understood as distinct types or forms of power; rather they represent analytically distinguishable features of a situation"[14]:

1. *Power-over* is "the ability of an actor or set of actors to constrain the choices available to another actor or set of actors in a nontrivial way."[15] These constraints may be intentional or unintentional. *Domination* is a concept within the concept of power-over that refers to: "the ability of an actor or set of actors to constrain the choices of another actor or set of actors in a nontrivial way and in a way that works to the others' disadvantage."[16]

2. *Power-to* is "the ability of an individual actor to attain an end or series of ends"[17] and can be thought of in terms of empowerment. *Resistance* is a specific way of exercising empowerment "to attain an end or series of ends that serve to challenge and/or subvert domination."[18]

3. *Power-with* is "the ability of a collectivity to act together for the attainment of an agreed-upon end or series of ends."[19] Power-with can bind together movements across difference based on common goals rather than identity politics. *Solidarity* is a subset of power-with in which collective action is "for the attainment of an agreed-upon end of challenging, subverting, and ultimately overturning a system of domination."[20]

All three senses of power may be present in the same situation.

Allen arrives at this multifaceted definition of power after rejecting command-obedience models of power as fundamentally repressive, instead borrowing Foucault's insight that power is relational, and that the productive and repressive aspects of power are complexly intertwined: "one is both subject to power and at the same time able to take up the position of a subject in and through power."[21] Butler clarifies the possibilities and limits of the agency of the subject by introducing the concept of the citation of social norms: "Since the norms must be cited by subjects in order to

13. Allen, *Power of Feminist Theory*, 127.

14. Allen, *Power of Feminist Theory*, 129.

15. Allen, *Power of Feminist Theory*, 123.

16. Allen, *Power of Feminist Theory*, 125.

17. Allen, *Power of Feminist Theory*, 129.

18. Allen, *Power of Feminist Theory*, 126.

19. Allen, *Power of Feminist Theory*, 127.

20. Allen, *Power of Feminist Theory*, 127.

21. Allen, *Power of Feminist Theory*, 119.

be reproduced, it cannot be the case that we are completely determined by them; but since we are compelled to cite the norms in some way or another, neither are we completely unconstrained by social forces."[22] Both Foucault and Butler present accounts of power that emphasize the individual and avoid normative questions. In contrast, Arendt provides a concept of power as communicative and collective that is anchored in the normative ideal of reciprocity and mutuality. This positive framing of power as solidarity is helpful yet must be balanced by Foucault and Butler's strategic conceptions of power that allow for analysis of domination and resistance.

Allen draws on Foucault, Butler, and Arendt to serve specific aims, identifying theoretical resources she can "cull" for the purposes of her project.[23] Likewise, I borrow Allen's theory of power in service of my project—an analysis of the power relations involved in Mennonite worship and the creation of *Voices Together*. I am working with Allen's theory because it has the capacity to illuminate the specifics of this case. Following Allen's methodological approach, I consider both the *foreground perspective,* in which "the aim is to describe the power relation that exists between individuals or discrete groups of individuals,"[24] and the *background perspective,* which "focuses on the complex social relations that ground every particular power relation," including "subject-positions, cultural meanings, social practices, institutions, and structures."[25] This distinction is analytical; the foreground and background are integrally connected.

Local Congregations: Power-over Worship

Local congregations have *power-over* Mennonite worship. While congregations collaborate around common goals through regional conferences, denominations, networks, and agencies, each congregation ultimately determines its own theology and practice, including worship practice. In the *foreground,* it is local leaders and local tradition that "constrain the choices available," intentionally or unintentionally. Congregations make a wide range of choices regarding liturgical leadership, worship structures and patterns, and whether and how to use resources developed beyond the congregation.

22. Allen, *Power of Feminist Theory,* 120.

23. Allen, *Power of Feminist Theory,* 87.

24. Allen, *Power of Feminist Theory,* 130.

25. Allen, *Power of Feminist Theory,* 131. The background perspective is extremely complex. This analysis can only begin to frame deeper questions that merit further exploration.

Each congregation must decide independently whether to use *Voices Together*. Congregations take a variety of approaches to making this decision that are accompanied by their own complex internal power dynamics. For example, some congregations conduct a community-wide consensus process or vote, while others delegate the decision to a small group of leaders, such as a worship committee. In either case, in the *foreground*, congregations have power-over whether *Voices Together* will be central to their worship.

At the same time, power is operative in the *background*, constraining the agency of congregations. Three examples: (1) Larger and wealthier congregations are better equipped to make the substantial investment required to purchase a congregational set of *Voices Together* than smaller congregations with fewer financial resources. (2) Congregations that worship exclusively in a language other than English would not find enough resources in *Voices Together* to support a robust worship life.[26] (3) Congregations that use the current denominational hymnal and its supplements are more likely to view the new hymnal as serving their worship practices than congregations that use older resources or that primarily sing projected contemporary worship music. *Voices Together* is a next step for those who have been tracking the trajectory of centralized resources; it is a big leap for those who have not, often for various structural reasons.

If a congregation chooses to purchase *Voices Together*, they must then determine how to use it. In the *foreground*, there is complete freedom in terms of implementation—local communities choose which worship resources and songs to use, and whether and how to adapt them. In practice, however, congregations are constrained by the interest, knowledge, and skills of leaders and the capacities of the community. On one level this is to be expected. For example, congregational song repertoires are limited to at most a couple of hundred songs and *Voices Together* includes 759 songs; no congregation is expected to engage all this material but rather to balance using the familiar with exploring new directions. On another level, in the *background*, the choices available to leaders and congregations are often constrained in ways that work to the disadvantage of congregations that are already marginalized, especially in terms of having fewer resources.

In addition, local congregations may *resist* centralized efforts to shape worship practices. For example, in 2018, feedback was requested on an early

---

26. Although *Voices Together* includes songs in more than forty languages, including twenty languages used in worship by Mennonites in North America, the hymnal only provides enough options for communities that worship in English.

draft of a "practical guidance" paragraph to accompany the communion worship resources in the *Worship Leader Edition*[27] of *Voices Together*:

> Communion may be shared in a variety of ways. Individuals may come forward in a line to receive from servers holding a common loaf and cup, or from multiple stations where servers distribute the bread and cup. Alternatively, people may gather in small clusters to serve one another or may serve one another in one large circle, passing the elements from person to person. Communion may be received by dipping the bread into the cup, or by first eating the bread and then drinking from the cup. Another option is to pass baskets of bread and trays with individual cups among those gathered; participants receive and wait to eat and drink together. Communion may also accompany a full meal. *Although there are a variety of options, communities are encouraged to discern a consistent local practice.*

Two reviewers who saw themselves as representing local congregations felt this statement was heavy handed and offered the following comments:

> The statement about encouraging a consistent local practice feels uncomfortable to me—somewhat authoritarian, plus I don't know that I agree with it. I would prefer a softer approach, such as: "Communities may find it helpful to discern a consistent local practice."

> Suggestion: [communities are encouraged to discern] how to balance consistency and variety in their local practice.

Those who reviewed the resource resisted this phrase as a perceived attempt of centralized resourcing to dominate the decision-making of local congregations (although no congregation is required to engage with this guidance in any way). A significant issue in Mennonite worship resourcing, therefore, is how to provide centralized resources that make substantial recommendations and that can be received by congregations that are inclined to resist such recommendations. The liturgical theologians creating this resource aimed to encourage congregations to recognize the value of repeated ritual and to advise that changing the method of distribution each time communion is celebrated to "keep it interesting" leads to participants focusing more on the logistics of how to receive the bread and cup than on the theological, spiritual, or embodied aspects of the practice. At the same time, if such a statement simply provokes resistance, it is unhelpful and weakens the capacity for further engagement with centrally developed resources.

27. Johnson, *Voices Together: Worship Leader Edition* (emphasis added).

In these dynamics of domination and resistance, there is an interplay between the foreground and the background. In the foreground, congregations have power-over worship. However, in the background, these choices are constrained by the nature of congregations, music and worship leaders within congregations, and their positions within the denominations and Canadian and American society. Furthermore, because local congregations have power-over worship, a new hymnal must offer resources that can be received and, as a whole, be a "saleable volume"—it must be a product that congregations desire to use since there is no way to require its use. In addition, to be a financially viable product for central agencies, it must be saleable to the largest possible number of congregations, or at least the congregations that have the capacity to purchase the largest number of copies. This perpetuates a pattern of centralized resources being directed toward the "broad middle" of the church rather than congregations on the margins.

Centralized Worship Resources:
Power-with and Power-to

Despite the constraints of congregational polity in capitalist society, the content of the collection is *not* simply determined by the desires of the most likely customers. One of the primary goals of centralized structures in Mennonite contexts is to accomplish aims that cannot be achieved by local congregations alone, such as operating universities and seminaries, international development agencies, and publishing houses. In this way, the centralized development of worship resources is a manifestation of *power-with*, "the ability of a collectivity to act together for the attainment of an agreed-upon end."

One aim of a centrally developed Mennonite hymnal and worship book is to give congregations the *power-to* worship in ways that they are unable to on their own, such as by selecting from among thousands of resources or bringing together writing teams from across the continent. Another equally important aim is to increase the capacity of local congregations to exercise *power-with* other local congregations—especially congregations very different from one another—toward a variety of common aims associated with God's just and peaceful reign, such as fostering mutual relationships between those on the margins of the denominations and those in the "broad middle."

In the foreground, *centralized worship resourcing is a manifestation of local congregations exercising power-with one another to give each local congregation the power-to make choices about worship that further increase their capacity to exercise power-with one another in service of God's reign.* I consider whether and how this ideal is manifest in *Voices Together* as a cultural object and in the process of creating the volume.

The Power of Mennonite Hymnals and Worship Books

Denominational hymnals are generational, and it is common for denominations to produce a new collection of music and worship resources every twenty to thirty years. *Voices Together* (2020) is the third denominational hymnal and worship book developed collaboratively by the community of congregations that now form MCUSA and MCCanada, building on *The Mennonite Hymnal* (1969) and *Hymnal: A Worship Book* (1992), as well as drawing on two well-received supplements, *Sing the Journey* (2005) and *Sing the Story* (2007).[28] All of these volumes include both songs and words for worship, such as prayers, Scripture readings, and resources to support practices like baptism, communion, child blessing, and funerals. The collections in their entirety are powerful forces shaping worship and song in the Mennonite tradition in Canada and the United States. Worship is formative as well as expressive. To borrow from Foucault and Allen, worship forms through the exercise of power that both produces and represses; it enables and constrains individuals and communities through power-to and power-over. Drawing on interviews with more than 100 Mennonites in Canada and the United States, Marlene Kropf and Kenneth Nafziger argue that singing in worship forms Mennonites in "three fundamental ways": (1) "our vision of God is formed," (2) "we are formed into Christian community," and (3) "our life is formed as people of the spirit in the world."[29]

The *theological commitments* communicated in worship are one dimension of the formative power of worship. These commitments are not only constructed cognitively, but anchored in relational encounter with the divine through the "sacrament" of song: "a personal encounter with the sacred in a way that engages the whole person: body, heart, and mind."[30] Caring for the vision of God expressed and encountered in worship through words, music, and images is critical.[31] The vision of God expressed in *Voices*

28. The General Conference and (Old) Mennonite Church collaborated on *The Mennonite Hymnal*; the Church of the Brethren joined these denominations in creating *Hymnal: A Worship Book*; the supplements were developed by MCCanada and MCUSA, *Sing the Journey*, *Sing the Story*.

29. Kropf and Nafziger, *Singing*, 110.

30. Kropf and Nafziger, *Singing*, 132.

31. Content analysis of Mennonite hymn singing for theological purposes includes Penner, "Mennonite Silences and Feminist Voices"; Tice, "Who Do You Sing

Together is one of the most widely disseminated, easily accessible, and emotionally resonant articulations of Mennonite theology that Mennonites in Canada and the United States will engage in the decades ahead.

More subtle and relational aspects of worship are also powerfully formative, particularly in the construction of individual identity and the *creation and solidification of communal identity*. Drawing on case studies in three Mennonite congregations, Jonathan Dueck argues that relationships nurtured through specific musical contexts, rather than theological principles or musical styles, are primary in commitment to and conflict over church music.[32] The importance of singing for "Mennonite identity" is a central theme in Kropf and Nafziger, and is closely linked to specific relationships, singing traditions, and resources:

> Mennonites who were interviewed were acutely aware of diverse strands of connection that happen when they sing—connections with the universal church, with people of the past, their sisters and brothers in the faith, parents and other family members, someone they just happened to sit next to, the sensuality of men's and women's voices in harmony, and the many layers of emotional and spiritual connectedness in the congregation. This awareness of connection was illustrated by a group of students from Goshen (Indiana) College who were studying abroad for a semester in China. After being there a few weeks, they sent an urgent message home: "Please send us some Mennonite hymnals. In this strange land, *we don't know who we are without our song books*."[33]

Drawing on ethnographic research in one Mennonite congregation, Katie Graber interrogates the relationship between singing from a hymnal and Mennonite identity:

> By continually singing and talking about singing, many Mennonites have collectively agreed that it is important to Mennonite identity. My answer to the question, "Can music make a person Mennonite?" is yes, though not in any simple way that claims "I sing, therefore I am Mennonite," or "I'm Mennonite, therefore I sing." Rather it is the complex interaction and layering of actions, objects, sounds, and words that construct what we together understand as Mennonite identity. *We understand our*

That I Am?"; Tice, "Singing Shapes Communion"; and Johnson, "Political Theology of *Hymnal*."

    32. Dueck, *Congregational Music, Conflict, and Community*.

    33. Kropf and Nafziger, *Singing*, 122 (emphasis added).

> *identity through the use of the hymnal,* as well as through those
> elusive moments when the ephemeral aspects of music and dis-
> course line up with our physical experiences.[34]

Hymns and hymnals are central to the construction of Mennonite identity and community in certain Mennonite congregations and contexts.

At the same time, many Mennonite congregations do not use a hymnal. Mennonites draw on music and worship practices from around the world and Indigenous traditions in North America, and many have adopted contemporary worship music,[35] all of which have similar capacities to form individual and communal identity.[36] The culturally bound format of a hymnal is particularly limiting in relation to these musical expressions, which were often never intended for Western musical notation or the printed page, but are best learned by ear. Extemporaneous prayer, physical movement and dance, architecture and art, and other aspects of worship are likewise challenging to acknowledge and celebrate within the constraints of a hymnal. The medium itself exerts a certain power-over what, and therefore who, can be included. Finding ways for centralized worship resourcing to move beyond the restrictions of this format is crucial.[37]

Nevertheless, hymnals continue to have a high degree of power-over Mennonite identity, especially in terms of determining who is included and excluded from the community that defines its identity in relation to these books. Therefore, a hymnal may also have the power-to change these boundaries. Through the material included in the collection, those who are at home in a hymnal may be empowered to see others as part of their community. Likewise, those who are not at home in a hymnal, through the material in the collection, may be empowered to see themselves as part of the Mennonite tradition in North America. How these boundaries are defined shapes how "our life is formed as people of the spirit in the world," how faith commitments and communal identity are *lived out in ways that do good or harm* within and beyond the church community. Worship and song are not neutral—both healing and hurtful outcomes are real, and likely simultaneous, possibilities. Recognizing that hymnals and worship books as cultural objects are powerful symbols of Mennonite identity and powerful forces in

---

34. Graber, "Identity and the Hymnal," 73 (emphasis added).

35. Graber, "Mennonite Voices."

36. Dueck, *Congregational Music, Conflict, and Community*; Myrick, "Relational Power, Music, and Identity."

37. A group of volunteers has developed a website curating and cataloging worship resources from an Anabaptist perspective called *Together in Worship* (www.togetherinworship.net).

the formation of community that have concrete implications for good and harm in the church and in society, a question the *Voices Together* committee asked often was: "*Who are we singing with?*"

Questions of identity and community are embedded in worship resources as well as songs. One example is resources for "Confessing Faith," such as creeds, affirmations of faith, and prayers of commitment. *The Mennonite Hymnal* includes four "Affirmations of Faith."[38] *Hymnal: A Worship Book* likewise incorporates a section of eight items titled "Affirming Faith." The *Hymnal Companion* discusses the different approaches to confessions of faith in worship in the Mennonite and Brethren traditions, the two traditions collaborating on the volume.[39] Personal conversations with both Mennonite and Brethren members of the *Hymnal: A Worship Book* committee reveal that this section was a compromise. For example, including the Apostles' Creed but not the Nicene Creed in the volume was a concession for both traditions that fully satisfied neither.

From the outset of the *Voices Together* process, the contents of the "Confessing Faith" section have prompted spontaneous and divergent feedback which may reflect their importance for defining identity and community.[40] A consulting process was established to invite advice from Mennonite

38. *Mennonite Hymnal*, 720–23. The *Mennonite Hymnal* offers the following introduction to this material: "Four affirmations of faith are given to provide an opportunity for congregations to express unitedly and in summary form the essentials of Christian belief. These affirmations do not represent official documents of any church body; but they are, in a sense, the church's answer to the Word of God. No one statement covers the entire range of Christian doctrine. The Nicene Creed and the Apostles' Creed are confessions that were developed from the fourth to the eighth centuries. A contemporary Affirmation of Faith (no. 4) was created by several leaders for *The Mennonite Hymnal* and was completed in 1967. Every hymn that a congregation sings is, in a sense, an affirmation of faith. Scripture readings can also be used a confession of faith."

39. *Hymnal: A Worship Book*, 710–17. "Brethren claim the New Testament as their only creed; thus they have not drafted confessions of faith during their history. . . . Reading affirmations of faith in a worship setting is an accepted practice. However, many Brethren are uneasy about using creeds. On the other hand, Mennonites have a long history of making confessions of faith to reflect their biblical beliefs and understandings, their tradition, and their current practice. . . . While Anabaptist/Mennonite confessions of faith have been used in worship rarely due to their length, other creeds, confessions of faith, and affirmations have been used frequently" (*Hymnal Companion*, 413).

40. Five theology faculty members at Mennonite colleges spontaneously commented on the Confessing Faith section, including one expressing surprise that the Apostles' Creed is included in a Mennonite resource, another insisting that the Apostles' Creed be included in the next hymnal, two strongly encouraging the return of the Nicene Creed, and one recommending an insertion into the creeds written by Jürgen Moltmann. In an initial testing of ideas at a Toronto Mennonite Theological Centre conference, the Apostles' and Nicene Creeds were the only resources a group of Mennonite systematic

theologians, pastors, and worship leaders on thirteen potential resources.[41] Certain points of consensus emerged.[42] However, at least one consultant was "not in favor" or "strongly opposed" to each of the other nine items. The Nicene Creed was the point of greatest divergence, with one theologian indicating it "absolutely must be included" and another being "strongly opposed to including this item." The "Immigrants' Creed" was another point of tension.[43] Discussion of the "Confessing Faith" resources among the Mennonite Worship and Song Committee was also characterized by strong and divergent perspectives. No congregation is required to use these items, and many will not. Those who do embrace these resources have the freedom to adapt them, or to frame them in creative ways, for example by juxtaposing traditional liturgical texts with more expansive language for God. Therefore, what is at stake here is not primarily what happens in worship in local congregations but how Mennonite faith and practice is defined in the highly symbolic space of a hymnal and worship book. *Who are we worshiping with? How are we connected to the past, the church worldwide, and the broader Christian tradition? Who are we, and who is part of this community?* This raises significant questions about who and what was involved in determining the contents of *Voices Together*.

Power in the Foreground of the *Voices Together* Process

When we consider power in the foreground of the process of shaping *Voices Together*, certain explicit power relations existed between groups

---

theologians could agree should be included, although these resources raised questions for other participants. In addition, a group of pastors who serve congregations with many new Canadians in Mennonite Church Eastern Canada recommended including "The Immigrant's Creed" by José Luis Casal.

41. Four Mennonite theologians, as well as four hymnal committee members with pastoral experience or theological training, participated in this process. Participants were invited to provide comments as well as to score each item:
    5 - You feel the item absolutely must be included
    4 - You strongly support including this item
    3 - You are indifferent, not opposed to inclusion
    2 - You are not in favor, you do not think the item merits wide circulation
    1 - You are strongly opposed to including this item.

42. No one opposed the inclusion of the Apostles Creed, the Shared Convictions of Mennonite World Conference, a Spanish language creed, or a Menno Simons quotation. These items are included in *Voices Together*, 923, 925, 927, 921.

43. Feedback was received by email in response to a sampler. Members of the coalition for Dismantling the Doctrine of Discovery were invited to comment. An article about this resource was published in the *Mennonite World Review* (Schrag, "Ancient Bones, New Flesh").

and individuals. In 2015, the *denominations*, MCCanada and MCUSA, empowered MennoMedia to pursue the creation of a hymnal and worship book. This decision was based on groundwork established in the 2005 and 2007 hymnal supplements and a 2011 curriculum resource and survey.[44] Denominational leaders were present at the first and final meetings of the hymnal committee to bless the project but did not have power-over what is included—their approval of the content was at no point required or requested beyond a general show of support.

MennoMedia, as the *publisher*, had power-over many aspects of the process, including finances, timeline, formal "marketing" decisions (such as the title and color of the book), and the project director, Bradley Kauffman, who was hired as a MennoMedia staff person for the duration of the project. The *project director* had the final word on decisions about what was included in *Voices Together*. All committee members signed a Memorandum of Understanding in which we committed to: "Defer to the Project Director and the Publisher to make final decisions if a conflict of interest arises."

The twelve members of the *Mennonite Worship and Song Committee* (MWSC) were volunteers, including the music, text, and worship resources editors, who received small honorariums.[45] The committee included: six women and six men; five Canadians and seven Americans from various geographic regions; and members ranging in age from an undergraduate student to a retiree. Specific steps were taken to ensure that the committee included people of color, leading to the appointment of one African American and one Korean American member. One member is a native Spanish speaker. Every member of the initial committee identifies as a musician, apart from me as the worship resources editor. About one year into the process, an additional committee member was added with a focus on worship resources and, around the same time, another committee member resigned. Between 2016 and 2020, this group of thirteen people had primary responsibility for determining the contents of *Voices Together*.

The MWSC aimed to exercise power-with the *broader church*. The first year of the process was dedicated to listening through surveys, focus groups, events, and an open submissions process. Recognizing that congregations that worship in languages other than English are less likely to engage

44. *The Heart of Mennonite Worship: Five Vital Resources* was developed by the no-longer-extant Mennonite Church Binational Worship Council.

45. The Mennonite Worship and Song Committee consisted of Bradley Kauffman (project director), Adam Tice (text editor), Benjamin Bergey (music editor), Sarah Kathleen Johnson (worship resources editor), Darryl Neustaedter Barg, Paul Dueck, Mike Erb, Katie Graber, Emily Grimes, Tom Harder, SaeJin Lee, Anneli Loepp Thiessen, Cynthia Neufeld Smith, and Allan Rudy-Froese.

in these spaces, a grant allowed three committee members to visit eleven congregations across Canada and the United States to hear stories about music and worship and to observe and film worship services and music rehearsals.[46] Samplers and events were used to test material at several points in the process.

In addition, expert *consultants* were engaged around many topics: songs and worship resources with connections to Indigenous communities, African American musical idioms, worship in Spanish-speaking congregations, music and worship resources from the Taizé community, sixteenth-century Anabaptist sources, texts and tunes from before the Reformation, an ecumenical core of texts and tunes, Russian Mennonite Kernlieder, German chorales, incorporating American Sign Language into the collection, interfaith resources, and more. In addition, separate volunteer structures were developed to work with the nonmusical aspects of the collection, including: creating and adapting resources for central practices like baptism, communion, child blessing, marriage, and funerals; selecting and arranging Scripture readings; curating a series of visual artworks; and screening submissions and published collections of resources. An effort was made to give power-to experts to shape the collection.

Determining the contents of *Voices Together* based on input from the committee, the church, and consultants within the tight space constraints was complex. Recognizing the time limitations of the process and the expertise of the editors, most final decisions were made by consensus by the *editorial team*. Although crucial qualitative and quantitative feedback were provided by all committee members regarding both the overall process and each song and resource at multiple points throughout that process, final selections and revisions were made by the editorial team rather than by direct committee vote. While aiming to exercise power-with the committee, editors had much power-over the content of *Voices Together*.

The project director empowered *editors* to finalize many decisions in collaboration with the tune, text, and worship resources subcommittees. While I was empowered to have power-over many worship resource decisions throughout the process, I attempted to give power-to others and to exercise power-with others, including the worship resources subcommittee, other committees, consultants, and via ongoing check-ins with the MWSC. Almost all decisions about worship resources were made through collaboration and consensus. At the same time, determining who was at the table, the structure of the process, and affirming the outcome were significant

46. Vital Worship Grant, Calvin Institute of Christian Worship. Graber, "Mennonite Voices."

exercises of power-over. For example, in relation to the "Confessing Faith" resources, at a certain point I had to carefully consider all of the consultation and discussion and make a proposal to the worship resources committee and then the MWSC, recognizing that the final selection of resources would not reflect a consensus.

The content of *Voices Together* is an expression of giving power-to and exercising power-with many contributors, not only the MWSC, the editorial team, or the publisher, although each of these groups exercised power-over certain aspects of the book. True to its name, the worship and song collection brings many "voices together." At the same time, some voices are more powerful than others and some voices remain absent.

Power in the Background of the *Voices Together* Process

Examining power in the background is more challenging than the foreground, especially because the MWSC and Mennonites in North America are enmeshed in subject-positions, cultural meanings, structures, and institutions far beyond those immediately visible in the process of creating centralized resources, particularly, but not only, in relation to questions of race, class, and gender. Therefore, I will focus on the background perspective of only two aspects of the process of developing *Voices Together*: (1) the formation of the committee through an open application process, and (2) relying on volunteer editors, committee members, and consultants.

An *open application process* for all positions on the committee initially appears to be an example of the mutuality and reciprocity associated with power-with, especially compared to committee members being appointed, as with *Hymnal: A Worship Book*. However, a major limitation of this approach is that applying to participate in such a project appeals to those who see a "hymnal" as immediately relevant to them: musicians in congregations that use hymnals. This closely correlates with white "ethnic Mennonite" identity and classical musical training.[47] Certainly this ethnic background and these skills are important to represent on the committee. However, given the significance of a hymnal for Mennonite identity—especially expanding what it means to be Mennonite in Canada, the United States, and worldwide in the twenty-first century—engagement with a broader cross-section of the church is required. Furthermore, due to the theological, historical, and pastoral weight the book carries, as well as the poetics of selecting and revising

---

47. Mennonite is an ethnicity in addition to a religious tradition. Various ethnic Mennonite identities are present in MCCanada and MCUSA, with Swiss-German and Russian Mennonite groups being dominant.

hymn texts, a wider range of skills is needed. Specific steps were taken to address these issues, including inviting additional applicants and engaging a substantial number of consultants. However, the mechanism through which the committee was formed in the background appears not only an instance of power-over, but also of domination: "the ability of an actor or set of actors to constrain the choices of another actor or set of actors in a nontrivial way and in a way that works to the others' disadvantage." The open application process facilitated the ongoing marginalization of nonethnic Mennonite identities, nonmusical dimensions of worship, and congregational song beyond classical repertoire. Again, the MWSC worked very hard to foster solidarity within these limitations, but the foundation of the process was not a solid starting point.

Relying on *volunteers* for both editorial and committee member positions limited who was able to accept these roles. On the most basic level, serving on the MWSC involved being able to spend more than fifty days within a three-year period attending in-person meetings. In addition, committee members were expected to spend ten hours a week working on the collection at home, and editors often worked twenty hours a week or more. This would simply not be possible for those in less flexible jobs or who need to be working those days and hours to make ends meet. Financial privilege was a prerequisite for serving on the committee. I could not have served on the committee if I did not have the privilege of being enrolled in a fully funded and relatively flexible doctoral program during this time. In addition, I took a one-year leave from my studies to work full time on Mennonite worship resourcing.[48] Working full-time on *Voices Together* was a tremendous privilege, and one that substantially increased my personal power in the process. The burden imposed on volunteers and the limitations that were placed on who was able to serve, particularly in the creation of a resource so central to Mennonite identity and community formation, is another instance of domination that limits the capacity of the collection to foster solidarity across class differences, and the associated differences in race, gender, geographic location, and theological orientation.

Finally, relying on volunteers means that the only thing those in leadership can say to committee members is "thank you." As Ammerman

---

48. My role included developing the worship resources for *Voices Together*, editing the *Worship Leader Edition*, pursuing the possibility of a worship resourcing website (now www.togetherinworship.net), and leading community and congregational events. This was financially possible only because I took the initiative to apply for a substantial grant from the regional church body that I am affiliated with, Mennonite Church Eastern Canada. I was fortunate that the funds were available and that I felt I had the power-to apply for them and was able to exercise that power with support from my networks within the church.

observes, leaders have "very few resources at their disposal" and "cannot offer rewards or threaten sanctions." As a result, there are those who consistently step up and do the work and those who do not. Every member of the MWSC dedicated thousands of hours to the creation of the collection. However, the hard work of creating *Voices Together* was not equally distributed—the women of the committee took on significant additional responsibility, especially between meetings, and particularly in relation to essential yet more administrative tasks. Although it is sometimes possible to point to differences in employment and life situation, these too are enmeshed in gendered social structures. Particularly sobering is the fact that two women of color resigned from the committee, one after the first year and another in the final months of the process when the collection was close to complete. A primary reason they gave for resigning was that they felt unable to keep up with the work between meetings in relation to changing life circumstances. Other white male committee members were likewise unable to keep up with work between meetings, and faced similar life circumstances, but did not feel compelled to resign. I do not point to these patterns to lay blame—I have complete confidence in the best intentions of every single committee member and those in leadership. At the same time, the gendered patterns associated with who carried the bulk of the work, and who resigned when they felt they could not continue on, reflect larger patterns of domination that shape this process. Perhaps this is unavoidable as human beings who, as Butler describes, are compelled to cite social norms, even when resisting them. However, it is especially lamentable when a primary objective of centralized worship resourcing is to foster solidarity in service of God's just and peaceful reign. Without clear-eyed attention to the multidimensional nature of power, Free Church worship risks reproducing relationships of domination present in our broader social context that are in violation of our ecclesiological commitments and eschatological vision.

Conclusion

Power "actively shapes church life, whether church members and leaders own, confront, deny, or ignore the extent of its influence within ecclesial settings."[49] This chapter aims to own and confront power in the process of shaping the worship of the church by applying Amy Allen's theory of power to the case of Mennonite worship in Canada and the United States and specifically to the development of the *Voices Together* hymnal and worship book.

49. Yoder Nyce and Nyce, "Power and Authority," 155.

Power is an unavoidable aspect of corporate worship because power is simply "the ability or capacity of an actor or set of actors to act," whether by constraining (power-over), empowering (power-to), or collaborating (power-with). Power is present both in the foreground, in observable relationships and formal authorities, and in the background, in often invisible subject-positions, cultural meanings, and structures. In sometimes strong and sometimes subtle ways, worship and worship resources are products of power that also exercise power, especially in defining individual and collective identity. The creation of centralized resources, like *Voices Together*, is necessarily enmeshed in complex power structures. Nevertheless, centralized resourcing has a crucial role to play in fostering solidarity, especially in empowering local congregations to exercise power-with a broader community. At the same time, in Free Church traditions, local congregations have ultimate power-over worship practices, including whether and how they engage centralized resources. I offer this analysis with the hope that those who shape Christian worship within and beyond Free Church traditions will find ways to avoid domination and foster solidarity in human relationships, trusting the power of the Spirit of God at work in the church at worship.

Bibliography

Ainlay, Stephen. "Mennonite Culture Wars: Power, Authority, and Domination." In *Power, Authority, and the Anabaptist Tradition*, edited by Benjamin Redekop and Calvin Redekop, 136–54. Baltimore: Johns Hopkins University Press, 2001.

Allen, Amy. *The Power of Feminist Theory: Domination, Resistance, Solidarity*. Boulder, CO: Westview, 1999.

Ammerman, Nancy. *Baptist Battles: Social Change and Religious Conflict in the Southern Baptist Convention*. New Brunswick, NJ: Rutgers University Press, 1990.

Castro, Jennifer, ed. *I've Got the Power! Naming and Reclaiming Power as a Force for Good: Presentations from the Women Doing Theology Conference*. Elkhart, IN: Women in Leadership Project Mennonite Church USA, 2018.

Dueck, Jonathan. *Congregational Music, Conflict and Community*. New York: Routledge, 2017.

Graber, Katie. "Identity and the Hymnal: Can Music Make a Person Mennonite?" In *Sound in the Land: Essays on Mennonites and Music*, edited by Marlene Epp and Carol Ann Weaver, 64–77. Kitchener, ON: Pandora, 2005.

———. "Mennonite Voices." *American Religious Sounds Project*. https://gallery.religioussounds.osu.edu/mennonite-voices-exhibit/.

Harrison, Paul. *Authority and Power in the Free Church Tradition: A Social Case Study of the American Baptist Convention*. Princeton: Princeton University Press, 1959.

The Heart of Mennonite Worship: Five Vital Resources. Scottdale, PA: Faith and Life Resources, 2011.

Hymnal: A Worship Book. Scottdale, PA: Mennonite Publishing Network, 1992.

Hymnal Companion. Scottdale, PA: Mennonite Publishing Network, 1996.

Janecek, Anna. "Gutierrez Is also a Mennonite Name: Issues in Identity and Hymnody in Southern Ontario Mennonite Churches." In *Sound in the Land: Essays on Mennonites and Music,* edited by Marlene Epp and Carol Ann Weaver, 143–58. Kitchener, ON: Pandora, 2005.

Johnson, Sarah Kathleen. "The Political Theology of *Hymnal: A Worship Book.*" Paper presented at Sound in the Lands conference, Conrad Grebel University College, Waterloo, Ontario, Canada, June 2009.

———, ed. *Voices Together: Worship Leader Edition.* Harrisonburg, VA: MennoMedia, 2020.

Kropf, Marlene, and Kenneth Nafziger. *Singing: A Mennonite Voice.* Scottdale, PA: Herald, 2001.

The Mennonite Hymnal. Scottdale, PA: Herald, 1969.

Myrick, Nathan. "Relational Power, Music, and Identity: The Emotional Efficacy of Congregational Song." *Yale Journal of Music and Religion* 3.1 (2017) Article 5.

Penner, Carol Jean. "Mennonite Silences and Feminist Voices: Peace Theology and Violence against Women." PhD diss., Toronto School of Theology, 1999.

Redekop, Benjamin, and Calvin Redekop, eds. *Power, Authority, and the Anabaptist Tradition.* Baltimore: Johns Hopkins University Press, 2001.

Schrag, Paul. "Ancient Bones, New Flesh." *Mennonite World Review,* September 16, 2019. https://anabaptistworld.org/ancient-bones-new-flesh/.

Sing the Journey. Scottdale, PA: Mennonite Publishing Network, 2005.

Sing the Story. Scottdale, PA: Mennonite Publishing Network, 2007.

Tice, Adam. "Singing Shapes Communion: The Progression of Eucharistic Theology in 20th-Century Mennonite Hymnals." *The Conrad Grebel Review* 24.3 (Fall 2006) 45–64.

———. "Who Do You Sing That I Am? The Life of Jesus in Twentieth-Century Mennonite Hymnals: A Case Study in the Use of Hymnody for Theological Research." Master's thesis, Associated Mennonite Biblical Seminary, 2007.

Voices Together. Harrisonburg, VA: MennoMedia, 2020.

Yoder Nyce, Dorothy, and Lynda Nyce. "Power and Authority in Mennonite Ecclesiology: A Feminist Perspective." In *Power, Authority, and the Anabaptist Tradition,* edited by Benjamin Redekop and Calvin Redekop, 155–73. Baltimore: Johns Hopkins University Press, 2001.

5

The Power of Ritual
to Authorize Leaders

Divine Agent in the Pulpit:
An Analysis of the Charismatic Power
of Korean Revivalist Preachers

Jaewoong Jung

After a preacher delivers *the sermon enthusiastically, congregants gather around the altar and pray to God fervently, kneeling on the floor and stretching their hands up to the cross. As their prayer grows deeper and their praying voice grows louder, the preacher moves toward the congregants and lays his hands on the head of individuals. In the meantime, if a couple of sick congregants are brought to the preacher, he presses his hands down on the head strongly and proclaims to expel demons and illness out of the sick persons in a shouting voice. Some of the praying folks fall down to the floor and tremble, as if they are entering into a trance. Those who believe that these experiences are truly from God and that the preacher is a genuine mediator of the divine grace would respect the preacher as a divine agent who has the divine power to reveal God's words hidden in the text and liberate them from the bondage to the evil which has troubled their lives. However, there are others who see the event from a different view. They wonder if what they are witnessing is truly*

96

from God or human manipulation. Depending on the answer to this question, the divine authority of the preacher can be accepted or rejected.

This is a description of a Korean revival meeting, a liturgical practice that is widely observed among Korean Free Churches, where the charismatic power of Korean revivalist preachers is formed, manifested, and accepted in a certain way. The participants at revival meetings, including preachers and congregants, consciously and unconsciously construct a power dynamic between them and manifest it through their ritual practices at the meeting. Although some of them might be keenly aware of unequal social status between preachers and participants and would sense vaguely that ritual practices have some relevance to such a power structure, it would be very hard to explain clearly how their ritual practices contribute to forming the power structure that defines their unequal status. Thus, most would believe that rituals do nothing with the formation of the preacher's power in worship, while some others would consider the charismatic power of the preacher purely a mysterious result of divine grace. However, a liturgical scholar who acknowledges that liturgy is a human work as well as God's work would not deem it as a pure mystery but approach it as a social phenomenon, recognizing the human side of the liturgical event as well as its divine side.

Based on this understanding, this essay attempts to analyze how ritual practices at revival meetings contribute to the formation of preachers' charismatic power. Here, the charismatic power of preachers is considered a result of social interaction rather than a spiritual gift conferred by God. This article argues the charismatic power of Korean revivalist preachers is constituted through a social process in which individual participants of unequal status recognize, resist, negotiate, and/or legitimate it. Drawing on the theories of practice, developed by Pierre Bourdieu and Catherine Bell, I argue that the charismatic power of revivalists is a symbolic power which is grounded on symbolic capital, working in a particular religious field, and legitimates the revivalist's domination over congregants. Meanwhile, I will show that rituals work to manifest, habituate, and reinforce the power relations of the ritual agents. Based on this theoretical framework, I suggest an alternative understanding of clerical power as the result of collaboration and complicity by all the agents, not the exclusive source of the preacher's power supported by religious illusion or human manipulation, which could alleviate the clerical authoritarianism in Korean Free Churches.

Historical Development of Ritual Practices at Korean Revivals

Before analyzing the practices theoretically, briefly sketching the historical development of ritual practices at Korean revivals in relation to the shift in revivalist preachers' power would be helpful to enhance non-Korean readers' understanding. A Korean revival meeting is a liturgical practice that has been widely used in Korean Free Churches. Because Korea is not Christendom, unlike European countries, but a secular and religious plural society, it is basically inappropriate to call any church in Korea a state church. Even if one defines Free Churches per its denominational tradition, except for the Anglican Church, Lutheran Church, and Roman Catholic Church, the majority of Korean Protestant Churches can be categorized as Free Churches, which advocate freedom of belief and conscience, separation of the church from state, dedicated discipleship, individual members' independence and autonomy, and noninstitutional clerical authority. Because most of them are rooted in North American and British revivalist movements from the nineteenth and twentieth centuries, revival meetings are widely used at Free Churches across denominations.[1] Another reason for widespread revivals in Korea is because they tend to consider the Great Revival in 1907 as the archetypal and ideal spiritual experience of Korean Protestants.

The Great Revival and *Tongsung Kido*

The Great Revival in Pyeong Yang was the event that offers Korean Christians the foundational experience of divine encounter in worship. The preachers at the Great Revival became the legend of Korean preaching and the preachers in the later revivals have sought to reenact this archetypical experience at the revivals by repeating the ritual practices at the Great Revival. Therefore, it is a good starting point to discuss what we want to talk about with this essay. Perhaps the most famous scene of the Great Revival should be *tongsung kido*. William Blair reports that it happened after the evening meeting on January 7th, 1907. After the sermon by Bruce Hunt concluded, Graham Lee requested the congregation to pray aloud simultaneously by saying, "Let us pray together," and the congregation began to pray aloud fervently but simultaneously audible in discernable voices, to a degree that William Blair was able to discern what individuals prayed.[2] This audible prayer later became known as *tongsung kido*. After the prayer

1. Joo and Kim, "Reformed Tradition in Korea," 485.
2. Blair, *God in Korea*, 66–67.

following the sermon, a couple of participants gave testimonies, confessing their sins, and all together sang a hymn. After that, the official meeting was over so that whoever wanted to go home was allowed to go. The remaining people began to confess their sins publicly and prayed for repentance.

In the report of the Pyeong Yang Revival, it is noteworthy that *tongsung kido* was not coerced by any clerical person but came spontaneously out of participants' piety and that the preachers were not described as a divine agent who possessed a spiritual power, given by God exclusively to them. That is, at this point, preachers were not considered the divine agent having charismatic power, and their power was not related to particular liturgical practices, as the spiritual experience at the revival was not a result of clerical mediation of divine grace but participants' faithful and spontaneous responses to the work of the Holy Spirt.

Although Sun-Ju Kil played an important role at the revival and became one of the most renowned revivalist preachers in Korea later, he didn't claim himself as a divine agent who kindled the spiritual great event and participants didn't consider him so at this point. While they responded to the sermon he preached and accepted that they experienced the powerful presence of the Holy Spirit who revealed their sins and embraced the sinners, it is hard to see that they attributed their spiritual experience to the charismatic power of Rev. Kil then. Also, *tongsung kido* was performed as a spontaneous expression of piety, which was not set up in the worship by a person of authority in the church. There was no preacher's hand-laying prayer during the Pyeong Yang Revival. so, when did Korean revivalist preachers begin to be considered divine agents?

Healing Revivals and *Ansu Kido*

It would be traced to the rise of divine healer preachers in Korean churches. Ik-Doo Kim, a Presbyterian minister, was the most prominent healing revivalist preacher in the 1920s. According to the report of his ministry, he led 776 revival meetings, preached around 28,000 sermons, and healed about 10,000 patients.[3] Because his healing ministry became so famous, many secular and Christian newspapers reported the healing events amid his revival meetings. Also, in order to check whether the healing really happened or not, Take-Kwon Lim interviewed those who claimed healing experiences at Kim's revival meetings and published these stories as *Evidence of Miracles in Chosun Christian Churches.*[4]

3. Kim, *History of Korean Christian Preaching*, 221–22.

4. Lim, *Evidence of Miracles.*

The notable elements of his healing meetings are his thorough preparatory fasting prayers and hands-laying prayer (Korean: *ansu kido*). After he prepared thoroughly through fasting prayer and praying in the mountains, he led revival meetings and prayed for patients by laying his hands on them. At first, he performed a hands-laying prayer for each patient at available times during the revival meetings, but later he had the patients sit together in one place according to their illness and prayed over them collectively. After that, at the dawn prayer meeting after the healing ritual the night before, he requested the patients to give testimony about their healing experience.

These ritual practices at his revivals distinguish his healing revivals from the other revivals, which focused on the exposition of the Bible. The typical revival meeting before the 1920s was the Bible conference (*sakyung-hoe*) or the revival-Bible conference (*puhung-sakyung hoe*),[5] which focused on teaching the Bible, Christian doctrine, Christian life, and management of the congregation. Although *tongsung kido* followed the sermon, it was not a central element of the revivals but rather a responsive practice to the preaching word. But, at healing revivals the focus shifted from the word to the rituals. Meanwhile, in terms of the preacher's role at revivals, the role of ritual performer became more highlighted than the role of the expositor. While exposition of the Bible was a primary focus at Kim's revivals, the participants, desiring divine healing, concentrated on receiving his hand-laying prayer as they believed it was a channel of divine healing. It was dangerous to him, because it could lead to a misunderstanding of his role in the miracle.

Therefore, he emphasized that healing is solely dependent on God, as Rhodes reported, "He told the patients that he can do nothing, and if something happens, it is the power of God who acts in the name of Jesus."[6] Similarly, Gale reports that Kim didn't claim he could cure the illness; instead, he knew the truth that if patients had a strong faith along with a pure heart, God probably would answer and many patients would get healed.[7] Ik-Doo Kim emphasized that he was only a channel of the divine grace and that healing was solely God's sovereign act. This understanding of healers can be found in a presbytery's report on Kim's healing, as written: "While God uses Rev. Ik-Doo Kim as a machine, the miracles of healing through prayer happened. The healed people were numerous in the country."[8]

---

5. Yun, "Study on Change," 123–46.

6. Rhodes, *History of the Korea Mission Presbyterian Church U.S.A.*, 290.

7. Gale, "Revival in Seoul," 4–5.

8. Report on Hwang Ui-rohoe's situation, 9th memoir of the Korean Presbyterian Church (1920), 87.

Kim's strong emphasis on the divine cause of healing, claiming that healing was not from himself but from God, showed paradoxically that he was recognized as a divine agent. The steeply growing number of participants at his revivals showed that many people came to recognize him as a special minister who had a spiritual power to mediate the divine grace of healing. At least it was widely accepted that he was used by God through his healing revivals. The reason why people recognized Kim as a person of God was their experience of healing at his revivals. It is also noteworthy that new ritual practices, like fasting prayer and hands-laying prayer, were performed at his revivals, unlike the previous Bible-conference-style revivals. It is hard to find evidence for what and how those ritual practices contributed to the recognition of Kim as a person of God, because there is no surviving record. However, as these rituals were practiced at revival meetings later, one could find a clue for the question.

Mystic Healing Revivals and Anchal

After Kim's healing revivals, public mass revival meetings in Korea became very hard to hold because of the political situations, including Japanese enforcement of Shinto worship and following persecution, and the Korean War after liberation. It was after the Korean War that revival meetings rose again vigorously. In the time of turmoil after the war, mystic revival meetings became popularized among Koreans who were in a state of mental chaos. Some of them were led by mystic sects, such as the Olive Tree Church (*Chŏndogwan*), which was founded by Tae-Seon Park, and the Yong Moon Mountain Prayer House (hereafter, YMPH), led by Woon Mong Na.[9] Particularly, YMPH was the center of the healing revival meeting. There, a new ritual practice began to be performed.

After the sermon, participants prayed ardently with *tongsung kido*, and the healing rituals followed, in which the preacher performed *anchal*, which is a ritual for healing or exorcism by rubbing, pressing, or slapping with palms on the sick part of the patient's body, while ordinary preachers just laid hands on the patient's head or shoulder (Korean: *Ansu*).[10] After receiving *anchal* or *ansu*, some participants fell into a trance or had fits, which is

9. Kim, "Heresy or Korean Christianity, 15–36.

10. Jung, "Korean Prayers," 128–29, 149–50. Because the practice of *anchal* has been criticized as nonbiblical and shamanistic practice, orthodox Korean churches strongly warn not to practice *anchal*. Only a few charismatic revivalist healers, standing at the far extreme of Pentecostal tradition or heretical tradition, practice it in unnormal ways, like hitting or scratching.

called *Ipsin* in Korean—a shamanistic term to describe the spirit's possession of a person. Also, amid the meeting, some participants danced freely, which some people criticized as being similar to a shaman's dance in ecstasy.

After charismatic spiritual experiences at YMPH, Tae-Seon Park began healing revival meetings, which gathered over tens of thousands people at public spaces in Seoul. Like the healing ritual at YMPH, Park performed *anchal*, claiming *anchal* caused the forgiveness of sins and the healing of disease. He argued whoever wanted to get healed should get *anchal* from those who had a strong spiritual power because the efficacy of *anchal* was dependent on the performer's spiritual power. In this vein, it is not surprising that he claimed himself the second messiah.[11]

Here, one can note that the shamanistic rituals at revivals emerged based on the shamanistic mindset. In addition to the truth that the ritual of *anchal* itself is very similar to shamanistic rituals for exorcism and/or healing (*kuta-beop*, a shamanistic practice of beating to expel demons), it should be noted that the shamanistic dualistic worldview, in which the invisible spiritual world is beneath the visible material world, works behind the ritual. Similarly, Park claimed that every problem in the material reality was directly related to the spiritual reality in realistic ways; thus, the disease was caused by demonic possession and the pain of a certain part of the body was because of the demon's affliction of that part.[12] Accordingly, he performed *anchal* under the belief that the best solution for the healing of the disease was to expel the demon which was beneath the sick part of the body.

His claim of charismatic power also came out of his shamanistic mindset. Shamanism argues that shamans can resolve the material issue, including illness, that is directly connected with spirits because they can mediate the material world and the spiritual world by using the spirit's power, which possesses him/her. Park emphasized the biblical basis of divine healing by giving examples of healing from the Bible. It is because he describes how illness can only be healed through a healer with charismatic power, and only a few special ministers have such spiritual power and can mediate it to make healing miracles. However, orthodox Christian churches teach that illness can be healed through anybody with true faith in God only if God wants to do so, because healing is solely the work of the sovereign God.[13]

---

11. Kim, "Heresy or Korean Christianity," 21–23; Lee, *Holy Spirit Movement in Korea*, 61–63. For this reason, he was condemned as a heretic.

12. Similar to Park, contemporary unorthodox healers teach of the mechanism of faith-healing based on such a shamanistic worldview. See Cho, "Healing in the Context of Korean Pentecostalism," 107–43.

13. Regarding the controversy over shamanistic syncretism in Korean Pentecostalism, see Kim, "Reenchanted," 278–83.

In addition, it is noteworthy that Park associates the efficacy of *anchal* with the spiritual power of the healer. As noted above, Park argued that the efficacy of *anchal* depends on the power of the agent, while the orthodox churches teach that it is solely dependent on God's will, regardless of the effectiveness of human agent. While some traditions underscore the human faith in divine healing, the initiative of the healing event is attributed to God. In contrast, because shamans should be highly trained ritual experts,[14] they play a decisive role in successful healing through shamanistic rituals. Therefore, Park's emphasis on the human agent in divine healing reflects on the shamanistic syncretism in his understanding of healing and charismatic power, which is clearly distinguished from Ik-Doo Kim's emphasis on the human agent's role as a pure channel of divine grace.

Ritual Indigenization in Korean Pentecostalism

In the meantime, Yong-Gi Cho began a Pentecostal revival movement, which was the foundation of Yoido Full-Gospel Church in Seoul (hereafter, YFGC).[15] From his own experience of survival from tuberculosis, he strongly emphasized divine healing throughout his ministry, and it became a main tenet of his fivefold gospel and threefold blessing. Also, based on his interpretation of 3 John 1:2, which was influenced by Oral Roberts, Cho taught that the fivefold gospel indicates Jesus as Savior, Blesser, Spirit Baptizer, Healer, and coming King, while the threefold blessing is the holistic salvation of spirit, soul, and body, which includes healing and wealth, as well as spiritual salvation.[16] Especially, as he stressed healing as an element of holistic salvation, he performed healing rituals frequently and integrated it into the Lord's Day service as well as revival meetings.

Although he preferred praying by laying hands on the patients who came up to the altar, he began to perform a sort of healing at a distance because his church members became so many that he couldn't make contact with all of them physically. To describe it, after preaching he would request congregants to put their hands on the sick part of their body and pray for healing with *tongsung kido*, which began with calling the Lord three times aloud, which is called *Juyeo-samchang* in Korean. After the *tongsung prayer* had ended, the pastor who led the worship would proclaim divine

14. Kim, "Reenchanted," 281.

15. For the historical and theological development of YFGC, see Lee, *Holy Spirit Movement in Korea*, 95–111.

16. Park, *Study on the Revival Movement in Korean Church*, 199; Ma, "David Yonggi Cho's Theology of Blessing," 144.

healing, saying, "Today God heals such and such diseases." His proclamation was not only indicative but also imperative. He would shout, "Dirty spirits, leave the saints!" or "Depressions, arthritis, insomnia, leave them!" Then, the congregation would respond to each proclamation of healing by saying "Amen" in loud voices.[17] This form of healing ritual is practiced at the Lord's Day service of YFGC and other branch churches, as well as the churches participating in the Holy Spirit movement, affiliated with other denominations.

Here, it is noted that *tongsung kido* evolved into a new form by adding a rite of calling "the Lord" three times in full voice.[18] As a preacher or a worship leader calls to do *Juyeo-samchang*, all the attendees call the Lord three times in a loud voice and begin *tongsung kido* collectively. During *Juyeo-samchang*, the congregants are usually requested to stretch their arms high. During the prayer, they express their piety freely by rocking back and forth, waving their hands in the air, clapping their hands, weeping with tears, and/or speaking in tongues. After the prayer, they might confess that their body has become lighter and their muscular rigidity has become softened; in some cases, they feel like their suffering or disease has been cured, regardless of the medical diagnosis. Although some are negative about *Juyeo-samchang* because they consider it a mechanical method to manipulate human emotion, it is widely used at Korean churches across denominations.

To this point, in view of the historical development of Korean revival meetings, I identified four rituals used at revival meetings: *tongsung kido, Juyeo-samchang, ansu kido,* and *anchal.* These ritual practices resulted from the inculturation of the practices that were introduced by Western missionaries. For instance, *tongsung kido* was introduced by Howard Agnew Johnston when he shared about the Welsh Revival and its characteristic practice of praying aloud simultaneously, as well as the Indian Revival at the Bible conference for missionaries in Seoul in September 1906.[19] J. F. Preston, one of the participants in that Bible conference, applied the practice of praying aloud simultaneously at the Bible conference in Mokpo in October 1906.[20] And then it was practiced at the Great Revival in 1907 and spread throughout the country. As praying aloud became a way of common spiritual expression by Koreans under sufferings and evolved into a different form that begins with *Juyeo-samchang*, it was transformed into *tongsung kido* as

17. Jung, "Korean Prayers," 194.

18. Regarding the origin of *Juyeo-Samchang*, see So, "Spirituality and Education," 116.

19. Clark, *Korean Church and the Nevius Methods*, 149.

20. Preston, "Notable Meeting," 227.

a unique form of Korean prayer, different from praying aloud by Western Christians. In a similar vein, *anchal* can be understood as an inculturated form of hands-laying prayer as Korean shamanism became incorporated with Christian practice.[21] Depending on the degree of indigenization, these practices were considered the hallmark of nonorthodox churches.

With regards to this study, one needs to see that ritual development could be relevant to the shift in revivalist preachers' charismatic power. It is doubtless that the other nonritual elements contributed to the construction of the charismatic power of revivalist preachers. They would include theological understanding of preaching, like preacher as herald and preaching as the word of God, and Korean cultural influence on the understanding of religious leaders as a person of paternal and/or shamanistic authority, including the Confucian hierarchy, military authoritarianism, and shamanistic spirituality.[22] However, one should note that rituals do something to construct the charismatic power of Korean revivalist preachers since rituals are social practices that embody the social relations of actors. In the next part, what rituals do with power at revivals will be investigated in conversation with Pierre Bourdieu and Catherine Bell.

An Analysis of the Charismatic Power of Korean Revivalist Preachers

Liturgy is a social action, as its Greek word, *leitourgia*, means the work of people. Thus, one should note that liturgy exhibits a social order that operates in the social relations of worshipers and helps them to make sense of their different social positions in the ritual community. In this sense, liturgy, a kind of ritual practice, is a social action that constructs power. So, how could we understand what ritual practices at revivals do with the power that operates in the social relation of participants? How do they create a power dynamic between preachers and congregants? These questions could be answered in light of the practice theory by French sociologist Pierre Bourdieu, who revealed the social aspect of practices in the application of sociological methods. Particularly, he is attentive to how practices work to constitute, manipulate, or resist positions of domination and subordination. Influenced by Bourdieu's theory, Catherine Bell, a renowned scholar of ritual studies, developed a theory of ritual practice, elucidating how rituals

---

21. For the debate over the Shamanism's influence on the Holy Spirit Movement in Korea, see Lee, *Holy Spirit Movement in Korea*, 111–15; Cho, "Healing in the Context of Korean Pentecostalism," 107–50; Jung, "Korean Prayers," 242–55.

22. Lee, *Korean Preaching*, 92–108; Kim, *Preaching the Presence of God*, 78–83.

construct power relations among agents through misrecognition, which Bourdieu used to explain how practices work to construct symbolic power. Thus, their theories offer a useful theoretical foundation to understand how ritual practices construct and exhibit the social relations of the agents.

Field, Practice, and Habitus

From the perspective of Bourdieu, a liturgical space can be understood as a social space, which is a system of relations that constructs the social positions of the agents and exhibits its structure. In Bourdieu's language, it is the field (*champ*), the symbolic system that works as a social space where the agents struggle in pursuit of desirable resources, or the exchange of symbolic goods or symbolic capital, or play a game in order to change their social position.[23] The social space supposes an asymmetrical social status among the agents that gives them an impetus to engage in the struggle or competition for better social status, as well as the pressure to comply with the rules operating in the field. Thus, within the field, the agents are inclined to act and react consciously and unconsciously per their social positions.

Practice is the way in which the agents act in the field according to their roles. Bourdieu explains how the practice works in the field as a dialectical relationship between a structured environment and the structured dispositions that lead them to reproduce such a structured environment.[24] That is, a practice constitutes a certain logic that determines the social relations between actors and the social order of the field (*habitus*) which the actors inhabit. The practice is performed according to the logic of practice that requires actors to act accordingly. Here, he names the principle of practice as habitus as follows:

> systems of durable, transposable dispositions, structured structures predisposed to function as structuring structures, that is, as principles which generate and organize practices and representations that can be objectively adapted to their outcomes without presupposing a conscious aiming at ends or an express mastery of the operations necessary in order to attain them.[25]

That is, habitus refers to the system of dispositions or the principles which are structured in the field and the generative schemes that function to structure the field so that it produces practices, thoughts, and perceptions,

---

23. Bourdieu, "Social Space and Symbolic Power," 16.

24. Bourdieu, *Logic of Practice*, 52. Cf. Bell, *Ritual Theory, Ritual Practice*, 78.

25. Bourdieu, *Outline of a Theory of Practice*, 72.

ultimately a sort of logic of practice or practical knowledge.[26] The agents come to know how to be in accordance with habitus in a field through practice. As each agent practices a certain ritual over time, s/he inscribes the logic of the practice and the social order in her/his body. Through a gradual process of inculcation by doing a certain ritual, each agent comes to embody the ritual practice subconsciously in the manner that the ritual community requires of her/him in the situation. For example, Asians greet a senior by bowing down, while Westerners may greet a senior by kissing her/him on the cheek. Through habitually practicing this greeting ritual, Asians inscribe a logic of practice in their bodies that is shaped by the social order at work between juniors and seniors. In this sense, habitus is the embodied and habituated logic of practice.[27]

Ritual practice is a kind of practice that Bourdieu takes into account. Catherine Bell is one of the representative ritual scholars who developed the ritual theory in the application of Bourdieu's theory of practice. In light of Bourdieu's theory, she notes rituals' function to construct power relationships, as she argues "ritual is a vehicle for the construction of relationships of authority and submission rather than a vehicle for the expression of authority."[28] Thus, she considers ritual "a performative medium for the negotiation of power in relationships" rather than a functional mechanism or expressive medium in the service of social solidarity and control.[29] That is, rituals do not function only to express the social positions of ritual agents and bond them together, as Victor Turner describes ritual process, but they also work to constitute such a power relation among the agents. Since ritual practices produce the power that enables the agent to control other agents, simply by participating in rituals the ritual agents involve a specific relationship of dominion and subordination; in other words, the hegemonic order constituted in the ritual.[30] So, how does ritual construct power relationships? It works through ritualization, which indicates a process where rituals lead ritual agents to engage in a process of negotiation in symbolic exchange, inviting the agents to consent or resist the hegemonic order.[31]

---

26. Bourdieu, *Outline of a Theory of Practice*, 95; Bourdieu, "Social Space and Symbolic Power," 19.

27. Thompson, "Editor's Introduction," 12–13.

28. Bell, *Ritual*, 82.

29. Bell, *Ritual*, 79.

30. Bell, *Ritual Theory, Ritual Practice*, 207–8.

31. Bell, *Ritual Theory, Ritual Practice*, 209, 218.

Symbolic Power and Symbolic Capital

Influenced by Karl Marx, Bourdieu describes the field as a kind of symbolic market where symbolic capital and symbolic goods are exchanged. Since the field is a social space where the agents of unequal status exchange, a certain power relationship works there while a new power relationship is constructed through the exchange. He names the power constructed in the field as symbolic power. Unlike overt power, the visible power (like physical violence or economic power) that is exerted in a direct and personal way, symbolic power is "the invisible power that can be exercised only with the complicity of those who do not want to know that they are subject to it or even that they themselves exercise it."[32] As symbolic power works with the agents in the field, it makes symbolic dominion operative, which is the tacit, almost subconscious modes of cultural and social domination occurring within everyday social habits.[33] So, how does symbolic power work?

Symbolic power rests on two conditions. The first condition is the possession of symbolic capital, and the second is the recognition of the symbolic power.[34] Briefly said, symbolic capital is the critical source of power and it is a form of credit, like honor and prestige, that includes cultural capital and social capital.[35] Symbolic capital is exchanged at the field where the agents compete to obtain their desired goods. If it is recognized that one has the symbolic capital that others would want to exchange in order to get what one wants, they will engage in a negotiation. If the negotiation is successfully completed, the one whose symbolic capital is recognized gains the symbolic power to govern the other agents.

For instance, salvation is the symbolic goods that people desire to gain in the religious field. To gain salvation goods, the agents engage in a negotiation or game to exchange symbolic capital with those who are recognized to have the symbolic capital for salvation goods. Such symbolic capital would include beliefs, dedication, spirituality, honor, and/or morality, among other things. Because not all the agents in the religious field have such symbolic capital, those who are recognized as having symbolic capital hold the initiative in the negotiation for power relations. To get the recognition, those who claim to have the symbolic capital should show it in a different form so others can make sense of its efficacy. Until symbolic capital is recognized, the symbolic capital, which the agent claims to have, remains at stake. If the

32. Bourdieu, *Language and Symbolic Power*, 164.

33. Bourdieu, *Outline of a Theory of Practice*, 183–91; Bourdieu, *Language and Symbolic Power*, 113.

34. Bourdieu, "Social Space and Symbolic Power," 23.

35. Bourdieu, *Outline of a Theory of Practice*, 179–81.

negotiation is completed through recognition of symbolic capital, the agent will attain symbolic power.

If a revival meeting is considered a field for symbolic exchange, one could understand how symbolic power is constructed through ritual practices there. People participate in the revival meeting because they are informed that the revivalists have the symbolic capital they can exchange for the symbolic goods, which can be named as salvation, divine healing, or divine grace. Revivalists claim that they have the spiritual power, a form of symbolic capital,[36] to mediate the exchange for salvation, the symbolic goods that the participants want to gain in exchange for their dedication. As the negotiation begins, the efficacy of revivalists' spiritual power should be presented in a recognizable way so that the participants can involve the exchange of symbolic capital for salvation good.

Like the clergies of state churches, revivalists present their institutional religious capital, such as ordination and theological education, as a form of objective symbolic capital. However, they seek to get endorsement for their charismatic power not by such institutional capital but by subjective symbolic capital, which is recognized by individual participants. As expository preachers also do, revivalist preachers seek to offer compelling and legitimate interpretations of biblical texts in order for hearers to perceive that they reveal the word of God hidden in Scripture. In addition, they attempt to be recognized for their spiritual power by presenting their extraordinary experiences, such as speaking in tongues, surviving long-term fasting prayers, and sharing testimonies of divine healing. If these examples of symbolic capital presented by revivalists are recognized as effective, they attain symbolic power.

Misrecognition and Ritual Practice

The remaining issue is how to get recognition of symbolic capital. Revivalists can exercise the symbolic power that affects symbolic domination only if it is recognized as legitimate. So, how do they recognize the invisible symbolic capital? What does ritual practice do with the process of recognition? It can be answered that symbolic capital or symbolic power is recognized through misrecognition that is generated by doing ritual practices.[37]

Misrecognition refers, similar to Marx's false consciousness, to the process whereby the agents perceive the power relationships in the field as

36. Bourdieu says symbolic capital is another name for charisma as described by Max Weber (*Logic of Practice*, 141).

37. Bourdieu, *Outline of a Theory of Practice*, 191.

legitimate, though they are not objectively legitimate, so that they take them for granted and accept them as they are. Within this process of misrecognition, the agent and those who are dominated do not and should not realize that they have contributed through their misrecognition to the establishment of the symbolic domination.[38] Since all the agents, those who dominate and those who are dominated, collaborate consciously and unconsciously to legitimate symbolic power or symbolic capital without recognizing that they have contributed to the legitimation of it, Bourdieu says that misrecognition is based on collective deception and/or legitimate imposture.[39]

In the process of recognition through misrecognition, ritual practice functions to show and construct the legitimacy of the agent's symbolic power. Bourdieu says, "for ritual to function and operate it must present itself and be perceived as legitimate, with stereotyped symbols serving precisely to show that the agent does not act in his/her own name and on his own authority but in his capacity as a delegate."[40] However, in view of the outsider, it is not legitimate because the logic of practice does not work for the outsider. Therefore, the outsider considers the recognition of symbolic power by the ritual agents a misrecognition.

To explain it with the case of revivals, a group of congregants receives *anchal* from a revivalist because they consider it legitimate, believing that the revivalist presides over it with the power of the Holy Spirit, not with his/her own knowledge or skills, and that *anchal* is the legitimate practice for them to receive divine grace. In the process of this recognition of the legitimacy of *anchal*, they share the testimonies of healing mediated by the revivalist while the revivalist denies his/her contribution to the divine healing. As a result, those who receive *anchal* respect the revivalist as the divine agent of charismatic power and submit to them. In this way, they all collaborate consciously and unconsciously to legitimate symbolic power and/or symbolic capital constructed through the ritual practice.

However, it would be a misrecognition for the outsiders, like non-Christians, Christians of other traditions, or bystanders at the revivals, because they have neither practiced *anchal* in their social space nor share the belief undergirding the practice. Accordingly, the outsiders neither practice *anchal* nor accept the divine authority of the revivalists that the practice supposes. They consider the testimonies of healing by congregants and the revivalist's denial of his contribution to healing as collective deception.

38. Bourdieu, *Language and Symbolic Power*, 116.

39. Bourdieu, *Language and Symbolic Power*, 214–16; Bourdieu, *Outline of a Theory of Practice*, 195.

40. Bourdieu, *Language and Symbolic Power*, 115.

Therefore, in view of the outsider, the recognition of the revivalist's symbolic power is a false consciousness constructed through misrecognition.

So, why do the ritual agents and the outsiders perceive differently what rituals do? Why do the outsiders consider the recognition by the ritual agents as misrecognition? Catherine Bell answers that it is a feature of practice. Drawing on Bourdieu's words, she says the context of ritual is never clear-cut but full of ambiguities.[41] It means rituals open an interpretive space in which individual ritual agents can perceive the phenomenon differently. The agents interpret the meaning of rituals by using their own hermeneutical scheme, which is constructed through their repetitive practice of rituals in different fields. Also, as they practice rituals, their habitus is constructed newly. In this sense, one can understand rituals through different interpretive frames that a participant of a ritual community or an outsider may hold consciously or subconsciously. While the participants receive the hands-laying prayer from the revivalist preacher, recognizing his/her charismatic power as legitimate, because their hermeneutical scheme has been structured through the practice, the outsiders consider it misrecognition and reject the belief or the social order undergirding the practice because they have never practiced it and haven't embodied the hermeneutical scheme, namely habitus, to make sense of the practice. Thus, practices construct a dialectical interpretive experience, the recognition through misrecognition.

In short, people believe it because they do it, while it is true that people do it because they believe it. Therefore, one should understand that the charismatic power of revivalists is not a mere illusion or something artificially manufactured or deliberately manipulated but a result of tacit collaboration by all the agents, not only those who dominate but also those who are dominated, based on recognition through misrecognition. It is not purely a theological claim but a result of the social process which is constructed through collaboration and complicity by all the agents, manifesting in and operating through the logic of practice.

Conclusion

To examine how the charismatic power of Korean revivalist preachers is constructed through ritual practices, this essay investigated the ritual practices of Korean revival meeting, identifying a couple of indigenous ritual practices, such as *tongsung kido, ansu-kido* (hands-laying prayer), *anchal-ki-do* (prayer with rubbing, pressing, or slapping), and *Juyeo-samchang* (calling the Lord aloud three times). These indigenized ritual practices evolved in

41. Bell, *Ritual Theory, Ritual Practice*, 207.

the liturgical space of Korean Free Churches through ongoing interactions between diverse Korean religious and cultural traditions and construct a unique habitus that operates the symbolic exchange for the symbolic power of the revivalists. In light of the theories of Bourdieu and Bell, I sought to show that these ritual practices have a constructive power to structure the hermeneutical scheme of practice.

As a result, I argue that the charismatic power of Korean revivalist preachers as divine agents is a result of the social consent that is made through practice, as the ritual practices construct the hermeneutical scheme for the ritual agents to make sense of their symbolic capital and symbolic power as legitimate. Accordingly, the revivalists must not claim that they have an exclusive power given by God nor abuse it to reinforce their domination, because they should recognize that their charismatic power is also a social product constructed by the congregants. I hope this study will help to alleviate the authoritarianism in Korean churches or other churches of similar tradition and prevent spiritual abuse due to misunderstanding of the clerical power. If the revivalists recognize that their charismatic power is sourced by both God's grace and congregational recognition, they should not claim superior status over congregants nor attempt to abuse their power to protect or reinforce their privilege. Instead, confessing humbly, "I am an unworthy servant" (Luke 17:10), they should serve the congregation of God with their gifts.

Bibliography

Bell, Catherine. *Ritual: Perspectives and Dimensions.* New York: Oxford University Press, 1997.

———. *Ritual Theory, Ritual Practice.* New York: Oxford University Press, 1992.

Blair, William Newton. *God in Korea.* New York: Presbyterian Church in the U.S.A., 1957.

Bourdieu, Pierre. *Language and Symbolic Power.* Edited by John B. Thompson. Translated by Gino Raymond and Matthew Adamson. Cambridge: Harvard University Press, 1991.

———. *The Logic of Practice.* Translated by Richard Nice. Stanford, CA: Stanford University Press, 1990.

———. *Outline of a Theory of Practice.* Translated by Richard Nice. Cambridge: Cambridge University Press, 1977.

———. "Social Space and Symbolic Power." *Sociological Theory* 7.1 (1989) 14–25.

Cho, Il-Koo. "Healing in the Context of Korean Pentecostalism, the 1950s to the Present: Historical and Ethnographic Approaches." PhD diss., Claremont Graduate University, 2002.

Clark, Charles Allen. *The Korean Church and the Nevius Methods.* New York: Revell, 1930.

Gale, L. S. "The Revival in Seoul." *Korean Mission Field* 17.1 (January 1921) 4–5.

Joo, Seung-Joong, and Kyeong-Jin Kim."The Reformed Tradition in Korea." In *The Oxford History of Christian Worship*, edited by Geoffrey Wainwright and Karen B. Westerfield Tucker, 484–91. New York: Oxford University Press, 2006.

Jung, Yong Kwon. "Korean Prayers: Evaluating the Prayer Phenomena at the Prayer Mountain Centers in Korea." PhD diss., Asbury Theological Seminary, 2002.

Kim, Eunjoo Mary. *Preaching the Presence of God: A Homiletic from an Asian American Perspective*. Valley Forge, PA: Judson, 1999.

Kim, Heung Soo. "Heresy or Korean Christianity: The Religious Movements of the Unification Church, the Olive Movements, and the Yong Moon San Prayer Mountain." *Religion & Culture* 23 (2012) 15–36.

Kim, Sean C. "Reenchanted: Divine Healing in Korean Protestantism." In *Global Pentecostal and Charismatic Healing*, edited by Candy Gunther Brown, 267–86. New York: Oxford University Press, 2011.

Kim, Un-Yong. *A History of Korean Christian Preaching: The Stories of Preachers in View of Narrative Innovation* [in Korean]. Seoul: Holy Wave Plus, 2018.

Lee, Jung Young. *Korean Preaching: An Interpretation*. Nashville: Abingdon, 1997.

Lee, Young-Hoon. *The Holy Spirit Movement in Korea: Its Historical Theological Development*. Oxford: Regnum, 2009.

Lim, Taek Kwon. *Evidence of Miracles in Chosun Christian Churches*. Seoul: Christian Literature Society, 1921.

Ma, Wonsuk. "David Yonggi Cho's Theology of Blessing: Basis, Legitimacy, and Limitations." *Evangelical Review of Theology* 35.2 (2011) 140–59.

Park, Myung-soo. *A Study on the Revival Movement in Korean Church*. Seoul: Institute of Korean Christian History, 2003.

Preston, J. F. "A Notable Meeting." *Korea Mission Field* II.12 (Oct 1906) 227–28.

Rhodes, Harry A. *History of the Korea Mission Presbyterian Church U.S.A,. 1884–1934*. Seoul: Chosen Mission Presbyterian Church U.S.A., 1934.

So, Tae Young. "The Spirituality and Education Which Is Implied in the Prayer Patter of 'Calling Lord Three Times' in the Full Gospel Church." *Journal of Youngsan Theology* 40 (2017) 107–40.

Thompson, John B. "Editor's Introduction." In *Language and Symbolic Power*, by Pierre Bourdieu, edited by John B. Thompson, translated by Gino Raymond and Matthew Adamson, 12–13. Cambridge: Harvard University Press, 1991.

Yun, Eunseok. "The Study on Change from Bible Class to Bible Class for Revival: From 1885 to 1919." *Korea Presbyterian Journal of Theology* 50.5 (2018) 123–46.

6

The Power of Tradition
over Biblical Theology

Raising up the Tabernacle of David: Pentecostal Memory in Praise and Worship Theology

Jonathan Ottaway

In the past seventy years, a new phenomenon called "Praise and Worship" has spread through countless churches, denominations, and movements, both in the US and globally.[1] Finding its initial impetus in the 1948 Latter

1. The fullest description of this historical and liturgical phenomenon is Ruth and Lim, *History of Contemporary Praise and Worship*. Ruth and Lim describe two different historical streams. The first is "Praise and Worship," a set of Pentecostal liturgical developments motivated by a new understanding of the manifest presence of God within praise. The second is "Contemporary Worship," a phenomenon within mainline Protestantism and Evangelicalism that sought to modernize worship to better communicate the Christian messages to contemporary audiences. Ruth and Lim argue that these two independent streams coalesced in the 1990s to become the modern form of "Contemporary Praise and Worship." While I agree with Ruth and Lim's assessment that these two distinct streams have increasingly blended, this has been a gradual and complicated process, worked out by myriad worshiping communities in myriad ways. Accordingly, in this paper, even though I focus upon "Praise and Worship Pentecostals," I do not describe this stream only as a past historical phenomenon that ended in the 1990s. There are many communities and organizations whose ethos continues to be largely influenced by the theological commitments and practices of Praise and

Rain revival (orchestrated by a group of independent Pentecostals), the practices and theologies of praise and worship were dispersed among classical Pentecostal denominations (who trace their history back to the early twentieth century), independent charismatics,[2] Free Church Evangelicals, and some Mainline Protestant churches (especially those impacted by the Charismatic Renewal). As it developed, evolved, and spread, praise and worship generated a vast and diverse body of literature that expressed the core tenets of its theology. This literature is diverse both because it exists in a multitude of genres and because it traverses chronologically, geographically, ethnically, and theologically diverse institutions and people. Its advocates teach praise and worship in diverse ways, using different theological paradigms and biblical ideas. However, at the center of this diverse body of theology is a common, primary theological authority—Scripture.[3]

From the outset, Scripture provided the impetus for the new teachings of praise and worship. Reg Layzell, the earliest praise and worship teacher, discovered a new biblical promise in Psalm 22:3—when Christians offer the sacrifice of praise, God must respond with his presence. In the following decades, as praise and worship became its own movement that spread beyond its original Latter Rain circles, its teachers began to develop a fuller biblical theology of praise.[4] These teachers sought biblical wisdom for praise, looking to Moses, David, Solomon, and the book of Revelation. They contemplated the Psalms and searched the numerous imperatives therein (for instance, Ps 100:4) for instruction on praise. As theologies of praise became more complex, biblical descriptions of Old Testament institutions such as the tabernacle of Moses and the tabernacle of David took on increasing theological significance as biblical types for Christian worship. Furthermore, praise and worship teachers began delving beneath the surface level of the biblical text, using concordances to conduct Hebrew and Greek word studies.[5] Later groups discovered new biblical themes and

---

Worship. It is, in part, my own experience growing up in communities such as this that gave rise to this research.

2. Various labels are used to describe this group throughout the scholarly literature, including neocharismatics, neopentecostals, pentecostal-charismatics, restorationists, and third-wave Pentecostals.

3. I use the word "authority" in this essay to describe the source which validates or authorizes theologies and practices. Accordingly, when I describe Scripture as a primary authority, I am describing how Praise and Worship Pentecostals seek to align themselves as closely as possible with their understanding of what Scripture teaches.

4. Even while Praise and Worship spread outside of the Latter Rain, Layzell's original tenet that God inhabits praise still formed the starting place for these fuller biblical theologies of praise.

5. Ottaway, "Seven Hebrew Words." This teaching has remained highly popular throughout the Evangelical and Pentecostal church.

ideas that they interwove with these preexisting teachings. For instance, in the 1980s, the Vineyard movement added the theme of intimacy between Christ and his bride in worship (based on their reading of Song of Solomon) to their understanding of praise. In the 1990s, a new concept of "Harp and Bowl" worship based on Revelation 5:8 emerged which became a critical teaching for organizations in the House of Prayer movement, such as the International House of Prayer in Kansas City (IHOPKC). Through all these various theologies of praise and worship, Scripture is the explicit authority. Marginalizing other theological authorities such as liturgical tradition or systematic theology, praise and worship Pentecostals have repeatedly turned to Scripture alone to authorize their theology and practices.

However, behind this sole reliance on Scripture, a set of theological and hermeneutical commitments exists. These commitments have influenced the nature, shape, and application of these theologies. While praise and worship Pentecostals see Scripture as their sole theological authority, there is a theological tradition that, while never explicit nor institutionally recognized, has implicitly influenced them. I describe this as tradition exerting power or influence over biblical theologies. This essay describes that tradition, naming the ways in which it acted and continues to act upon biblical theologies of praise and worship. In particular, I describe how tradition *directs* (channeling theologians towards certain biblical themes instead of others), *governs* (establishing the rules for licit theology), and *frames* (setting the biblical theologies into a narrative tradition or historical context) biblical theologies of praise and worship.

It may seem antithetical to describe tradition in relationship to praise and worship. After all, the Free Church has historically been defined by its freedom *from* tradition (usually emphasizing freedom from liturgical tradition).[6] This sensibility is especially true among Pentecostals. From the outset, Pentecostalism saw itself as a return to the faith and practice of the apostolic era in contrast to the church catholic that they saw as marked by apostasy and nominalism.[7] However, despite the Pentecostal rejection of tradition, recent scholarly literature has begun to define the shape of the implicit tradition present beneath Pentecostalism. This exploration commonly relies on Alistair MacIntyre's definition of tradition as an "historically extended socially embodied argument."[8] Scholars have drawn upon

6. See for example, Ellis, *Gathering*, 25–30.

7. Dayton, *Theological Roots of Pentecostalism*, 25–26. The return to apostolic faithfulness was not just an element of the early Pentecostal tradition but has remained the clarion call of subsequent Pentecostal revivals (Chan, *Pentecostal Ecclesiology*, 1).

8. Alistair MacIntyre, quoted in Chan, "Tradition," 96. See also Waddell and Althouse, "Living Tradition of Pentecostals and Charismatics," 173–75; Archer, "Pentecostal Story," 36–59.

this definition to discuss the Pentecostal tradition as a stable community that has accumulated a "collective memory expressed in its core beliefs, shared values, stories and practices."[9] It is this definition of tradition that I use in this essay.[10] I argue that beneath the biblical theologies of praise and worship there is a communal memory that holds certain values, narrates a certain view of history, and encourages certain hermeneutical choices for their theology.

Rather than describing one facet of tradition's power over multiple biblical theologies within the praise and worship movement, this essay will instead explore multiple dimensions of tradition's power over just one of the many praise and worship theologies—the restoration of the tabernacle of David. This teaching has been one of the most influential theologies within the praise and worship movement. While the teaching did not become widespread until the 1970s (and there was a significant minority of praise and worship advocates who rejected this theology), the tabernacle of David quickly moved to the center of praise and worship discourse.[11] For praise and worship Pentecostals, it provided a key scriptural link between the Old and New Testaments that organized all of the forerunning teachings on praise.[12] As the 70s and 80s were a period of dramatic dissemination of the praise and worship teaching beyond the domain of independent charismatics, the tabernacle of David became the primary biblical idea through which they imbibed this new theology. Accordingly, practices that arose out of the theology of the tabernacle of David, especially the musicalization of praise and the emphasis upon the musical leader as a primary liturgical leader, have also become mainstays of liturgical practice in contemporary praise and worship (see footnote 1). Moreover, the tabernacle of David has continued to find new proponents today. Many organizations in the House of Prayer movement, like IHOPKC, Burn 24/7, and David's Tent DC (among many others), see themselves as direct embodiments of the tabernacle of David.

9. Chan, "Tradition," 96.

10. Throughout this essay, I capitalize the word "Tradition" when referring to the specific Pentecostal "collective memory" that has influenced Praise and Worship theology. I use the lowercase "tradition" when referring to tradition as a general concept.

11. Throughout this essay, these earlier, foundational writings on the subject will be the primary focus. However, I also reference later instances of Tabernacle of David theology to show ongoing continuity among proponents of this teaching.

12. Perez, "All Hail King Jesus," 212.

While this paper focuses on one of the biblical theologies that was present in the praise and worship movement, I suggest that other biblical theologies in praise and worship were influenced by tradition in a similar way. Of course, the praise and worship movement as a diverse and global phenomenon was far from theologically monolithic. However, as the movement evolved over time, its constant was the method of biblical theology. There was a common set of biblical themes and Scriptures that shaped the core theology of the movement, not least of which was the notion of God's manifest presence in praise connected to Psalm 22:3. Furthermore, biblical theologies of praise and worship tended to express a similar set of theological, hermeneutical, and methodological assumptions about theologies for worship. Accordingly, my description of the influence of Tradition over the theology of the tabernacle of David provides a window into how Tradition established the broad contours of praise and worship theology and practice.

The Tabernacle of David in Praise and Worship Teaching

The importance of the tabernacle of David for praise and worship was first suggested at a conference for Latter Rain leaders that was held in Nelson, New Zealand in 1962. One of the conference speakers, David Schoch (a close friend of praise and worship pioneer Reg Layzell), spontaneously spoke about the tabernacle of David during his sermon. Although Schoch's extemporaneous word was perfunctory, it would go on to have a great impact. This event was a "divine seed"[13] that inspired both Kevin Conner and Graham Truscott—the two earliest and most important authors on the topic—to spend years in meditation, prayer, and biblical study on the topic.[14] By 1969, Truscott had developed and published a full biblical teaching for the doxological restoration of the church, entitled, *The Power of His Presence: The Restoration of the Tabernacle of David*. Truscott's book gained immediate popularity and went through five printings and three translations by 1982. However, it was Conner's 1976 book, *The Tabernacle of David: The Presence of God as Experienced in the Tabernacle*, that proved to be even more enduring. This is partly due to Conner's influence as a teacher at Portland Bible College, a key educational institution of the Latter Rain that

---

13. Conner, *Tabernacle of David*, iii.

14. Although Truscott was working as a missionary in India at the time, Schoch recounts that Truscott received a tape of the teaching from the Nelson conference. David Schoch, interview by Vivien Hibbert, September 3, 2001, transcript contained in Vivien Hibbert, email message to Lester Ruth, May 12, 2017.

helped to disseminate praise and worship teachings more widely, where his work was featured as the standard textbook.

Two key Scripture passages provide the foundation upon which teachings on the tabernacle of David for praise and worship are built. In Amos 9:11–12, the prophet states: "In that day will I raise up the tabernacle of David that is fallen, and close up the breaches thereof; and I will raise up his ruins, and I will build it as in the days of old" (KJV). This passage is quoted by James at the Council of Jerusalem in Acts 15:13–17. In its context, James's quotation of Amos was part of a larger discussion about whether gentiles who were joining the Christian faith should undergo circumcision. However, praise and worship Pentecostals saw far more in this quotation. Crucially, they saw parallels between Amos's promise of a restoration and the spiritual restoration that they were witnessing through contemporary movements like the Charismatic Renewal.[15] For them, these two Scripture passages promised a grander restoration: the "building up of a glorious habitation for the Spirit of God, to bring a harvest of souls to Christ."[16]

While the typological link between Amos and Acts may seem to provide scant information about the practice of Christian worship today, for praise and worship Pentecostals, these verses functioned as a key that opened other Old Testament Scriptures about the tabernacle of David.[17] Particularly important were the descriptions of David's tabernacle in 1 Chronicles 15:1—16:43 and the Psalms, which they read as descriptions of the words and practices used within David's tabernacle. These biblical passages demonstrated that David had inaugurated a new liturgical form within his tabernacle that was fundamentally musical in nature. Its *telos* was a heartfelt expression of praise. In contrast to the Mosaic tabernacle, whose liturgy was centered on strict forms and animal sacrifices, in David's tabernacle the Israelites worshiped the Lord by singing, playing instruments, thanking, praising, clapping, rejoicing, shouting, dancing, raising their hands, and saying "Amen."[18]

The tabernacle of David was more than just the location of a new set of liturgical practices that the Israelites carried out. These new practices were a response to the mighty acts of God in their midst. Not only had God restored the ark of the covenant to the Israelites after it had been captured by the Philistines, but God had caused the ark (that contained God's manifest

15. Restoration was the primary theme that undergirded the other theological and spiritual innovations of the Latter Rain revival from which Praise and Worship emerged (Faupel, "New Order of the Latter Rain," 239–64).

16. Truscott, *Power of His Presence*, 6.

17. Conner referred to this as the "Key of David" (*Tabernacle of David*, ii).

18. Truscott, *Power of His Presence*, 75–76.

presence) to be placed in the middle of David's tabernacle. Previously in the Mosaic tabernacle, the ark of the covenant had been cloistered within the holy of holies where only the high priest could access it. In David's tabernacle, God made his presence freely and graciously available. For the first time, "the Glory of God was visible to all people."[19] Accordingly, the Israelites responded with worship that was exuberant, unstructured, continuous, joyful, and intimate.[20] This created a blueprint for praise and worship Pentecostals. Responding to the manifest presence of God, Christians were to respond as the Israelites had responded with heartfelt expressions of musical praise.

Theological Tradition and the Tabernacle of David

Having named the broad contours of how praise and worship Pentecostals saw the tabernacle of David as a template for Christian worship, the next section considers how the Pentecostal theological tradition shaped this theology. For its advocates, the tabernacle of David was the clear teaching of Scripture. It was the normative ideal of Christian worship that David received in the Old Testament and which God promised to restore in the age of the church. Its narration in the Old Testament provided a clear template for Christian liturgical practice today. However, a glance at Christian history will reveal that the tabernacle of David has never been a clear or universal guide for liturgical practice. Indeed, it is unique to twentieth-century praise and worship Pentecostals. This suggests that we need to understand how tradition shaped the ways in which praise and worship Pentecostals did biblical theology so that, for them, the tabernacle of David became the primary teaching of Scripture on worship.

Tradition Directs Biblical Theology: The Legacy of Evangelical Typological Theology

One of the most important ways that tradition guided biblical theologies of praise and worship has been in how tradition predisposed its teachers to see the importance of certain biblical ideas rather than others. I describe this as tradition *directing* biblical theology. Like a river that follows a preexisting channel in the ground, tradition carved out familiar biblical topics, ideas, and themes which theologies of praise and worship flowed along. Thus,

19. Conner, *Tabernacle of David*, 151–55; Truscott, *Power of His Presence*, 75.

20. Simultaneously, the sacrificial requirements of the Mosaic law continued to be carried out on the brazen altar that was located on Mount Gibeon (1 Chr 16:39–40).

praise and worship teachers of the latter twentieth century often inherited a set of biblical topics and ideas which they newly applied to theologies of praise. The theology of the tabernacle of David helpfully illustrates this. This theology did not emerge *ex nihilo* in the 1960s. Instead, it inherited several centuries of Evangelical theology and piety that were deeply typological and intensely fascinated with the Old Testament tabernacles.

Catholic and Mainline theology of the nineteenth century increasingly adopted historical-critical methods of biblical exegesis that marginalized the tradition of figural biblical interpretation. It was only in the 1940s that Catholic theologians again turned to figural biblical interpretation,[21] particularly buttressed by the *ressourcement* project most associated with Henri de Lubac and Jean Danielou.[22] However, Evangelical theology of the same period was fascinated with typological and spiritual interpretations of Scripture. This robust and continuous tradition provided a foundation for the theology of the tabernacle of David. Rejecting many of the assumptions present in historical-critical exegeses, Evangelicals continued to read the Old Testament as a reliable historical record which disclosed important spiritual truth. This is reflected in the body of Evangelical publications during the nineteenth century that displayed a particular fascination with typology and, notably, with the typological significance of the Old Testament tabernacles.[23]

The interest in the Old Testament tabernacles was not just a nineteenth-century phenomenon. It remained a continuous area of exploration in Fundamentalist, Evangelical, and Pentecostal theology in the twentieth century. Indeed, the prominent Fundamentalist system of dispensational theology was unworkable without interpreting the Old Testament as both literally true and typologically significant. Books from this period, such as

21. This historical narrative of biblical theology is described in Fritsch, "To Antityphon," 100–107, and Lampe, "Reasonableness of Typology," 9–38. Both authors discern a renaissance and rebirth of typological exegesis occurring across the Western hemisphere in the 1940s. Examples of new works from the 1940s which are indicative of a return to typological reading include Phythian-Adams, *People and the Presence*; Herbert, *Throne of David*.

22. A helpful overview of this history can be found in Hughes, "Deep Reasonings," 32–45.

23. See Taves, *Fits, Trances and Visions*, 235–37. Taves provides an extensive list of books published in the early nineteenth century on the subject of the Old Testament Tabernacles, including Rhind, *Tabernacle in the Wilderness*; Nisbet, *Tabernacle*; Cooke, *Shekinah*; Newton, *Jewish Tabernacle*. A wider tradition of typological readings of Scripture in Evangelical circles exists which extends beyond Jewish forms of worship and their application to the present. Gordon Hugenberger provides a brief overview of this literature in the nineteenth century in his chapter, "Introductory Notes on Typology," 331–41.

Philip Mauro's *The Hope of Israel* (1929) or W. H. Offiler's *God and His Bible: The Harmonies of Divine Revelation* (1946), demonstrate that a rich vein of typology was present in this theology during the early twentieth century.[24] The Latter Rain itself also provides a helpful indication of the continuing prominence of typology in their theological reflection and teaching. Many of the most significant early Latter Rain publications were focused on the typological significance of Old Testament institutions for present Pentecostal practice and experience. Particularly important volumes include *The Feast of Tabernacles* (1951) by George Warnock, *The Path of the Just: The Tabernacle of Moses* (1963) by Maureen Gaglardi (Reg Layzell's assistant), and *The Tabernacle of Moses* (1975) by Kevin Conner. Published volumes by themselves do not convey the full extent of how prominent this theme was in Latter Rain teaching though. The published works are just a small component of a much larger body of teaching contained in sermons, songs, and other oral teachings.

More than just their published and oral theologies, Evangelicals, Fundamentalists, and Pentecostals made typology a deeply internalized element of their piety. From even as early as the late eighteenth century, typology provided Evangelicals across numerous traditions with imagery and vocabulary through which they framed their experience in the world and the church. Early Methodists in particular drew freely on biblical events, institutions, and practices from the Old and New Testament to describe their meetings.[25] Through the nineteenth century, typology continued to provide a rich biblical language through which even the most mundane activities could be reframed.[26] Significantly for the focus of this paper, a key image that came to form part of this typological piety was the image of the tabernacle. In the latter nineteenth century, Holiness and Baptist groups increasingly described their camp meetings as "tabernacles."[27] By this they sought to describe a place where they experienced God's presence. This framing of camp meeting events was carried over into early Pentecostalism and even remained common parlance in the Latter Rain revival.[28]

24. These works also provided theological resources that Praise and Worship theologians drew upon. For instance, Mauro's book was a key theological resource that Kevin Conner consulted in *Tabernacle of David.*

25. Ruth, *Worship at Early Methodist Quarterly Meetings,* 104–13.

26. See for instance, Taves, "Camp Meeting," 119–31. Taves quotes at length from the diary of Zilpha Elaw, a participant in Methodist camp meetings in the nineteenth century, to demonstrate how biblical language that drew heavily on the Old Testament framed the events of her day.

27. Taves, *Fits, Trances, and Visions,* 235–40.

28. For instance, Reg Layzell commonly referred to places where prayer or worship

The above discussion indicates that the tabernacle of David arose out of an ecclesial context where the stories, places, and institutions of the Old Testament formed a major component of their theology and piety. Praise and worship teachers were deeply typological thinkers and were predisposed by their theological tradition to dwell on the significance of the tabernacles of the Old Testament as locations where God's presence dwelt. Thus, praise and worship Pentecostals did not read Scripture alone but inside a broader historical community that guided them toward certain topics.

Tradition Governs Biblical Theology: The Influence of Early Pentecostal Hermeneutics

Throughout the body of praise and worship literature, Scripture is the voice of theological and liturgical authority. Praise and worship Pentecostals read Scripture intensively and cited it extensively as they wrote their theology.[29] While they occasionally cited other theological sources, these citations never function in an authoritative manner but only serve to illustrate those things which are clearly found within Scripture.[30] However, under this explicit reliance upon Scripture, a set of hermeneutical rules and assumptions governs the interpretation of Scripture for theology. These rules and assumptions are rooted in the broader Pentecostal theological tradition. Ultimately, tradition legitimates or governs biblical theologies of praise and worship.

The praise and worship method of scriptural interpretation was strongly influenced by early Pentecostalism. While the mid-twentieth century had witnessed classical Pentecostal theologians make a definitive shift toward Evangelical hermeneutics, these independent Pentecostals rejected this development (if not explicitly, then at least implicitly).[31] Their hermeneutic and theological method, like early Pentecostalism, was formed in the crucible of the Modernist-Fundamentalist divide of the late nineteenth century. While Modernists, influenced by evolutionary scientific theories, moved toward "an expressivist theory of religious language" where the interpretation of Scripture did not rely on historical claims, Fundamentalists doubled down on both their affirmation of Scripture's absolute factuality

---

were carried out as "tabernacles" (Layzell, *Pastor's Pen*, 18). This language is evident in other early Pentecostal sources as well (Taves, *Fits, Trances, and Visions*, 337–41).

29. As a representative sample, chapter 8 of Conner's *Tabernacle of David* contains over sixty distinct scriptural references, citations, and quotations in just five pages of prose.

30. For instance, Truscott, *Power of His Presence*, xiv, 1, 55, 124, 185, 215, 237, 243.

31. I trace some of this history in Ottaway, "Seven Hebrew Words."

and their adherence to commonsense realism as their interpretive model.[32] This model saw truth as singular, static, and not influenced by culture. Like the Modernists, early Pentecostals appealed to the importance of experience as data for theology. However, Pentecostal theology had much more in common with Fundamentalism. Early Pentecostals affirmed the Fundamentalist belief that Scripture was *simply* the thoughts and words of God.[33] They continued to adhere to commonsense realism as the foundation of their scriptural interpretation. Accordingly, the common theological method of early Pentecostalism—the Bible-reading method—was heavily informed by Fundamentalist prooftext methods.[34]

Expressions of tabernacle of David theology reflect many of the early Pentecostal hermeneutics described above. At its foundation, the theology of David's tabernacle assumes the absolute factuality and historicity of the Old Testament. The descriptions of David's tabernacle are read as simple and literal descriptions. This is especially important in relation to the typological nature of David's tabernacle. For both Conner and Truscott, the typological connection between the events and institutions of the Old Testament, the New Testament, and the contemporary church is neither literary nor abstract in nature. Instead, the typological connection is between a material, historical reality that was described in the Old Testament and a material, literal restoration of that tabernacle in their day. Their trust in the historicity of Scripture extended further than the text itself and encompassed extra-textual considerations such as the ascriptions of authorship in the Psalms. Accordingly, both Conner and Truscott treat the Psalms (especially those ascribed to David) as reliable descriptions of the historical context, piety, and practices of David's tabernacle.

Also in line with earlier Pentecostal theology, the theology of the tabernacle of David assumes the absolute clarity of Scripture. Demonstrating the influence of commonsense realism, teachers of the tabernacle of David expected that other faithful readers of Scripture would reach the same fundamental conclusions as them. Truscott displays this well when he first introduces the Amos-Acts typological link as an obvious doctrine that requires no further contextualization: "Here are two of the most important Scriptures about God's promised Restoration in the whole Bible. Read them through prayerfully. Meditate on them."[35] For Truscott and Conner,

---

32. Archer, *Pentecostal Hermeneutic*, 48–55; Marsden, *Fundamentalism and American Culture*, 55–61.

33. Wacker, *Heaven Below*, 72–76; Oliverio, *Theological Hermeneutics in the Classical Pentecostal Tradition*, 79.

34. Archer, *Pentecostal Hermeneutic*, 99–102.

35. Truscott, *Power of His Presence*, 4. Truscott argues that he reached his

the question was not whether Scripture clearly taught this doctrine; the question was whether Scripture was read faithfully or not. While neither Conner nor Truscott made explicit claims about Scripture's perspicuity, their use of Scripture everywhere assumes it. Their theology does not rely upon close exegesis of Scripture to persuade their readers. Instead, the persuasiveness of their biblical theology relies upon quantity of Scripture rather than quality of interpretation. Their writings omit the theological methods that Evangelical and classical Pentecostal theologians were using in this period but abound with biblical citations.

As a close hermeneutical relative of Scripture's clarity, theologies of the tabernacle of David also assumed that they had uncovered the singular true archetype for Christian worship. The tabernacle of David was not just *a* biblical suggestion for liturgical practice. Instead, David's tabernacle embodied the singular, normative, biblical practice of worship that God intended the church universal to embody. As Conner argued, Scripture contains the "divine order of worship" that described "how, when, where, and why we are to worship Him"; this is what Jesus meant when he stated that "the Father God seeks those who are true worshipers who would 'worship Him in SPIRIT and in TRUTH.'"[36] This truth is understood to be self-evident in Scripture. God's instruction on worship is singular, static, nonculturally bound, and available to all faithful readers of Scripture. Even later proponents of tabernacle of David theology continue to refer to it as a singular divine ideal. For instance, at IHOPKC, while their understanding of the tabernacle of David has evolved the theology, they still argue that the worship of David's tabernacle was an historical expression of God's divine will. They argue that David received a similar vision to John's Apocalypse that enabled him to understand God's divine liturgical ideal.[37]

The theology of the tabernacle of David relies upon many of the hermeneutical assumptions and ideas that have been inherited from the Pentecostal theological tradition. While many of these teachers were not aware of a theological tradition that shaped their biblical theology—after all, they were just presenting Scripture's clear teaching—their theology was undergirded by a set of assumptions about licit use of Scripture. This ultimately acted to govern their theology.

---

understanding of the Tabernacle of David independently through biblical study and meditation (cf. xii). This assists his implicit argument that important scriptural truths can be discerned through deep reading of Scripture.

36. Conner, *Tabernacle of David*, i–ii (emphasis original). See also 103, 130, 151–58. Conner also uses the phrase "Davidic order of worship" to similar effect (cf. v, 49, 150).

37. Bickle, *Harp and Bowl Handbook*, 8.

Tradition Contextualizes Biblical Theology: The Restorationist Metanarrative in Praise and Worship Theology

Thus far, I have narrated the way in which tradition influences the activity of theologizing from Scripture, arguing that tradition directs and governs the task of biblical theology. Tradition also influences the use or application of the biblical theology once it has been formulated. In particular, tradition provides an historical narrative that contextualizes and frames biblical theology. The Pentecostal tradition contains a distinct communal narrative that provides the essential framework into which Scripture is read. This narrative is one of the elements that has unified Pentecostals into a coherent and definable theological tradition even if the nature of that narrative is contested.[38]

The essential narrative tradition that underpinned the emerging praise and worship theology of the latter twentieth century focused on the theme of restoration. In continuity with the belief embodied in the Latter Rain movement that church history was "a series of sequential restorations of truths formerly lost,"[39] praise and worship Pentecostals saw their new understanding of the biblical doctrine of praise as God's eschatological restoration of a lost biblical practice. This narrative freed Latter Rain Pentecostals to explore novel theological concepts and doctrines, unworried that the long heritage of Christian theology had not taught those concepts and doctrines. God was now revealing God's divine will that had long been contained but ignored in Scripture. This emphasis on restoration as the primary explanation of novel doctrine and practice was not an innovation of the Latter Rain revival. Instead, they merely renewed the metanarrative that had existed in early Pentecostalism.

In his description of the early Pentecostal narrative tradition, Archer argues that the core of the early Pentecostal narrative was the "Latter Rain" motif.[40] This motif described the powerful work of the Holy Spirit as God's divinely initiated fulfillment of Joel 2—the promise to pour out the latter rain.[41] The contemporary fulfillment of the latter rain within Pentecostalism

---

38. Some scholars have focused on the personal testimonies "into which persons became caught up as they encountered Christ in the Spirit" (Coulter, "On Tradition, Local Traditions, and Discernment," 1–3). See also, McDonnell, "Function of Tongues in Pentecostalism," 332–54. Other scholars have focused on Pentecostalism as a communal narrative that collectively embodies a certain view of Christian history (Archer, "Pentecostal Story"; Archer, *Pentecostal Hermeneutic*, 128–71).

39. Ruth and Lim, *History of Contemporary Praise and Worship*, 16.

40. Archer, *Pentecostal Hermeneutic*, 136–40.

41. This passage is crucially recapitulated in Acts 2.

was to prepare the church to bring in the end-time harvest ahead of Christ's imminent return. While this narrative stresses God's divine initiation of the latter rain, the motif also had elements of human agency admixed. This restoration was the sign that the church (particularly, the Pentecostal Church) had returned to the practice and faith of the apostolic era. The Pentecostal belief in a "full gospel message" that believed in Christ not only as Savior but as the Baptizer in the Holy Spirit, enabled the new work of the Holy Spirit to be released among them. As we will see, this narrative that emphasized God's eschatological work of restoration among Christians who have returned to true biblical faith forms the core metanarrative behind tabernacle of David theologies.

In the earliest writings on the tabernacle of David, both Truscott and Conner frame their biblical theology through a decline-restoration narrative. Both see the Davidic worship as the liturgical form of the apostolic faith that had been lost but was now being restored to the church. Like the earliest Pentecostals who saw the eschatological fulfillment of Joel 2 in their experience, later Pentecostals saw the prophetic promise of Amos 9:11–12 as fulfilled among them. Truscott, though, went even further than this. He viewed the restoration of the tabernacle of David as a restoration that surpassed Pentecost: "while the book of Acts most certainly records the commencement of this Restoration, it is obvious that in the book of Acts the Restoration was neither completed nor perfected." Instead, Truscott argues that Amos and James "look down the corridor of time to an age when there will be a complete Restoration of the Tabernacle of David."[42] Thus, the restoration motif for Truscott leads him to see the antitype of Amos' prophecy of restoration as fulfilled in twentieth-century Pentecostalism. For later proponents of the tabernacle of David, such as IHOPKC, a similar narrative underpins their adherence to tabernacle of David theology.[43]

In answering the question of why had the liturgical practice that was commanded during the Old Testament and practiced during the New Testament fallen into disuse, Truscott and Conner express a narrative that would have been familiar to early Pentecostals: after the apostolic period, the church had been unfaithful and blind; accordingly, they lacked the glory, power, and holiness of the earlier period. For instance, Conner describes

---

42. Truscott, *Power of His Presence*, 5. Elsewhere, Truscott continues to reinforce his view that the gift of the Holy Spirit was coming to fuller fruition than at Pentecost (cf. 18).

43. See for instance, Bickle, "Tabernacle of David." In IHOPKC's later theology, they have increasingly attempted to distance themselves from this earlier view that saw the fulfillment of Amos 9:11–12 in the global prayer movement. See, for instance, International House of Prayer, "Affirmations and Denials."

Christian history as an initial long period of decline (that mirrored Israel's decline in the Old Testament): "decline and apostacy set in even as in Israel's history. The Church departed from the faith once delivered to the saints . . . Spiritual death settled on the people of God."[44] For Conner, the turning point in this decline was the Reformation. Ignoring some of the basic theological contributions of the Reformation, Conner argued that it was the return of apostolic musical practices that turned the church toward renewal: "Now the Church is coming out of Babylon, 'religious confusion,' and her captivity is being turned. Once again the songs of Zion are being heard in the earth."[45] The completion of this renewal is seen in the Latter Rain movement where true, expressive, biblical praise in the model of David's tabernacle was restored to the church.

Like early Pentecostalism, this narrative encoded within the tabernacle of David theology has an eschatological dimension to it. The restoration of the church's vocation as a holy priesthood is being restored as a sign of, and in preparation for, the final days.[46] This eschatological expectation was mapped back onto the biblical narrative of David's initial establishment of his tabernacle. Just as David's tabernacle was the temporary inauguration of a new liturgical form that was then incorporated into the permanent locale of Solomon's Temple, so the Latter Rain practice of praise was a prophetic revelation of the praise that will form the basis of the church's eternal, heavenly song. It is this new practice of praise that has been released just prior to Christ's return and establishment of this new liturgical form in his eschatological kingdom. By contrast the liturgical worship of other Christian traditions was representative of the former Mosaic covenant which is passing away.[47]

Scripture and Tradition in Dialogue in Free Church Worship

Throughout the Free Church tradition, Scripture has historically been the primary authority. This is especially true for Evangelical traditions within the Free Church. Their reenvisioning of their liturgical practice has often

44. Conner, *Tabernacle of David*, 148.

45. Conner, *Tabernacle of David*, 149.

46. David Blomgren, a later teacher on the Tabernacle of David, saw this as Amos's reference to closing up the breaches of David's Tabernacle; God restored the Tabernacle of David at Pentecost but closed its breaches in the Latter Rain movement (Blomgren, in Nation, "Hermeneutics of Pentecostal-Charismatic Restoration Theology, 172).

47. Truscott, *Power of His Presence*, 74.

been their attempt to better embody Scripture's witness about Christian worship and what it should be and do. However, this paper suggests that there are no biblical theologies of worship that are not influenced by their broader network of ecclesial communities. These ecclesial communities embody common narratives, theological assumptions, and values that I have described as a tradition. In turn, these traditions shape biblical theologies of worship by establishing the contexts within which biblical theology takes place. Tradition exerts influence over theology by suggesting biblical themes, governing licit theological methods, and narrating the doctrines uncovered in Scripture. Even where tradition is explicitly rejected, tradition continues to shape theology, even if unseen, implicit, or unauthorized.

This should invite us to consider the ways in which our traditions predispose us to understand Christian worship. It is both warning and gift. It is warning in that it should encourage us towards a position of epistemic humility as we understand that what we see as clear and universal in Scripture may not be clear and universal to all. It is gift because understanding how different groups have read Scripture to inform their worship can also provoke us to consider how our own ways of reading Scripture as a guide for Christian worship may be limited. Whether recognized or not, our reading of Scripture is formed by our contexts, communities, and traditions, and this shapes our understanding of Christian worship.

Bibliography

Archer, Kenneth. *A Pentecostal Hermeneutic: Spirit, Scripture and Community.* Cleveland: CPT, 2009.

———. "Pentecostal Story: The Hermeneutical Filter for the Making of Meaning." *Pneuma* 26.1 (2004) 36–59.

Bickle, Mike. *Harp and Bowl Handbook.* Kansas City: Forerunner, 2020.

———. "Tabernacle of David." Sermon, Over 30s Retreat, March 12, 1999, transcript.

Chan, Simon. *Pentecostal Ecclesiology: An Essay on the Development of Doctrine.* Dorset, UK: Deo, 2011.

———. "Tradition: Retrieving and Updating Pentecostal Core Beliefs." In *The Routledge Handbook of Pentecostal Theology,* edited by Wolfgang Vondey, 95–105. New York: Routledge, 2020.

Conner, Kevin. *The Tabernacle of David: The Presence of God as Experienced in the Tabernacle.* Rev. and exp. ed. Portland, OR: Christian City, 1986.

Cooke, William. *The Shekinah, or, The Presence and Manifestation of Jehovah, Under the Several Dispensations, from the Creation of Man to the Day of Judgment. With Dissertations on the Cherubim and Urim and Thummim.* 2nd ed. London: Hamilton, Adams and Co. 1877.

Coulter, Dale M. "On Tradition, Local Traditions, and Discernment." *Pneuma* 36.1 (2014) 1–3.

Dayton, Donald. *Theological Roots of Pentecostalism*. Grand Rapids: Baker Academic, 1987.

Ellis, Christopher. *Gathering: A Theology and Spirituality of Worship in Free Church Tradition*. London: SCM, 2004.

Faupel, D. William. "The New Order of the Latter Rain: Restoration or Renewal?" In *Winds from the North: Canadian Contributions to the Pentecostal Movement*, edited by Michael Wilkinson and Peter Althouse, 239–64. Leiden: Brill, 2010.

Fritsch, C. H. T. "To Antityphon." In *Studia biblica et semitica: Theodoro Christiano Vriezen qui munere professoris theologiae per XXV annos functus est, ab amicis, collegis, discipulis dedicate*, 100–107. Wageningen, The Netherlands: H. Veenman en zonen, 1966.

Gagliardi, B. Maureen. *The Path of the Just: The Tabernacle of Moses*. Vancouver: New West, 1963.

Herbert, Arthur G. *The Throne of David: A Study of the Fulfilment of the Old Testament in Jesus Christ and His Church*. London: Faber and Faber, 1946.

Hugenberger, Gordon. "Introductory Notes on Typology." In *The Right Doctrines from the Wrong Texts*, edited by G. K. Beale, 331–41. Grand Rapids: Baker, 1994.

Hughes, Kevin. "Deep Reasonings: *Sources Chretiennes*, *Ressourcement*, and the Logic of Scripture in the Years Before—and after—Vatican II." *Modern Theology* 29.4 (2013) 32–45.

International House of Prayer. "Affirmations and Denials." https://www.ihopkc.org/about/affirmations-and-denials/.

Lampe, G. W. H. "The Reasonableness of Typology." In *Essays on Typology*, edited by G. W. H. Lampe and Kenneth J. Woollcombe, 9–38. London: SCM, 1957.

Layzell, Reg. *The Pastor's Pen: Early Revival Writings of Pastor Reg Layzell*. Compiled by B. Maureen Gagliardi. Vancouver: Glad Tidings Temple, 1965.

Marsden, George. *Fundamentalism and American Culture*. 2nd ed. New York: Oxford University Press, 2006.

Mauro, Philip. *The Hope of Israel: What Is It?* Boston: Hamilton Brothers, 1929.

McDonnell, Kilian. "The Function of Tongues in Pentecostalism." *One in Christ* 19.4 (1983) 332–54.

Nation, Garry D. "The Hermeneutics of Pentecostal-Charismatic Restoration Theology: A Critical Analysis." PhD diss., Southwestern Baptist Theological Seminary, 1990.

Newton, Richard. *The Jewish Tabernacle and Its Furniture in Their Typical Teaching*. New York: R. Carter, 1874.

Nisbet, James. *The Tabernacle: Its Literal Uses and Spiritual Applications*. London: James Nisbet, 1853.

Offiler, W. H. *God and His Bible: Or, The Harmonies of Divine Revelation*. Seattle: Bethel Temple, 1946.

Oliverio, L. William. *Theological Hermeneutics in the Classical Pentecostal Tradition: A Typological Account*. Boston: Brill, 2015.

Ottaway, Jonathan. "The Seven Hebrew Words for Praise: Pentecostal Interpretation of Scripture in Liturgical Theology." *Worship* 97.1 (2023) 10–30.

Perez, Adam. "All Hail King Jesus: The International Worship Symposium and the Making of Praise and Worship History, 1977–1989." ThD diss., Duke University, 2021.

Phythian-Adams, William J. *The People and the Presence: A Study of the At-one-ment*. London: Oxford University Press, 1942.

Rhind, William G. *The Tabernacle in the Wilderness: The Shadow of Heavenly Things.* London: Bagster and Sons, 1844.

Ruth, Lester. *Worship at Early Methodist Quarterly Meetings.* Nashville: Abingdon, 2000.

Ruth, Lester, and Lim Swee Hong. *A History of Contemporary Praise and Worship: Understanding the Ideas That Reshaped the Protestant Church.* Grand Rapids: Baker Academic, 2021.

Taves, Ann. "The Camp Meeting and the Paradoxes of Evangelical Protestant Ritual." In *Teaching Ritual*, edited by Catherine Bell, 119–31. Oxford: Oxford Scholarship Online, 2007.

———. *Fits, Trances and Visions: Experiencing Religion and Explaining Experience from Wesley to James.* Princeton: Princeton University Press, 1999.

Truscott, Graham. *The Power of His Presence: The Restoration of the Tabernacle of David.* San Diego: Restoration Temple, 1969.

Wacker, Grant. *Heaven Below: Early Pentecostals and American Culture.* Cambridge: Harvard University Press, 2001.

Waddell, Robby, and Peter Althouse. "The Living Tradition of Pentecostals and Charismatics: Nostalgias, Shibboleths, Histories and Identities." *Pneuma* 37.2 (2015) 173–75.

Warnock, George H. *The Feast of Tabernacles.* Springfield, MO: Bill Britton, 1951.

7

The Power of Claiming Biblical Authority

We Practice "Biblical Worship": A Southern Baptist Vision of Liturgical Authority

Emily Snider Andrews

The Southern Baptist Convention (SBC) lands squarely in the category of Free Church worship and comprises the largest evangelical Protestant group in the United States. Like the wider evangelical body of which they are a part, the contributions to a scholarly defined "church theology"[1] by Southern Baptists have been narrow, producing scholarship on worship that is largely insular and generally situated within Baptist spheres of life. While that audience is widening, the trend still continues, limiting their role in wider scholarly and ecumenical contexts. This essay addresses that gap by describing notions of liturgical authority among Southern Baptists in order

---

1. That is, the approach rooted in the academy and embodied by those who study "liturgical theology." As used by liturgical theologian Graham Hughes, this approach includes the work of notables like Alexander Schmemann, a number of Lutherans, and the Methodist Geoffrey Wainwright. Hughes claims the categorical term was inspired by Frank C. Senn, also a member of the "churchly" theologians. See Hughes, *Worship as Meaning*, 222.

to offer a sympathetic, yet clarified, interpretation of the group's prioritizing "biblical worship."

My approach is, at once, from the perspective of both insider and outsider. I was raised in the Southern Baptist tradition, but I left the denomination in my early twenties. My association with them continues though through my teaching at a private Christian university in the southeastern United States whose history and mission privileges the Southern Baptist tradition.[2] My work there entails regular collaboration and even leadership among and with Southern Baptist entities and persons. Further, I aim to highlight insider perspectives, a particularly Baptist understanding of liturgical authority, by focusing on primary sources and voices privileged by the group.

At the same time, I am an outsider. I no longer worship in and with a local church associated with the convention.[3] What is more, I will aim to describe this SBC vision to other outsiders in order to provide clarity to others studying the phenomenon. In bringing these angles together, I am in the position of insider-as-researcher, attempting to speak from perspectives within the community while also retaining a more objective stance through application of scholarly perspectives.

After providing a brief overview of the current state of public worship in Southern Baptist life and describing the influence of the Gospel-Centered Movement (GCM) on the denomination, I will address the issue of liturgical authority among Southern Baptists by exploring their priority of "biblical worship." Southern Baptist leaders regularly laud their "biblical worship" and its "biblical leadership." On the one hand, this is unsurprising given the group's self-proclaimed "biblicist" status. On the other hand, this language obscures clarity among outsiders who wonder what is notably "biblical" about Southern Baptist worship. This paper seeks to clarify the concept by describing the tradition's own values of public worship that is

---

2. Samford University, Birmingham, Alabama, was founded by Alabama Baptists in 1841. In 2018, the university elected to reduce its anticipated budget allocation from the Alabama State Convention to zero, effectively ending its formal relationship; however, as then-President Andrew Westmoreland reiterated publicly on a number of occasions, "The relationship between Alabama Baptists and Samford remains crucial to the mission of Samford and the ongoing work of Baptists in Alabama and Christians throughout the worl" (Poole, "Samford University Volunteers to Forego," para. 4).

3. In full disclosure, I was ordained for ministry by a Baptist congregation affiliated with the Cooperative Baptist Fellowship (CBF), whose identity was especially shaped by its opposition to the conservative takeover during "The Controversy" dispute within the SBC, which began in 1979. I spent several years ministering among CBF congregations before resigning my leadership position to participate as a lay worshiper. I currently worship with a congregation affiliated with The United Methodist Church.

"gospel centered, musically relevant, and pastorally focused," as one large SBC seminary puts it.[4] How do SBC worship leaders describe and practice these concerns? What is the theological vision undergirding these authoritative values? Concluding observations describe these efforts as increasingly "churchly" developments that may contribute to an ecumenical flourishing in a denomination known for its insularity.

Worship in the SBC and the Gospel-Centered Movement

Certainly, no single depiction will do justice to a faithful description of liturgical life in the SBC. There exists much diversity, and Southern Baptists themselves do not agree on the proper liturgical heritage of their historical predecessors.[5] Still, as Eric Mathis has demonstrated, since the 1979 Controversy, which pitted conservative Southern Baptists against their moderate counterparts,[6] the conservative Southern Baptists leading the convention

4. As described in the mission of The Southern Baptist Theological Seminary's (SBTS) "Department of Biblical Worship." See The Southern Baptist Theological Seminary, "Department of Biblical Worship." SBTS is especially invested in the term, also housing their "Institute of Biblical Worship," which aims to "equip God's people to sing the gospel by helping church leaders plan, prepare, and present biblical worship." See http://biblicalworship.com/.

5. One Baptist historian memorably describes the diversity present in Southern Baptist history as a heritage which comes "from sophisticated cities like Charleston and from rustic crossroads like Sandy Creek. We came educated and uneducated. We came with evangelism, and we came with educational institutions. We came with the local church and the universal church. We came with Calvinistic theology, Arminian theology, and no theology. We came applauding confessional statements, and we came deploring confessional statements. We came affirming culture and rebuking culture." Today, one would find Southern Baptists who argue a privileging of a single side of each of these poles as the "authentic" Baptist identity (See Shurden, "Southern Baptist Synthesis," 11).

In particular, and as it relates to public worship, Southern Baptists disagree on whether or not the group especially belongs to the "Sandy Creek" or "Charleston" tradition. The Sandy Creek tradition is rooted historically in eighteenth-century Sandy Creek, North Carolina, a tradition which "expressed itself in individualism, congregationalism, Biblicism, and egalitarianism. Sandy Creek congregations released a devotion to freedom which is without parallel in Baptist history" (Shurden, "Southern Baptist Synthesis," 4). By contrast, the "Charleston" tradition is more closely akin to the Separatist and Puritan tradition of worship. "For Southern Baptists," writes Eric Mathis, "the Charleston tradition became a tradition of order; theologically, ecclesiologically, ministerially and liturgically." While both traditions took root in the local churches affiliated with the SBC, the post-1979 Controversy decades saw a cementing of the freer Sandy Creek tradition as the proper liturgical expression of Southern Baptist faith (Mathis, "Campaigning in the House of God," 259).

6. A number of scholars from both the "fundamentalist" and "moderate" perspective

have largely rallied around a liturgical tradition rooted in liturgical historian James White's "Frontier worship" in an attempt to ritually distinguish themselves from their moderate Baptist counterparts and other assumed "liberal" Protestant groups. These conservatives expressed an inherent skepticism of "liturgical worship" and "high church music," while prioritizing evangelism efforts to "reach the lost." One Southern Baptist pastor, Bailey Smith, preached the message memorably in 1982 at the annual Southern Baptist Convention meeting. His sermon highlights the tendency among Southern Baptists to claim a divine revelation and a resulting liturgical practice that is at once unique, evangelistically relevant, countercultural, and above all, biblical:

> If Southern Baptists ever try to escape the absolute priority of evangelism and the authority of the infallible, inerrant Word of God, we will not be able to escape the mediocrity of other mainline denominations. . . . They [mainline institutions] are conservatories of culture instead of lighthouses of Gospel truth. . . . [T]here are some marriages that will not work. We cannot wed missions to liberalism; evangelism to liturgical worship; spiritual power to high church music . . . We must preach the Bible, live the Bible, and obey the Bible. We must . . . [be] Bold, Believing, Bible Baptists.[7]

The convention entered the twenty-first century with a greater openness to, and association with, the wider evangelical body, leaving room for the importation of liturgical theologies and practices that were not particularly "Baptist." Rising leaders like David S. Dockery and Albert Mohler embodied a convention that increasingly identified a need to more thoroughly engage with culture in order to effectively convey its conservative message. This coincided with an affirmation of theological themes highlighted by certain Reformed sectors within the wider, conservative evangelical body, including an emphasis on substitutionary atonement, predestination, divine sovereignty, and a disdain for themes that might be interpreted as "liberal," including topics such as social justice, the environment, ecumenism, and gender equality. These SBC leaders increasingly leaned into a particular niche of evangelicalism, a self-described "movement" operating under the auspices of several titles, including the "young, restless and Reformed movement," the "New Calvinists," and the "neo-Reformed" or "neo-Puritan"

---

have documented "The Controversy." For a fairly comprehensive and clarifying look, see Ammerman, *Baptist Battles*.

7. Smith, "Southern Baptists' Most Serious Question," 72.

movement." More recently, this arm has preferred the "Gospel-Centered Movement" (GCM).

The GCM is not led exclusively or even primarily by Southern Baptists, although several leading Southern Baptists ascribe to it, and there are a few Southern Baptists identified as key, influential leaders of the group.[8] Its central authoritative voices include J. I. Packer, R. C. Sproul, John MacArthur, John Piper, and Timothy Keller, among others. There is no universally accepted definition of the movement. Common descriptions are a bit circular, with statements promulgating a faith life that is "biblically mandated" and "gospel centered." The Gospel Coalition, a central promoter and resource of the movement, states that its primary purpose is "to propagate a robust understanding of the gospel's content and to encourage gospel-centered ministry . . . [that] flows from Jesus and the gospel."[9] "Scripture," as Timothy Keller argues, "is the starting point for everything," including worship.[10]

The influence of the GCM on the SBC means that many leading Southern Baptist voices tend to be "Reformed-ish" and are generally recognized as leaders and participants in the movement. This connection is worth noting, as it is thinking from this group that has especially shaped an SBC understanding of "biblical worship," guiding denominational leaders toward its aims of worship that is "gospel centered, musically relevant, and pastorally focused."

SBC Worship Is Gospel Centered

Biblical worship is fundamentally about the gospel, SBC leaders suggested at a Southern Seminary "Think: Worship" conference. This claim is made often. What does it entail? While, as was stated previously and which bears repeating, there is no universally accepted description, SBC proponents advocate a vision for gospel-centered worship that fundamentally shapes

8. Jared C. Wilson, director of content strategy at Midwestern Baptist Theological Seminary and author of a number of "gospel-centered" books, including *The Gospel-Driven Church*, identifies Southern Baptist Convention leaders Al Mohler (president of Southern Baptist Theological Seminary), Russell Moore (former president of the SBC's Ethics and Religious Liberty Commission), David Platt (currently pastor of McLean Bible Church and former president of the SBC's International Mission Board), Timothy George (ordained SBC minister and founding dean of Beeson Divinity School, Samford University), Thom Rainer (former president of LifeWay Christian Resources), and a number of Southern Baptist pastors, to name a few (Wilson, "Top 125 Influences").

9. The Gospel Coalition, "Gospel-Centered Ministry," para. 2.

10. Keller, *Serving a Movement*, 11.

both worship's message and content as well as structures its delivery and leadership.

In keeping with the wider evangelical body, an SBC understanding of gospel-centered worship is rooted in the Christ-event, particularly Jesus' death and resurrection. However, as evidence of the Reformed-leaning influences of the GCM, many SBC leaders insist on a more particular message of worship, one that is in keeping with theologies of atonement, soteriology, and divine sovereignty promulgated among the "New Calvinists," such as those fueling The Gospel Coalition.[11] SBC pastor and educator Matt Boswell describes this vision as embodying the "biblical truth" that should ground worship's message:

> If we knew nothing of God, His greatness, His holiness, His goodness, His gospel, we would have no reason to worship Him. If we don't believe in the substitutionary death of a sinless Christ, we have no reason to worship Him.... It is vital for worship leaders to have a robust and growing theology.... Without a deep and growing understanding of biblical truth, our worship will be uninformed and weightless. Infused with Scripture . . . the worship of God will be . . . gospel-soaked and powerful.[12]

In this view, gospel-centered worship makes central a particular proclamation and teaching of Christ's death and resurrection that is believed to best encapsulate "the gospel." For Baptist leaders, this focus is often featured in the sermon and song lyrics of worship, although it also contributes to an overarching theology of worship. For instance, gospel-centered preaching is understood to counter a contemporary penchant for other approaches that might be more fittingly described as contextual, life-situational, evangelistic, or narrative. Sermons that give focus to current events, societal transformation, personal or family therapy, general morality, or those exclusively directed to "the lost" are not in keeping with this understanding of gospel-centered worship in that they fail to properly focus on the message of Christ's death and resurrection.

Jared Wilson, author of a teaching series on the "gospel-shaped church," proposes a more fully orbed theology of worship for the practice of "gospel-shaped worship." First is the recognition that the worship gathering is a service for the church and is thus primarily for believers whose focus is on worshiping the Lord. This counters the notion suggested by some that

---

11. GCM leader Timothy Keller identifies the doctrine of substitutionary atonement as "at the heart of everything." It is "the single most consoling and appealing atonement theme" (Keller, *Center Church*, 131).

12. Boswell, "Doxology," 13.

SBC leaders have largely replaced believers' worship with evangelism or missions. Second, the service should utilize the sermon as a chief tool that focuses the life of the worshiper on "the gospel," particularly as espoused in the substitutionary atonement models noted above. Finally, the worship service is for sending worshipers on mission, Wilson's explicit connection of the worship gathering to the daily life of the believer. Overall, the "way in which . . . regular services happen" should reflect "clear statements of the gospel facts, promises and commands."[13] This embodies an overarching theology of worship that reflects the gospel.

Gospel-centered worship focuses the message of worship, but it also shapes the structuring delivery. In this, the role of the worship leader is vital, a responsibility envisioned as extending beyond the task of music. The worship leader should "think theologically . . . so that the people of God can recover gospel-saturated worship."[14] Since the worship leader's theological convictions serve as a foundation for worship, what the particular leader believes, especially about the Bible, is important. "Worship leaders ought to come," Boswell writes, "to lead the people of God with a guitar in one hand, a Bible in the other, and know how to use each weapon well."[15]

Boswell frames his understanding of the worship leader through the same lens in which he interprets the New Testament roles of "overseers" and "elders," claiming that the worship leader, too, is tasked with the sacred duties of shepherding, leading, and teaching God's people, a functional "elder" in the local church.[16] In the context of SBC life and its teachings on gender roles, this is a weighty statement on the gendered nature of worship leadership and its related dynamics of power and authority. While the SBC has reported a significant increase in the number of female students seeking an SBC seminary education preparing them for ministerial service, including service in the church's worship ministry,[17] SBC leaders continue to identify men as the ones biblically called to leadership. As Boswell and others have argued, the teaching and shepherding role, now understood as vital for the

13. Wilson, *Gospel Shaped Worship*, loc. 1065 of 1873.

14. Boswell, "Introduction," 2. Boswell goes on to write that the worship leader must maintain a "vivid belief in the inerrancy and sufficiency of the Word of God" ("Doxology, Theology," 12).

15. Boswell, "Doxology, Theology," 10.

16. Boswell, "Qualifications of a Worship Leader," 24. This is in keeping with Boer's study, which found that 55 percent of the job descriptions for full-time worship leaders in SBC local church contexts describe the position as one for a "pastor or elder," with 66 percent of those descriptions clearly delineating a male candidate (Boer, "Comparative Content Analysis," 116–17).

17. Roach, "'Remarkable' Number of Women."

worship leader, means that worship in the local church should be overseen by men. Biblical, gospel-centered worship, then, is a means of addressing the gender debate that has been at the forefront of SBC life for many decades now. It structurally situates worship leadership within a larger picture of what is understood by adherents as "biblical."

SBC Worship Is Musically Relevant

The SBC's increasing affiliation with the wider evangelical body means that the practices of contemporary worship have come to especially define the normative liturgical ethos of the group, concretely evidenced by the robust inclusion of contemporary worship songs in the denomination's recently published hymnal, *The Baptist Hymnal* (2008). While musical diversity continues among SBC congregations, one early motivating factor behind the SBC's adoption of contemporary worship music remains rooted in the 1979 Controversy, with conservatives publicly criticizing their "liberal" counterparts who were said to value more "liturgical" forms of worship alongside "traditional" or "high church" styles of music.[18]

Today, the more divisive motivations have diminished, with leaders settling into contemporary worship music as the assumed and largely unquestioned model. It is presumed, as Boswell puts it, that "worship leaders ought to come to lead . . . with a guitar in one hand . . ."[19] Younger Southern Baptists and the denomination's "cosmopolitan" adherents from which many of the denomination's chief leaders are drawn, often located in urban areas and especially in large, megachurch-status congregations, trend toward contemporary worship music and practice.[20] In 2015, one study found that only 15 percent of SBC congregations with over 1,100 attendees would describe their worship gatherings as "traditional."[21] Another study found that today's SBC worship leaders are increasingly expected to speak a musical language that is outside the "formally-learned traditional" one.[22] The general expectation is that the worship leader should be conversant in a number of band-associated instruments, particularly guitar and drums,

---

18. Mathis, "Campaigning in the House of God," 202.

19. Boswell, "Doxology," 10.

20. Trevin Wax, director for Bibles and References at LifeWay Christian Resources, an entity of the SBC, describes the diversity within SBC via the categories of "conventional" and "cosmopolitan" cultures (Wax, "Southern Baptists").

21. Boer, "Comparative Content Analysis," 39.

22. Gillis, "Contemporary Practices," 667.

further evidence of the deep roots of contemporary worship practice among SBC congregations.

For musical relevancy, some leaders have been guided by a seeker-service mentality, looking for practical ways to grow their local congregations through efforts of appealing to the masses with popular music practices. However, as described above, there are indications that simply "reaching the lost" is no longer the primary motivating factor behind the SBC's widespread use of contemporary worship music.

In their vision for "biblical worship," the accoutrements of contemporary worship music better facilitate an "artistic" and "creative" model of worship leadership. This is understood to fulfill a biblical mandate, one in which Christians are called to serve as culture-creating artists "who are creating and expressing . . . our worship of God."[23] The worship-leader-as-artist cultivates a creative community in the local church, attempting to "empower creatives in our own context" since "authentic creativity is grass roots."[24] Churches leading these efforts are known for calling and employing artists who contribute to unique and contextualized worship offerings, which often culminate in the production of a music album featuring talented church members.[25]

Mike Cosper suggests that this model is prescriptive, that SBC pastors should "learn to empower creatives (as opposed to importing creativity)," thus enabling the "congregation to lead worship through word, symbol, music, visual art, and architecture that uniquely reflects our tribe—our unique, local context."[26] This is a vision of "musically relevant" worship not often associated with the SBC due to its historic emphasis on evangelism and outreach. The worship leader leading as artist is envisioned as "contextualizing in the best possible sense" since those efforts demonstrate that "the gospel has impacted our lives," and that "we respond with our . . . proclamation of

---

23. As described by former director of worship for LifeWay Christian Resources Mike Harland (*Worship Essentials*, 94). Southern Baptists certainly are not alone in this vision and related efforts. For instance, Makoto Fujimura, CEO of Culture Care Creative Inc., identifies "culture care" as a "movement toward renewal born from the integration" of art and Christianity. He describes this "movement" as an "alternative to 'culture wars,'" and "a philosophy that offers the creation and conservation of beauty as antidote to cultural brokenness" (see para. 1. at https://culturecarecreative.com/home/).

24. Cosper, "Worship Leader and Creativity," 141.

25. Travis Cottrell, worship pastor at Englewood Baptist Church in Jackson, Tennessee, and Mark Willard, worship pastor at Sherwood Baptist Church in Albany, Georgia, are two notable examples of SBC worship leaders and congregations who have led these efforts.

26. Cosper, "Worship Leader and Creativity," 147.

that changeless gospel."[27] Musically relevant worship, then, is best embodied in contemporary worship musical styles, but not simply for popularity's sake. The relevancy especially resides in the relational capital developed through localized, grassroots efforts of music-making and music-sharing. These communal musical practices, centered in the congregation's public worship, further catalyze the community toward biblical worship that embodies the gospel.

SBC Worship Is Pastorally Focused

While Southern Baptists have certainly not diminished the prominence of evangelism and missions, the recent emphasis on worship that is pastorally focused indicates a renewed theology of worship that understands the public gathering as one that is by and for believers, rather than maintaining the typical evangelistic impulses often associated with SBC worship.[28] This is stated explicitly in Wilson's popular teaching series. There he states, "The church gathering is primarily for believers. Non-Christians should be made welcome, but evangelism mainly takes place *outside* of the gathering."[29] In a rejection of seeker-service models that have, at times, guided the worship of SBC congregations and garnered criticisms from their "liturgical" counterparts who have read in that model the authoritative guides of pragmatism, church growth, evangelism, and fellowship,[30] pastorally focused worship is among believers. This model is further understood to support the denomination's missional efforts and is "attractive to outsiders" since it "shows the gospel at work."[31]

27. Cosper, "Worship Leader and Creativity," 147.

28. The kind of worship that, historically, culminates in the ritual of an "altar call" among Southern Baptists. To be clear, many Southern Baptist congregations still maintain the practice of an altar call in their gatherings. However, it is no longer the climactic ritual moment in many SBC congregations, especially in ones employing contemporary worship models.

29. Wilson, *Gospel Shaped Worship*, session 4, loc. 992 of 1873 (emphasis original).

30. As in Gordon Lathrop's criticism of contemporary worship practice. He characterizes the rituals found in that liturgical body as having been "transformed into signs of human decision . . . [so that the worship] meeting will not really be around God . . ." (Lathrop, "New Pentecost or Joseph's Britches?," 533).

31. Wilson, *Gospel Shaped Worship*, session 4, loc. 1037 of 1873. Most SBC leaders would still reject some of the more "liturgical" forms and rituals classically associated with "believers' worship." Even while insisting that worship is for believers, Wilson teaches, in seeker-service fashion, "Don't assume that people know what to do. . . . Explain the meaning of words and don't use Christian jargon without defining it. . . . The only obstacle to joining in and belonging should be the gospel" (session 4, loc. 1065 of 1873).

This vision has not been adopted by all and was recently debated by SBC leaders. In a 2016 debate on "Leadership, Preaching, and Cultural Engagement," Andy Stanley, senior pastor of North Point Community Church, a mega, multisite church in the metro Atlanta area, called for renewed emphasis on a seeker-service approach, insisting that worship gatherings should especially aim to reach nonbelievers. Stanley's goal for preaching, he explained, is for unchurched people to be excited by what they hear so that they will want to come back with their friends. "If your church people are not comfortable bringing their unchurched friends to church," he warned, "you just need to think about that."[32] Russell Moore, president of The Ethics & Religious Liberty Commission of the Southern Baptist Convention at the time, engaged Stanley in the debate, insisting on an alternative approach, one that is in keeping with a believers' worship model. Moore stressed the gospel-shaped content of the sermon and worship gathering: "[I]t's important that what we're approaching people with is an encounter with the risen Christ who speaks through His Word."[33] Moore is recognized as a leader of the GCM and has articulated his support of the movement's central teachings. When imagining himself as the "Pope of Evangelicalism," Moore stated that the first change he would initiate among the group would be for its leaders to "seek a consistent confidence in the Bible as the Word of God . . . among church leaders as they're speaking both to the church and to the world."[34] This is in keeping with the gospel-centered efforts identified above as among the distinguishing characteristics of worship promoted by SBC leaders.

Evidence that Stanley's view is no longer mainstream in the SBC is revealed in a simple Google search related to this debate. Many in the SBC were critical of Stanley's positions. He was called everything from a "liberal" to a "heretic," leading Stanley to issue a formal response to the criticism in which he reiterated to the group that he does, in fact, believe "the Bible is without error in everything it affirms."[35] The debate, though, seemed to invigorate a more robust response by SBC leaders in Moore's camp. Worship that is pastorally focused ultimately rejects the seeker model because of

32. Stanley and Moore, "Leadership, Preaching, and Cultural Engagement," 11:35–11:43.

33. Stanley and Moore, "Leadership, Preaching, and Cultural Engagement," 17:02–17:10.

34. Stanley and Moore, "Leadership, Preaching, and Cultural Engagement," 46:00–46:15.

35. See Stanley, "Why 'The Bible Says So,'" para. 1. Two of the more considered criticisms of Stanley came from David Prince. See Prince, "Andy Stanley's Statements," and Umstattd, "On the Road to Emmaus."

their privileging of the gospel. "The only thing the Bible calls power," writes Wilson, "is the gospel of Jesus Christ."[36] Without this priority, worship becomes "upside down."[37]

Biblical Worship: Jesus, Singing, and Mission

A summary vision of biblical worship as gospel centered, musically relevant, and pastorally focused is found in a brief essay on the subject by SBC songwriter and worship leader, Matt Papa.[38] Papa articulates an understanding of worship in which believers' worship sits at the heart of the Christian mission in the world. True worship is centered on Jesus, especially his death and resurrection. The work of "missions" is especially rooted in the church's worship, in contrast to its external, evangelistic efforts. In expounding on the characteristics of biblical worship, Papa reiterates the music-centric approach that is typical of contemporary worship, that worship is faithfully embodied in corporate musical practices, the "true praise" of worship. When Christians engage this praise in public worship, they are subsequently formed to be missionaries. In Papa's vision, becoming a "missionary" is an inherent result of the sanctifying process of believers' worship.

While singing is a privileged element of worship for Papa, he reiterates an overarching claim of the GCM: biblical worship is put "on display through the Gospel."[39] In keeping with more classical theologies of worship, the dichotomy between believers' worship and evangelism is shunned, since believers' worship is naturally enacted for the sake of both the church and the world. It will be "filled with the passionate celebration of the gospel. We must preach the gospel. We must sing the gospel. Our songs must be saturated with the gospel."[40] When the worship of believers embodies the true gospel, people "will fall in love with Him [God]. People who are in love do crazy things, like change the world."[41] Biblical worship as gospel centered, musically relevant, and pastorally focused is understood to support an overarching Christian vision in which worship sits as the fueling center for the entire life of Christian discipleship. This brings together for SBC adherents the two poles of worship and evangelism, efforts sometimes understood as

36. Wilson, "Is Your Worship Service Upside Down?," para. 7.

37. Wilson, "Is Your Worship Service Upside Down?," para. 1.

38. Papa, "Worship Leader and Mission."

39. Papa, "Worship Leader and Mission," 88.

40. Papa, "Worship Leader and Mission," 88.

41. Papa, "Worship Leader and Mission," 89.

polarities even within SBC circles, in a vision that situates the church's missional efforts as stemming from true, "biblical" worship.

Concluding Remarks

By attending to the perspectives of SBC insiders, I hope to have clarified an SBC vision of biblical worship as being authoritatively positioned as gospel centered, musically relevant, and pastorally focused. One notable observation arising from this study is the identification of GCM as an authoritative resource for many SBC leaders. That movement has guided the SBC toward a theology of worship diverging from its own historical models while maintaining the biblicism that has been a chief identifying marker for the group.

Consequentially, drawing from a resource such as the GCM has also sparked ecumenical efforts in the SBC, at least where conversations on worship are involved, with leaders finding support in the theologically conservative sectors of the wider evangelical sphere. While SBC scholarship and discourse remain largely insular, there is a growing body in their ranks participating in, and even leading, broader conversations on evangelical worship, particularly among others valuing the "biblical" and "gospel centered" moniker. Vibrant SBC relationships with other ecclesial communities, especially the Presbyterian Church in America, the Anglican Church in North America, and the charismatic Calvinists of C. J. Mahaney's "Sovereign Grace" network evidence the ways in which "biblical worship" can serve as a starting point for ecumenical relationships and dialogue. What's more is the potential for growth on this point, since many Christian worshiping and ecclesial communities value the Bible as an authoritative source for faithful worship. While those further from these conservative, (largely) Reformed, and evangelical centers might contest many of the particulars, there is evidenced here opportunities for deepening dialogue with churchly theologians outside the SBC network.[42] Other widening opportunities especially result from the denomination's current focus on the public worship gathering as one for and among believers, rather than the anthropologically centered categories of church growth and evangelism, the latter being an association that has hindered ecumenical dialogue.

---

42. One recent contribution to this effort was made by Scott Aniol, associate professor of church music and worship at Southwestern Theological Seminary, who invoked the hermeneutical theories of Kevin Vanhoozer and Nicholas Wolterstorff to articulate how Scripture may provide concrete aesthetic guidelines for contemporary worship music in his unpublished paper, "From Text to Expression."

At the same time, some outsiders remain skeptical that the SBC's leaning into the GCM and related resources indicates any substantive ecumenical effort. Admittedly, one may read some of these developments, and even the attempt to name what they do and teach as that which constitutes "biblical worship," as furthering the insularity for which the denomination is sometimes known. Identifying something as "biblical" connotes implicitly, and even explicitly in some cases,[43] that there are certain practices and teachings rightfully understood as "not biblical." However, nearly all Christian traditions value the Bible as Scripture and are, in some sense, "people of The Book." Yet Southern Baptists seldom acknowledge that reading Scripture itself involves interpretive acts that are in themselves discursive and culturally mediated, rather than straightforward and divinely given, practices. A focus on the Bible as propositional revelation objectively communicated by God may effectively prevent the opening of a dialogue on the subject and further support insular readings.[44] This closure of the discussion is particularly evident in their situating the office of "worship leader" as exclusively male, a point offered regularly by the narrow body of white males who speak authoritatively for and among the group, and an aspect that is highlighted to further support the SBC complementarian position on gender roles and its "biblical" vision of male headship. In this, describing a teaching as "biblical" is a direct means of identifying particular practices, and perhaps more significant in relation to the concrete power dynamics of a local worshiping body, particular persons, as rightfully authoritative and others as inevitably sliding down a slippery slope towards (unbiblical) "liberalism."

Finally, it's worth noting that not all, including some in the SBC itself,[45] will support the particular vision of what constitutes "biblical" worship

43. An example here is Wax's description of preaching approaches that are not "gospel-centered," some of which are widely utilized among Christians of various theological traditions (Wax, "Gospel-Centered Preaching").

44. Grenz and Franke describe the view officially maintained at SBC seminaries as "viewing the Bible as primarily a storehouse of theological facts," a position in which adherents "set out to amass the true statements of factual propositions they believed were taught in the pages of Scripture . . . so as to bring together what they concluded the Bible 'teaches' about any given topic. And by bringing these biblical teachings together in a systematic whole, their goal became that of compiling the one, complete, timeless body of right doctrines" (Grenz and Franke, *Shaping Theology*, 62).

45. For instance, those among what Wax describes as the "conventional" arm of the SBC are less comfortable with any connections outside those explicitly tied to the denomination itself. Regarding worship, conventionals are more likely to maintain explicit forms of the revivalistic "Sandy Creek" worship tradition, including the altar call, than their more Calvinistic "cosmopolitan" counterparts. Ecumenical dialogue is not prioritized, if welcomed at all, among some "conventional" SBC adherents (Wax, "Southern Baptists").

described here. This is especially worth noting in a volume such as this and further evidences the messiness of theological work among Free Church worshiping traditions, a process in which liturgical authority and public worship's power structures are more frequently contested, negotiated, and reconsidered as compared to their mainline counterparts.[46]

In the end though, untidy processes such as these may better facilitate the sustainability and potential growth of a group like the SBC in a contemporary, evolving world, one in which the inroads of a postmodern insistence on localized narratives and aesthetically impactful experiences are increasingly valued. The regular contestation and negotiation of precisely what constitutes "biblical worship" permits the group a flexible mode of constructing and anchoring the community's authorities on public worship, even if the concrete work of construction remains largely unrecognized.[47] The ability to interpret and promote relatively new liturgical teachings and practices, such as those associated with contemporary worship music, the effort toward "creative communities," and the GCM movement more broadly as "biblical," allows SBC leaders to identify authoritative guides in the evolving cultural resources available to them. This versatility may ultimately contribute to the denomination's future viability and its ability to enter other ecumenical spaces.

Bibliography

Ammerman, Nancy Tatom. *Baptist Battles: Social Change and Religious Conflict in the Southern Baptist Convention*. New Brunswick, NJ: Rutgers University Press, 1990.

Aniol, Scott. "From Text to Expression: 'Fittingness' as a Guideline for Biblically Informed Worship Music." Academic presentation, Christian Congregational Music conference, August 2021, asynchronous virtual.

Boer, Kenneth Alan. "A Comparative Content Analysis of Worship Leader Job Descriptions and Undergraduate Worship Leader Curricula in the Southern Baptist Convention." PhD diss., The Southern Baptist Theological Seminary, 2019.

Boswell, Matt. "Doxology, Theology, and the Mission of God." In *Doxology & Theology*, edited by Matt Boswell, 5–22. Nashville: B&H, 2013.

46. For instance, the need to regularly negotiate these definitions and values is already evidenced in the questioning among some insiders of the "gospel-centered" trend. See, for instance, Leeman, "What's Wrong?"

47. By this, I mean that such work may be perceived as divinely initiated or given without substantial human effort. For instance, Floyd, former CEO and president of the SBC Executive Committee, recently described the "biblical" effort in pure, unmediated terms: "Southern Baptist[s] . . . need to be having biblical conversations about cultural matters. What we think really does not matter . . . what God thinks . . . is exactly what this world needs to hear" (see Floyd, "Will Southern Baptists Practice?," para. 9.)

———. "Introduction." In *Doxology & Theology*, edited by Matt Boswell, 1–4. Nashville: B&H, 2013.

———. "Qualifications of a Worship Leader." In *Doxology & Theology*, edited by Matt Boswell, 23–42. Nashville: B&H, 2013.

Cosper, Mike. "The Worship Leader and Creativity." In *Doxology & Theology*, edited by Matt Boswell, 139–48. Nashville: B&H, 2013.

Floyd, Ronnie. "Will Southern Baptists Practice Biblical Conservatism or Acceptable Progressivism?" *Kentucky Today*, December 5, 2020. https://www.kentuckytoday.com/stories/will-southern-baptists-practice-biblical-conservatism-or-acceptable-progressivism,29410.

Gillis, Leslie Myers. "Contemporary Practices in Southern Baptist Church Music: A Collective Case Study of Worship, Ministry Design and Music Education." DMA diss., Boston University, 2013.

The Gospel Coalition. "Gospel-Centered Ministry." https://www.thegospelcoalition.org/publication/gospel-centered-ministry/.

Grenz, Stanley J., and John R. Franke. *Shaping Theology in a Postmodern Context.* Louisville: Westminster John Knox, 2001.

Harland, Mike. *Worship Essentials: Growing a Healthy Worship Ministry without Starting a War.* Nashville: B&H, 2018.

Hughes, Graham. *Worship as Meaning: A Liturgical Theology for Late Modernity.* New York: Cambridge University Press, 2003.

Keller, Timothy. *Center Church.* Grand Rapids: Zondervan, 2012.

———. *Serving a Movement: Doing Balanced, Gospel-Centered Ministry in Your City.* Grand Rapids: Zondervan, 2016.

Lathrop, Gordon W. "New Pentecost or Joseph's Britches? Reflections on the History and Meaning of the Worship Ordo in the Megachurches." *Worship* 72.6 (Nov 1998) 521–38.

Leeman, Jonathan. "What's Wrong with Gospel-Centered Preaching Today?" *9Marks Journal*, March 31, 2020. https://www.9marks.org/journal/whats-wrong-with-gospel-centered-preaching-today/editors-note/.

Mathis, Eric Lawrence. "Campaigning in the House of God: How Worship Shaped the Ecclesiology of the Southern Baptist Convention in the Controversy of 1979." PhD diss., Fuller Theological Seminary, 2013.

Papa, Matt. "The Worship Leader and Mission." In *Doxology & Theology*, edited by Matt Boswell, 75–92. Nashville: B&H, 2013.

Poole, Philip. "Samford University Volunteers to Forego Alabama Baptist Funding Allocation Starting in 2018." *Samford University*, July 7, 2017. https://www.samford.edu/news/2017/07/Samford-Volunteers-to-Forego-Alabama-Baptist-Funding-in-2018.

Prince, David. "Andy Stanley's Statements about the Bible Are Not Cutting Edge—They're Old Liberalism." *Prince on Preaching*, September 7, 2016. http://www.davidprince.com/2016/09/07/andy-stanleys-statements-bible-not-cutting-edge-theyre-old-liberalism/.

Roach, David. "'Remarkable' Number of Women Reported at SBC Seminaries." *Baptist Press*, September 22, 2017. http://www.bpnews.net/49585/remarkable-number-of-women-reported-at-sbc-seminaries.

Shurden, Walter B. "The Southern Baptist Synthesis: Is It Cracking?" *Baptist History and Heritage* 16.2 (April 1981) 2–11.

Smith, Bailey. "Southern Baptists' Most Serious Question." In *Going for the Jugular: A Documentary History of the SBC Holy War*, edited by Walter Shurden and Randy Shepley, 72–75. Macon, GA: Mercer University Press, 1982.

The Southern Baptist Theological Seminary. "Department of Biblical Worship." https://www.sbts.edu/bgs/biblical-worship/.

Stanley, Andy. "Why 'The Bible Says So' Is Not Enough Anymore." *Outreach Magazine*, May 20, 2018. http://outreachmagazine.com/features/19900-the-bible-says-so.html.

Stanley, Andy, and Russell Moore. "Leadership, Preaching, and Cultural Engagement." *The Ethics & Religious Liberty Commission of the Southern Baptist Convention*, August 25, 2016. Video. 50:40. https://erlc.com/resource-library/event-messages/leadership-preaching-and-cultural-engagement.

Umstattd, Rustin. "On the Road to Emmaus: A Response to Andy Stanley's Sermon 'The Bible Told Me So.'" *Echoes from the Plot Twist*, September 5, 2016. https://echoesfromtheplottwist.wordpress.com/2016/09/05/on-the-road-to-emmaus-a-response-to-andy-stanleys-sermon-the-bible-told-me-so/.

Wax, Trevin. "Gospel-Centered Preaching." *The Gospel Coalition*, May 11, 2010. https://www.thegospelcoalition.org/blogs/trevin-wax/gospel-centered-preaching.

———. "Southern Baptists and Conventional and Cosmopolitan Cultures." *The Gospel Coalition*, May 15, 2017. https://www.thegospelcoalition.org/blogs/trevin-wax/southern-baptists-and-conventional-and-cosmopolitan-cultures/.

Wilson, Jared C. *Gospel Shaped Worship*. Charlotte: Good Book, 2015. Kindle.

———. "Is Your Worship Service Upside Down?" *The Gospel Coalition*, June 23, 2016. https://www.thegospelcoalition.org/blogs/jared-c-wilson/is-your-worship-service-upside-down/.

———. "The Top 125 Influences on the Gospel-Centered Movement." *The Gospel Coalition*, January 26, 2018. https://www.thegospelcoalition.org/blogs/jared-c-wilson/top-125-influences-gospel-centered-movement/.

PART 3

Claiming Power through Practices

8

The Power of Testimony

"Gon' Ahead and Testify": Black Baptist Women's Testimony as a Reimagination of Liturgical Authority

CHELSEA BROOKE YARBOROUGH

"DOES ANYBODY WANT TO tell how the Lord has been good to you this week?" Ten o'clock in the morning on the dot, and we all knew that it was time for testimony. In this Black Baptist church in the middle of Baltimore, Maryland, testimony was the norm. One of the deaconesses or deacons would grab the mic to open up the floor for the testimony service. After that initial opening, the movement and offerings were in the hands of those present. As a kid, I thought this was a time to listen to who could outdo their elaborate stories of trials and tribulations from the previous week. As an adult, I now realize the moment of testimony was a rare space where all voices were heard and every story mattered. Regardless of how elaborate a story was, it belonged to the speaker. It didn't matter who the speakers were, they were given a space to speak and contribute to worship. Women spoke who would otherwise not speak outside of singing and announcements. Children were encouraged to give reports on how school was going or to name their accomplishments from extracurriculars. Even when someone's story was met with a few rolled eyes because it got too long or felt too elaborate for some, they were still able to take up space and speak.

Testimony was a time of witness and a time of sharing with the public community to which you belonged something that had happened in private. Once testimony service—or, as some called it, predevotional time—began, the microphone would pass from person to person. In some cases, people would simply stand up and begin their story. Those present lifted up sacred stories of the week as they spoke about where they witnessed God moving in their lives. There were praise reports, intertwined with prayer requests, alongside Scripture passages, threaded with personal narratives that would acknowledge God's movement with a "But God!" to connote the turn of events.

When something was particularly impactful to those present, often a bodily healing or deliverance from something thought otherwise impossible, the musicians would chime in with the undercurrent of sonic pushes to incite the charismatic expression of spirit often known as "the shout." Even if that particular expression of praise didn't occur, members of the community offered "mmmhmm" and "tell the story" to those who were speaking. Although anyone could speak during the time of testimony, it was particularly special in my Black Baptist church because it was one of the few times outside of announcements and singing that I saw women with the microphone—and often, more women speaking than men. Black women who were not often given formal power in the pulpit would use this time to tell their stories and to align their narratives with the gospel narrative and God's intervention in their lives. If someone was struggling as she spoke, someone else would go and care for her in the moment. As they each spoke of God's goodness, it was normal for them to intertwine Scripture and theological assertions of who God was. This is where I first saw women preach, and a space where women were the leaders of the worship—not from pulpits or podiums but from their seats, bearing witness to their experience with Jesus through their life stories. When something got really good, one of the elder mothers who always sat in the back with a bag of candy for us kids would tell us to be quiet, throw her hand up and exclaim, "Gon' ahead and testify." This is where the practice of testimony begins for me. It is a place where authority is given back to the people and the gospel narrative is a living, breathing one, still actively at work within the community.

Black Baptist women used testimony in church as a place of communal authority, weaving stories with assertions about who God is and what Scripture said. These women would conduct space with the rise and fall of their tone, weaving hymns into their narratives and reminding all who were present about the God they were talking about. By considering the testimony practices of Black women within the Black church traditions, we are able to see a different proclaiming practice and expanded sense of liturgical authority within the worship service. These proclaimers have no formal training or authoritative body that offers them unction or authority to speak. Instead, those things come from God (as many themselves say), and the self.

Testimony requires a reimagination of liturgical authority, away from a hierarchical positionality to one that is shared in the community. Black women's testimony is both a practice of proclaiming and an act of listening for voices that would otherwise be present but silent or given lesser roles denoting the hierarchy of the space. By learning from the underlying implications of the practice of testimony, we can lean into more expansive practices within our liturgy, resisting exclusive ideologies and hierarchical systems in worship. The expansive understanding of liturgical authority that can be extracted from testimonial practice helps us consider how authority is used and wielded both in and beyond the Black church where I have located testimony service. This chapter provides a brief overview of the practice of testimony, and more significantly offers an invitation to reimagine what liturgical authority emerges when we put Black women's testimony at its center.

Testimony

Testimony as a historical liturgical movement in some Black churches subverts the normative authority primarily rooted in the pulpit, which is most often a male-dominated space. In many Black church traditions, formalized positions of power have often been dominated by Black, cisgender, heterosexual men. These positions excluded Black women (alongside others who didn't fit within the normative authority framework) not only from the titles, but also from the authority to preach in the spatial demarcation of the pulpit. In Black church traditions, the pulpit is not only sacred but the locus of liturgical authority, alongside the director of music. However, these exclusions didn't stop women from proclaiming and finding space to wield liturgical authority. Testimony is rooted in a type of transparency that is dependent on the agency and consent of the speaker. They decide how to shape their narrative and, in general, how long they plan to bear oral witness. Though the speech is extemporaneous, this doesn't leave the moment without some form or structure. The speaker expresses gratitude for what is happening, often coupled with either a story of how God's intervention made a situation possible, or a story about what is currently going on and the anticipated in-breaking of God's presence that will the disrupt the present difficulty. However, within that loose framework is a vast array of possibilities as to how someone might tell their story and offer their testimony.

Testimony can in itself be a worship service, or be set within the larger Sunday morning worship. It is a time when authority is given to the whole, not just the one. It is a time when people experience the good news as a collective sharing, not merely listening to the rhetoric of the pulpit preacher. Cheryl Townsend Gilkes asserts that testimony is one of the four pillars of Black worship. In *If It Wasn't for the Women* she writes, "In any pre-devotional session, one can hear a litany of the social problems that affect black women: abandonment, assaults, aging, poverty, violent crime, single-parenthood, and their children's futures. Testimony may also be responsible for the ideology of sisterhood among black women. It sometimes serves as an instrument of reconciliation."[1] Through the use of story and shared narratives, collective care practices emerge and community is formed. These sacred moments of weaving the particularities of one's personal narrative with the interventions of God, which adds to the God story of a congregation, create a textured ritual of storytelling. Unlike the pulpit or other formalized spaces where the speaker is prescribed beforehand, the testimony service is a space where anyone can speak if they feel led to talk on that day. Authority in these spaces is shared and rooted in the God narrative, not in the spatial demarcations of pulpit or formal authorization by ordination or title.

Testimony service or a time of testimony can take on different forms within Black church traditions, however the root telos is the same: to listen for the activity of God as heard through the lived experiences of everyday people within the community. Black women's testimony is a practice where Black women are given free space to speak, share, and lead. Testimonies are liturgical conductors. These testimonies invoke music from the director, and the ecstatic shout of charismatic congregations ensues after hearing someone's particular "But God" narrative. Therefore, the deliverer of testimony, if only for a minute, becomes the conductor of the symphonic layers of the Black liturgical experience. By situating testimony as an interlocutor with liturgical authority, notions of "authority" have to expand. The worship space moves beyond the confines of a prescribed order of worship and beyond the realities of exclusive leadership hierarchies that would exclude the voices who find freedom within testimony.

---

1. Gilkes, *"If It Wasn't for the Women . . .,"* 138.

Expanding Liturgical Authority through Testimony

Liturgical authority is often rooted in a hierarchical structure that depends on a system that formalizes ministerial authority within ecclesial settings, or is affirmed by a particular community within that space. This is not an inherently problematic system until the structures require exclusionary practices in order to maintain who has power in the space and whose voices matter most. In "This Is My Body—This Is My Blood: Inventing Authority in Liturgical Discourse and Practice," Andrea Bieler argues that the invention of authority was inherently created to exclude women.[2] I add that authority was created to exclude all people who didn't fit the prescribed status quo for formal leadership in worship—a status quo that definitely leaves out women. Thus, it is critical not only to talk about liturgical authority, but to interrogate its nature and consider how to move liturgical practices away from the exclusive exercise of power that is often upheld by that authority.

In talking about liturgical authority Bieler asserts, "I take as basis the following understanding: the invention of authority is a dialogical event in which the claim that a particular text or ritual action is of special significance for the formation of religious identity is accepted and affirmed by individuals and/or groups who engage in the same ritual practice."[3] At best this works as a communal effort, but far too often systems of power prevent communal participation. In this explication, Bieler asserts that authority is created in community and the navigation of that authority is also within community. When a ritual is experienced over time, the rules of engagement and the practices of authority are created and re-created as a part of this dialogical event, meaning that authority is shared. For example, in testimony there is a leader who starts the service and they also decide when it is over. While much of the rest of ritual is loosely determined by the participants, the communal acceptance of the leadership to open the ritual space is a way that authority is utilized. With this in mind, I aim toward a reinvention of authority that is best understood dialogically, communally, and as equitably as possible—all of which are characteristics of the liturgical practice of testimony at its best. This type of authority isn't ascribed to one person who has been affirmed by the community, but is spread throughout the community, offering space for the moment to be shared in practice as well as in intention. Testimony as a practice of Black women offers us a lens into an expanded sense of liturgical authority.

2. Bieler, "This Is My Body—This Is My Blood," 143.

3. Bieler, "This Is My Body—This Is My Blood," 143.

As stated, testimony is a practice that shifts authority. For Black women, whose access to formal authority ascribed by the ministerial office was limited, testimony was a place to reclaim space as participant leaders within a congregation. In *Preaching as Testimony*, Anna Carter Florence posits, "The tradition [of testimony] calls us to rethink our assumptions about what it is to preach and what it takes to become a preacher. . . . It shifts the locus of authority away from the ministerial office and places it with the one who testifies: that is, the one who has seen and believed the liberating power of God's Word and who then risks proclaiming the truth of the gospel."[4] This practice of proclaiming via testimony marks an expansion of liturgical power. Black women's testimony is a subversive response to liturgical authority in Black church traditions. The expansive nature of testimony allows liturgical power to be shared among all those who, whether they have spoken or not, have borne and can bear witness to the movement of God present within and beyond their lives. The ways and reasons Black women testify in Black Baptist spaces expand limited liturgical authority to shared liturgical power. I posit that the practice of testimony historically found in Black Baptist churches offers three invitations to resist normative liturgical authority. Testimony from Black women invites us to resist hegemonic positioning of power within worship, it invites us into the work of collective care as a liturgical practice, and it invites us to consider the necessity of proclaiming from particularity and not universality.

Invitations of Black Women's Testimony

Resisting Hegemonic Power

Black women's testimony practice invites us to consider what it means to resist a hegemonic positioning of power. This liturgical practice pushes against normative ideals of ecclesial power, such as who is called to speak and the type of formalized ordination that gives one credence to offer a word about who God is and what God has done. Black women's testimony resists and actively moves away from a hierarchical practice of liturgical authority and into a shared ritual of liturgical influence. Collective liturgical influences offer everyone a space to speak while uplifting the reality that each person's story is sacred, particularly those whose stories are often ignored or left out of the conversation of God's holy activity. The dominating presence in testimony is the collective. Whether situated within a larger worship service or as its own service, testimony is the unfolding of narratives that speak to how

4. Carter Florence, *Preaching as Testimony*, xxvii–xxviii.

God moves in minute and major ways from week to week. The aesthetic of Black women speaking about who God is and what God has done in their lives, with their voices carrying through the physical space, causes a necessary upset to any ideology that would claim their voices to be less significant and unable to enter into spaces like the pulpit. Cognitively, this causes a disruption in what it means to preach and who has the authority to manage liturgical movements.

Black women's testimony, then, is a ritual of resistance. In her article, "Dismantling Domination through Womanist Rituals of Resistance," Lorena Parrish argues that womanist rituals of resistance are "religious practices . . . and other elements of worship that foster truth-telling, spiritual flourishing, hope in a liberating Jesus, and opposition to theological notions and ways of being that buttress exceptionalism, white supremacy, misogyny and the trivialization of the lived experience of black women."[5] She articulates that such womanist liturgies offer Black churches ways to remember that there are gender-expansive traditions within Black church spaces, and if we begin there the liturgy at large can develop more inclusively. Testimony stems from a practice of truth-telling, rooted in the real, lived experiences of everyday people. By speaking their truth aloud, Black women articulate their place within the liturgical space—which is everywhere anyone else can be. However small it may appear, centering this practice creates friction for practices of domination that aim at more exclusive notions of power, authority, and agency within the liturgical setting. This makes testimony a critical practice to consider. Testimony creates an opportunity for shared power and dispersed authority, such that the experience within the liturgy is a space of collective witness and an expansion of the voices that carry the good news—and even the voice of God.

Creating a Call to Collective Care

Black women's testimony invites us to consider how we hear from those whose stories aren't inherently woven into the fabric of our liturgy and whose voices aren't often at the tables of leadership and authority. Liturgical practices that stem from power and not the people reinforce hegemonic systems of power outside of the worship environment, as well as making collective care a difficult task for the community. Testimony operates as a new image of care for the collective within the liturgy, because it opens up the whole to the experiences of the individuals. If something needs to be and can be addressed by the community, there is room to speak to those

5. Parrish, "Dismantling Domination," 13.

needs in real time to those who can provide care. At its best, testimony is a space where transparency is valued, and the community can participate in God's movement in a person's life.

Shared authority is a form of care because the actual needs of congregants can be addressed as a part of the liturgical moment, not as an addendum to it. While certain details of one's experience may not always be named in the public forum of testimony, expressing a story creates a communal synergy that allows for everyday relationships to be built within the congregational community, and people can get and share needed resources. This orientation to liturgical practice as a place of collective care removes the hierarchy of authority and imagines a space where concerns are both heard and responded to through the love and resourcefulness of a given community. Black women's testimony provides a space for the needs of Black women to be heard and addressed in a world where Black women are often left out of narratives of care—beyond being the caretakers.

Proclaiming from Particularity

Finally, testimony requires that people tell their own story. Oftentimes in preaching, prayer, and music, which are some of the other pillars of African American worship, more general narratives are woven together into the Christian narrative. In testimony, the depths of particularity (as opposed to generality) allow for specific voices to be heard that wouldn't be otherwise, leading to surprising and unexpected gospel narratives and interpretations being offered to the collective. In pulpit preaching, the gospel narrative is threaded through the story of community and, in Black churches, often the historical collective. The liturgical movements of prayer, song, and other forms present in the space mirror that intention. They often aim to impact the individual alongside the community through a wide and overarching conversation about God's activity. Testimony takes on a different tenor because it starts from the particularity of the individual and moves out to the crowd.

Black women's testimony is a reclamation of storytelling as sacred proclamation and a liturgical practice that pushes against a generalized, universal identity that often upholds rigid ideas of authority and hierarchy. When these women speak from their specificity, engaging the complicated narratives of their existence, speaking the truth of their problems and also being transparent about their joys, the gospel emerges from the specificity of their witness of themselves, not from a general narrative they apply to themselves. In this case, Black women's testimony invites us to consider not just the authority of other people in the liturgical space, but what texts, ideologies, and doctrines we hold as absolute but which aren't in alignment with the everyday experiences of those who testify.

Conclusion

The practice of testimony in my Black Baptist church growing up taught me that stories are sacred and that everyone's story was an important part of the narrative. Black women witnessed and proclaimed in that space, pushing against the demarcations of authority more prevalent in the other worship environments of the church, and the limitations of who was allowed to preach. I know now that this practice taught me that authority wasn't only a position and title, but a posture even just for a moment. When people claim their narratives aloud, inviting others into their narrative alongside God's, they are wielding liturgical authority. They are inviting us into dialogical and communal creation of authority as we listen to, acknowledge, and learn from their witness of who God is in their life. Black women have been silenced in many formal pulpits, yet this practice is a way where voices are heard and the good news as seen by God's activity within our lives is shared through the larger body of believers. Black women's testimony moves us to reimagine liturgical authority through the lens of community, and invites an expansive view of how liturgy can live as a practice within community, not simply one in which the community comes to observe and follow.

Testimony challenges the notion of liturgical authority by offering an expansive invitation. This invitation is not without risk, as we know that authority exists within the space. Testimony is best practiced with openness to all, and those participating must be prepared to ensure that all voices are welcomed and adjust if some are still left out of the ritual. At best liturgical authority is shared and liturgical influence is passed throughout the space during testimony so that the worship is actually a collective effort and witness to the ways that God is operating in the lives of the gathered community. By pushing against hegemonic ideas of power, cultivating a call to care, and pushing us to imagine the necessity of particularity, the normative sense of hierarchical liturgical authority is disrupted and a new dynamic of communal influence is placed at the center. Black women's testimony resists rigid authoritarian postures in the liturgical setting and other restrictive liturgical movements that adhere to exclusionary practices that don't serve the voice and liturgical movement of the whole.

Black women's testimony creates a new aesthetic for whose story is uplifted and whose voice is considered sacred within the canon of proclaimers.

It moves the worshiper beyond the confines of hierarchical authority and embraces the possibility of collective power and communal influence. With this in mind, liturgical practitioners at large might consider the ways that Black women's testimony as an interlocutor invites them to reimagine their own systems and expand their practices.

First, we might consider how hegemonic power is operative in the spaces and what practices might resist hierarchical enforcement of power. Whose voices are heard, and how do those voices offer a new, imaginative identity for what it means to have influence and place within the liturgical movement? When power as a marker of liturgical authority is present and uninterrogated, it mimics the very ill systems that create injustice in all areas of our world. If we want worship to be a space of inbreaking that invites people into something beyond these systems, then the testimony practice of Black women is a helpful place to begin.

Second, questions about care as a liturgical practice emerge. How can the needs of those present, spoken in their own words and voices, become a practice of worship rather than something that is addressed later in the church's week? Do we simply hear those needs in the moment, or can liturgy be a space to also respond to those needs?

Finally, where is the space for particularity to be present, especially for those on the margins of a community? Testimony is an opportunity to create space for all to be heard, and this practice can be critical for any community of faith.

Reimagining liturgical authority through the lens of Black women's testimony means releasing a rigidity of authority. Engaging together today in the testimony practices I witnessed as a child may be an invitation to create more extemporaneous approaches to the liturgy. Black women continue to push the envelope, creating new spheres and circles of authority to make room not just for their voices, but also for the voices of those who find themselves on the margins. Considering testimony as a central part of the liturgy makes room for an expansive approach to authority and gives credence to Black women as progenitors for new and amazing things. Gilkes writes, "Testimony transforms the collective worshippers into a community. Oppression and suffering make testimony important for psychological survival. Testimony does not resolve black problems but does transform them from the private troubles of distressed individuals into the public issues of a covenant community."[6] In short, Black women's testimony is a strategy to resist normative liturgical authority in Black church traditions that focus on pulpit as power and to instead invite a larger range of voices to participate.

6. Gilkes, *"If It Wasn't for the Women . . .,"* 137.

Other traditions might consider how testimony functions within their liturgical spaces and how authority might be shared when the mic is passed. Perhaps, as authority is shared, we might create more equitable liturgical practices for all worshipers.

Bibliography

Bieler, Andrea. "This Is My Body—This Is My Blood: Inventing Authority in Liturgical Discourse and Practice." *Yearbook of the European Society of Women in Theological Research* 12 (2004)143–54.

Carter Florence, Anna. *Preaching as Testimony*. Louisville: Westminster John Knox, 2007.

Gilkes, Cheryl Townsend. *"If It Wasn't for the Women . . .": Black Women's Experience and Womanist Culture in Church and Community*. Maryknoll, NY: Orbis, 2001.

Parrish, Lorena. "Dismantling Domination through Womanist Rituals of Resistance." *Liturgy* 35.1 (2020) 10–18.

9

The Power of Everyday Spirituality
Spiritual, but Authoritative?: Pentecostal Women and Liturgical Authority

Dorothy Mendez, Tanya Riches, Andrew Davies

Tia Loli Proaño

Blanca Dolores Proaño, better known to her family as Tia Loli, is the third-born out of seven children in a single-mother family. She was born and raised in Ecuador, deep in poverty and with little to no opportunity for social mobility. Tia Loli's life was defined by her name, *Dolores,* meaning "pain." Her story epitomizes the Latina lament or what Ada María Isasi-Díaz describes as *la lucha* ("the struggle"). Her life is an example of how one can overcome societal and religious limitations.

From the young age of six, she worked as the maid for a family that treated her harshly; she was repeatedly beaten and deprived of food. At seven, she suffered third-degree burns when a gas stove she was using exploded. She was hospitalized in intensive burn care for over eighteen months, and during that time, only once was her mother permitted to visit her. During that time, Tia Loli went through several painful skin grafts and surgeries. However, despite these painful experiences Tia Loli testifies that she was never completely alone; God was with her.

At the age of fourteen, after returning to the loving environment of her mother's home, Tia Loli started searching for this God. Several seemingly unconnected events contributed to Tia Loli's spiritual transformation. Her journey started with making friends with the local village nuns.

"They were modern nuns," Tia Loli laughs, as she shares how she was initially attracted to this group of religious women because they were different from what she perceived and nontraditionalist. She said to herself, "I'm going to be a nun, but I'm going to be a modern one."

Later, a man from the village gifted their family with a Bible. Every night next to a kerosene lantern, Tia Loli and her siblings read the Bible together even though they did not understand its message.

At eighteen, the nuns invited Tia Loli to join their mission, where they visited throughout the village and taught people how to recite the Lord's Prayer. Tia Loli enjoyed the mission work. Slowly her search for God unfolded. She approached the nuns about completing her education, as well as that of her younger siblings. In their village, school classes were only available up to year six. The nun found another school for them in Quito, the capital city of Ecuador, where they could live onsite in a small room. In exchange for their room and board, they were responsible for the cleaning of the entire property. Thus, she again left her mother's home and her small village in the mountains and moved to Quito with her four younger siblings. In just a year she was able to complete her schooling.

Though things in her life were improving, Tia Loli still felt a great sense of emptiness. When she was around twenty years of age, Tia Loli would often listen to Argentinian evangelist Luis Palau's regular radio broadcasts, and one day she decided to write a letter to him, asking about everything she was feeling in her heart. She later received a return letter from Palau, which read,

"Dear young lady, I have your letter on my desk. What you are going through is the consequence of sin, it is sin that produces hatred . . ." Of this, she recounts:

> But here in this letter, he told me I could ask Jesus to be my personal Saviour and that everything was going to change, that God was going to give me a new life. In that letter, they sent a prayer. I said that simple prayer in the kitchen of our little apartment and as I did, I started crying and crying and crying. It was like rivers of tears and now I realize that it was the Holy Spirit that was touching me. It was the Holy Spirit leading me to Jesus

and showing the love of God. The time I had there with God, . . .
now that changed my life.

In Tia Loli's testimony of faith, she describes her childhood pain and suffering as the catalyst for her search for purpose and meaning in life. It was in that moment when she prayed that she found hope, healing, and transformation.

Turning to faith inspired Tia Loli to pursue a life of mission and ministry. Soon afterward, Tia Loli and her younger brother met a group of missionaries from an organization called *Cristianos En Accion* (Christians in Action) who invited them to a special outreach event. This included a youth basketball competition, which Jorge, Tia Loli's fifteen-year-old brother, was keen to take part in. So, against the demands of their older brother, they closed their small shop early for the day and went to what turned out to be a youth revival meeting. At this event, Jorge gave his life to the Lord and decided that he too was going to pursue a life of ministry following the calling of God. From this time, Tia Loli also began praying to God, "Dear God, I want to be a missionary, so that I can serve you and help people."

Her commitment to an incarnational message of salvation and healing afforded Tia Loli the strength to leave her home and travel to Colombia to attend ministry school. Tia Loli and her younger brother first studied at a mission-focused Bible college. Excluded culturally from any position of power yet still wanting to respond to what she felt was the Spirit's calling, Tia Loli was forced to leave her home, her country, and her family's preference in order to follow this calling. As the eldest sister, she was by now the matriarch of her family, traveling to Colombia as a young woman, to pursue "the call" to ministry. Thus, she needed to be accompanied by her younger brother. Without the covering or protection of a male, she may have been excluded from the opportunity to study. Since then, however, she has persistently refused to be excluded from participation.

After being forced to return to Ecuador due to changes in immigration laws, missionary pastors took care of them and helped them stay faithful to God. Though returning to life with their family, things had changed.

Tia Loli recalls, "We were different; we were people with a calling, and we would never be the same again."

Tia Loli and her brother worked to try to save enough money to return to their mission training in Colombia. Although she served and volunteered with her local church and pastors, Tia Loli still felt a strong desire to be an international missionary. However, she did not have the financial means or resources to do so. One day when she was praying, Tia Loli felt God spoke to her through the passage in Revelation that speaks about God opening doors that no human can close. In many ways there were too many obstacles, and Tia Loli was ready to move back with her family. However, the day she decided to return home, she received an anonymous letter which contained an invitation to attend a Bible school in Guatemala, and it contained the boarding passes for her flights. She recalls that it was God who made all these things possible.

Leaving home and becoming a missionary in Guatemala during a time of civil war did not provide any social stability. Tia Loli was still a single woman living in a foreign country and working in remote villages. But it was here in Guatemala that Tia Loli developed her God-given gifts. Her lack of ordination certificate could not impede her from caring for people in need, teaching Sunday school to children, leading worship, counseling and training leaders, and teaching people to read the Bible. She said of her life as a missionary:

> I learnt to do what was needed: preach, teach, sing, I even helped a woman deliver her baby, I baptized people . . . In the morning I would be in one village, and in the evening, I would minister and serve in another . . . sometimes I went with a group and other times I travelled on my own and learnt to build teams in those villages.

In some of these villages and townships there were also local pastors or American missionaries. However, when there was not a pastor, the women missionaries were sent to lead the services, to preach, and run the children's ministry. There was never any question of their ability or spiritual authority to do so.

Tia Loli later married, and after eighteen years as a missionary in Guatemala, she and her husband returned to Ecuador. There they planted their first church. They later moved to El Salvador and planted another church. Together, Tia Loli and her husband today pastor churches in both Ecuador and El Salvador. The spiritual authority that so distinguishes her life is immediately evident to anyone meeting her. Her deep spirituality is what authorizes her to participate in the ministry of preaching the gospel, to disciple others, and to teach and lead from the pulpit. This participation is not authorized by her marital status, ordination, or any kind of formal recognition within the ritual or liturgy of her church. Conservative readings of the Pauline texts among her community and denomination have meant that Tia Loli's participation and ministry experiences are not sufficient to lead to her ordination with its accompanying formalized liturgical authority. Still, Tia Loli continues to exercise spiritual authority through her participation in both formal and informal roles in the liturgy. While her authority and gifting are recognized by her church and community, the gendered social and religious structures mean these are not always formalized. However, this does not stop her from creatively and energetically pursuing her calling.

As a leader in her community and church, Tia Loli learned to meet the needs of the people she was serving as they were presented. For example, if there was no pastor in one of the village church-plants, she would preach. If there was a need for a children's schoolteacher, she would minister to the children, and if they needed a worship leader, she would lead the congregation in singing. It is her response to "the call" to ministry that authorizes her on the ground. She is trusted by her community, and they consider her spiritual "mothering" in the streets as irrefutable. Dorothy, who knows her well, can recall her stopping countless times to speak with someone she recognized on the street. She would proceed to encourage them whether to return to the things of God, to commit to attending a church, or to set aside whatever their destructive habits were. In these moments she would pray for them, encourage them with a Bible verse, and tell them that God loves them. She was never prescriptive in her practices or response; it seemed innate to her. Affectionately, Dorothy would say to her, "Tia, you have the gift of 'strong encouragement!'" (Some might call it rebuke.)

Though Tia Loli is a remarkable example, she is one among many determined, influential, and dedicated women who model this typically Pentecostal subversive authority. Within many Pentecostal contexts "the call" of the Holy Spirit, as well as spiritual gifts, authenticates spiritual authority within formal liturgical spaces. In Tia Loli's case, her spiritual authority is unquestionable, actioned in her "mothering" the streets. Her lived-faith experiences authenticate her spirituality and leadership within the liturgy of her tradition. Ultimately, her community, family, and congregation uphold her as a spiritual mother, mentor, and deacon. Similarly, her apostolic missionary involvement, church-planting, and "spiritual" encouragement are drawn from her interpretation of New Testament Scriptures. As such, she demonstrates spiritual authority beyond her official title or position.

Her life story exemplifies and illustrates both *la lucha* and the ways in which women move beyond traditional roles to participate in a missional praxis of everyday faith. She was the first person to convert to Pentecostalism in her family. Within her story, even as a young girl we see the example of a Latina who looked beyond her cultural hindrances and socially disadvantaged status and grew to evidence a spiritual authority that moved far beyond the formal roles traditionally afforded to women. Although she lacked the authorization of male permission for her spiritual calling, she would testify that it was her encounter with God that authorized her service and participation in the proclamation of the gospel message of transformation, healing, and liberation.

Spiritually Authoritative, but Liturgically Authoritative?

Even though ecclesial and social structures may seek to place boundaries on the liturgical authority of women like Tia Loli, their spiritual authority often and persistently contests this hierarchy. In this essay, we describe how Pentecostal Latinas navigate attempts to exclude women in liturgical spaces and identify strategies they use to circumvent problematic gendered ecclesial and social norms. We are specifically arguing that spiritual authority a) is different from liturgical authority; b) comes from (among other things) a woman's commitment to her calling; c) can be as impactful as liturgical authority; and d) can open doors for liturgical opportunities even in churches and cultures where these would otherwise not be allowed.

A contrastive dialogue between pulpit and people has defined Pentecostal liturgy from its beginning, and this highlights an important distinction we see between what we label as "spiritual" and "liturgical" authorities. By "spiritual authority" we have in mind the dynamic evidence of an individual's empowerment by the Spirit for a particular moment, task, or role. This can be demonstrated in the proclamation of a prophetic word, in the quiet sharing of a Bible verse, or giving a message of encouragement to a struggling fellow believer. It can also be seen in counseling, in public prayer, and in responding to and thus catalyzing the response of others to the Spirit's presence in sung worship and the preaching. The shouted "amen" and "preach it" which often characterize congregational responses to Pentecostal preaching are in themselves demonstrations of a spiritual authority to draw others in, strengthen their focus, and encourage them to be responsive to the work of the Spirit.

However, "liturgical authority" is solidly anchored in the pulpit and all the official and ecclesial structures that the pulpit signifies. Though liturgical authority may be temporarily delegated to a worship team during sung worship, undoubtedly, the pulpit is the focal point of the public gathering in terms of liturgical authority. Those with the liturgical authority of the pulpit narrate and interpret the Spirit's renewal activity as part of the framing of Pentecostal public worship even while it is more fundamentally the work of the Spirit amongst the congregation that demonstrates God's active presence and gives opportunity for the demonstration and outworking of spiritual authority. Therefore, even though ecclesial and social structures may seek to place boundaries on the liturgical authority of women like Tia

Loli, Latinas' evident spiritual authority often and persistently contests this hierarchy.

Our essay draws on Tia Loli's story and ethnographic research conducted amongst Latina women in Canada in order to highlight women's roles in the formal but also informal liturgies of the Pentecostal church. Women do participate in both formal liturgies (preaching and teaching from the pulpit in the main church service) as well as informal rituals in most Pentecostal churches, but their formal participation is generally at the invitation and under the spiritual "covering" of men (as interpreted from 1 Cor 11:12).[1] However, our research demonstrates that in contexts which prioritize patriarchal readings of Pauline texts, place restrictions upon women, and limit or deny access to ordination or the opportunity of participating freely in their own right within the formal liturgies as pastors, the evidence of a Latina's spiritual authority is still seen among the congregation and in the streets. This spiritual authority provides a clear argument for their liturgical authority, and it often facilitates their increased liturgical participation. Tia Loli's ministry and accompanying spiritual authority have granted her access to participate in formal liturgies even without the credentials of ordination. This is not to say that these spaces are completely open to her, but that she *does* preach even despite the formal structures attempting to prevent her from doing so.

These stories of the key dimensions of transnational Latina experience among the women interviewed, of which we highlight Tia Loli's story as representative, opened our eyes to these processes of spiritual authority which are demonstrated via vocalization, spontaneity, participation, and inclusion—all essential characteristics of Pentecostal worship. To illustrate our argument, we situate the story of Tia Loli's spiritual authority in the context of gender and authority in Pentecostal traditions and Pentecostal liturgical practice. We then consider how transnational Canadian-Latina Pentecostal women subversively lay claims to liturgical authority by means of spiritual authority and reflect on the implications of this upon worship in the Pentecostal tradition and beyond.

Gender and Authority in Pentecostal Traditions

Liturgical authority has always been of importance to Pentecostals who have sought to ensure the experience of the Spirit's voice as authoritative

---

1. In more conservative readings of 1 Corinthians 11:1–12, Paul is interpreted as prescribing male authorization over any women who seek to participate in the liturgy (in this passage Paul references prayer and prophesy).

within worship. However, the structural limits upon authority are also and have also always been important. Viewing Pentecostal practice through the lens of gender provides one useful way to think through this issue. Latin America offers an excellent illustration of what sociologist Bernice Martin calls the "Gender Paradox" of Pentecostalism.[2] Although Pentecostalism is a male-dominated movement, women comprise the majority in their congregations by very significant proportions in many contexts. Martin argues Pentecostalism acts as a "women's movement" that is preferential to the poor, marginalized, and those classed outside of the "circles of power."[3] However, she notes that shifts toward the equality of men and women are tolerated within the movement only as long as the social structure of men publicly exercising power is upheld.[4] The issue of gender in Pentecostalism is complex and nuanced.

Several recent feminist authors highlight the complex status of Pentecostal liturgy as both repressive and also liberating for women. To examine this tension requires reading the liturgy with attention to subversion and unauthorized expression. Our reading is twofold and intentionally focuses on blurring the definitional edges. First, scholars must consider the ways in which women's spiritual authority and liturgical participation often defy any formalized restrictions and policies implemented by official ecclesial bodies; the gender divide is often blurred within formal liturgical spaces. Second, Pentecostal liturgy is always happening informally outside the primary assembly, and the spiritual authority exercised in these other settings can also be seen in some sense as liturgical. In other words, the practices of encouragement and prayer in the streets have always been rituals requiring and invoking spiritual authority of equal value to any corporate worship service. This dynamic is evident in Pentecostal literature.

In *Gender and Pentecostal Revivalism: Making a Female Ministry in the Early Twentieth Century*[5] Leah Payne notes that feminine authority "to lead, perform rites, discern and interpret the divine, and instruct congregants was in question perpetually."[6] Payne engages important American Revivalist women who defied social norms to take their place at the pulpit, drawing on the ritual lens of Catherine Bell to explain that the construction of the authority for women to lead was via "the call" to ministry but ultimately maintained via the congregation. This liturgically orientated analysis is

2. Martin, "Pentecostal Gender Paradox," 58.

3. Martin, "Pentecostal Gender Paradox," 54.

4. Martin, "Pentecostal Gender Paradox," 54.

5. Payne, *Gender and Pentecostal Revivalism*, 6.

6. Payne, *Gender and Pentecostal Revivalism*, 19.

useful for engaging worship and gender (or maleness) as the key attribute that revivalist America used to authorize public participation.

Joy Qualls, in her volume *God Forgive Us for Being Women*, outlines the role of women in the founding and growth of the largest Pentecostal denomination of the Assemblies of God (AGUSA).[7] She notes increasing resistance from the denomination against the feminist movement despite their inclusion of female preachers. She also notes a history of women able to exercise cultural authority via a "prophetic" role, proclaiming the Spirit's message.[8] However, the accompanying ordination and the pulpit ministry was a "priestly" form of ministry in which male dominance was institutionally authorized via the rhetorical use of the biblical text.[9] Thus, in her view, the symbol of authority overcame service within the AGUSA tradition.[10]

Kate Bowler's *The Preacher's Wife: The Precarious Power of Evangelical Women Celebrities* outlines a "precarious" authority held by women in Pentecostal and evangelical churches, but particularly by "megaministry" celebrities.[11] She reviews the historical development of female evangelical authority in light of conservative theological commitments, noting that women identify, "little moments of encouragement or discouragement that nudge them toward a sense of being acceptable."[12] In response, they form particular relationships with men who can provide their "covering," or spiritual authority. Strong limitations within a church may also serve to move women to self-promote in the marketplace to utilize commercial appeal to authorize their participation in church alternatively through mechanisms such as celebrity, at times on a global scale.[13]

The Practice of Pentecostal Worship

Pentecostalism from its earliest days was a global phenomenon, arising contemporaneously in all corners of the world, with missionaries sent out across the world. It has retained its characteristic as a transnational movement through its history until today. While these individual revivals all had their own local color and distinctive features, there are four values that

---

7. Qualls, *God Forgive Us for Being Women*.

8. Qualls, *God Forgive Us for Being Women*, 183.

9. Qualls, *God Forgive Us for Being Women*, 9.

10. Qualls, *God Forgive Us for Being Women*, 28.

11. Bowler, *Preacher's Wife*.

12. Bowler, *Preacher's Wife*, ix.

13. Bowler, *Preacher's Wife*, ix.

connect these varied manifestations of Pentecostal worship: vocalization, participation, inclusion, and spontaneity.[14]

First, early Pentecostal worship was *vocalized* rather than internalized. In other words, there was little room for quiet personal reflection, or whispered prayers alone in a corner. The gathered community expressed its faith by speaking out *aloud* the praises of God and giving voice to its requests. Pentecostalism was vividly expressionist.

Second, early Pentecostal worship was *participatory*. There was no presiding oversight to conduct or direct the service—indeed, at Azusa Street, there was literally no platform or pulpit. The shared experience of worship required every participant to be active and to play their part, and not only as a voice in the crowd.

This leads us to the third observation: anyone was invited. This participation was *inclusive* and open to everyone, with cultural barriers broken down by this simple act of worshiping together. Race, gender, class, age, or disability were no barrier to full participation in worship. Authority was vested not only in middle-class elites but those that contemporary society would marginalize and overlook.

Fourth, early Pentecostal worship was *spontaneous* and sought to be Spirit-led. It was most unusual for these global revival services to be dominated by the guidance of a single leader up front. Rather they sought above all to discern the presence and voice of the Holy Spirit within the gathering. The community sought to allow the Spirit to speak and work within the moment, inspiring them to speak out and giving them the words to say. Prayers were extemporized rather than read, and those who spoke did so in response to what they believed to be the Spirit's prompting, rather than from any instruction by leadership. Any congregation member could start the singing of any hymn or sacred song or share a biblical reading or prophetic word, as they felt inspired. Such spontaneity might be seen as the inevitable result of the inclusive and participatory nature of the worship, but it is vital to note that this was an ideological move and not principally a practical one. Pentecostals at their origin were committed to recognizing and appreciating the priesthood of all believers, cherishing the ministry of the Spirit within the people as well as their leaders.

Whilst Pentecostal worship may lack the formal and traditional elements of, for example, a standardized eucharistic prayer or formal call to worship, it is not correct to think of Pentecostalism as nonliturgical. As Wolfgang Vondey rightly observes, for Pentecostals, "While worship as embodied spirituality can be ritualized, the process of formalization and

14. Daniels, "'Gotta Moan Sometime,'" 5–32.

structuring is slow. In this sense, the term liturgy always remains closer to spirituality and worship and resists formal structure, whether imposed by church or culture."[15] A more accurate, if more complex, description might be to suggest that Pentecostals continue an informal, encultured, and orally transmitted liturgy which is motivated by their commitment to discern the work and guidance of the Holy Spirit, and that is framed by these four values of vocalization, participation, inclusion, and spontaneity. These values have remained key elements to Pentecostal worship over some 120 years now, with little evidence of their importance abating.

Although Pentecostalism has retained its informal liturgy, the Pentecostal service is often now very highly structured and carefully scheduled (not least for practical reasons such as broadcast, split-site multicasting, and the need to host multiple services—and now, especially amidst the global Coronavirus pandemic, for livestreaming). In many Pentecostal churches, a more prominent role for an up-front worship leader and preacher has appeared with not as much contribution from the congregation. Like threads in a tapestry, different emphases emerge and fade into and out of greater prominence through time; however, to relegate the congregation to the status of an observer would be to fundamentally misunderstand the values of Pentecostal worship. The pulpit is not the only source of power in contemporary Pentecostalism. Pentecostal worship is still very much vocalized, participatory, inclusive, and spontaneous, even if in sometimes less obvious ways.

Those four values of Pentecostalism's liturgy are evident in Tia Loli's story in ways that hearken back to early Pentecostal liturgical history. Pentecostalism gave priority and room for participation to those who contemporary society classifies as marginal. In Tia Loli's story, she exercises authority first in her obedience in following the Spirit's call, and then her participation in ministry. She embodies a liberative praxis that subverts interpretations of biblical texts that would deny her participation in formal liturgies, and she takes her faith to the streets. In this way her spirituality is lived and vocal. She will take any and every opportunity to encourage, pray for, or give to people on the streets in her community. Her authority is expressed outside of the formal structures of church meetings. Her spiritual practices are not forced or prescriptive, in that sense; they are spontaneous and empowered by the Spirit. She is inclusive of people from different social backgrounds and classes. She is welcoming to the unbeliever and not shy to embrace those who, as she once did, exist outside positions of power and social mobility.

15. Vondey, "Making of a Black Liturgy," 150.

The Spiritual Authority of Transnational Canadian Latina Pentecostals

To more fully understand the contestation of liturgical authority through spiritual authority, particularly within the context of the intersection of Pentecostal liturgical values and yet unfolding patriarchal, ecclesial, and social histories, it is helpful to consider ethnographic research conducted amongst Latina women from two Pentecostal Spanish-speaking churches in Calgary, Alberta, Canada.

In much the same vein as Tia Loli's story, this research describes how spiritual authority is not restricted even in contexts where liturgical authority (at least as seen in the traditional role of a pastor as the one who preaches and teaches from the pulpit) is limited. Transnational Canadian-Latina Pentecostalism provides a fascinating case study between Western and non-Western cultural spaces that reveals insights into the complexity of spiritual authority in worship. Canadian-Latin American culture does not allow open advocacy for the public authority of women in the church, and transnational Latinas rarely seek any such authorization or liturgical authority from the pulpit. However, they have subtly contested this authority as they lay claim to their own spiritual authority. Spiritual authority opens doors for women to access liturgical authority, though these contexts remain governed and controlled by men.

In Christ and through the power of the Holy Spirit, Latinas "re-image" themselves as the redeemed, *santos* (sanctified), called to witness to God's salvation and redemption for all of creation.[16] This is despite the culturally constructed and religiously enforced *machismo* of patriarchal tradition. This representation mirrors the imagery of God as described by the prophet Hosea as a mother bear who protects her cubs from harm.[17] This can be witnessed both in the participation of Latina members in the liturgy and in the community of believers via what is described as *familia y la iglesia* (family and church).

The term *familia y la iglesia* in the Canadian-Latina Pentecostal context describes more than a gathering of people or a set of traditions and community practices. Our ethnographic research suggested that *la iglesia y la familia* represents belonging to a group of people sharing a story; it

16. Virginia Nolivos and Eloy H. Nolivos argue that Latin Americans go through a process of a "re-imaged" self, first in Pentecostalism, because "they are being freed from the image of God of those who have exploited and oppressed them" (Nolivos and Nolivos, "Pentecostalism's Theological Reconstruction," 205, 218; see also Martell-Otero et al., *Latina Evangélicas*, 33–34).

17. Hos 13:8.

provides love and support to those sharing in *la lucha*. Here the Eucharist is evocative within the incarnational reality of Latin American traditions embedded in *la familia y la casa* (the family and the home). The migrant narrative adds another layer to sharing in the Eucharist. For those who have left their countries of origin and "started over" in Canada, faith and *la familia* are necessary for survival. Faith and *la familia*, as represented in *la iglesia*, provide a sense of safety and security amongst those sharing language and traditions. Thus, in the liturgy of the vocalizing, giving thanks, and breaking of bread, we see the proximity of these lived experiences. Similarly, within the Pentecostal tradition, sharing one's testimony of faith amplifies the narrative of overcoming *la lucha* and encourages others to do the same.

As was previously introduced, at the heart of these migrants' stories is a shared experience of transnational Latina women, named "*la lucha*" by Catholic Cuban-American theologian Ada Maria Isasi-Díaz.[18] *La lucha* not only describes the obstacles one must overcome when leaving a country of origin, but it also embodies the struggle of women to overcome the cultural and religious barriers against their free participation in communities of faith. *La lucha* is very much in evidence in the way it frames and develops a woman's spiritual authority, and in the way that she is able to use that spiritual authority to access a measure of liturgical authority even when she is excluded from formal positions of power. In Calgary, Latinas are the marginalized and underclass and, although removed from the context of Spanish colonialism and popular Catholicism, they are directly impacted by the influence of colonial thinking and cultural elitism.

Bernice Martin argues it is the very fact of Pentecostalism's emphasis on the doctrine of the Holy Spirit that allows women to move beyond the identity of "marginalized victim" to form a new identity, thus creating a "re-imaged" narrative.[19] In one sense, this is their story of survival as a migrant, overcoming abuse and victimization. Their faith also allows them to look beyond traditional views and reimage authority; they give testimony to the transformative power of the Holy Spirit. The growth of Pentecostalism in Canada is largely attributed to migrants bringing, establishing, and sharing (evangelizing) their traditions in Canada.[20] Regardless of the social and cultural limitations these Latina migrants face when trying to integrate into a primarily Anglo-Western society, their will to overcome in the struggle, to participate in their communities, and to vocalize the stories of overcoming

18. *La lucha* is both the external reality of social oppression and injustice and the internal struggle for one's own dignity and equal humanity (Isasi-Díaz, "Lo Cotidiano," 8).

19. Martin, "Pentecostal Gender Paradox," 54; Nolivos and Nolivos, "Pentecostalism's Theological Reconstruction," 205, 218.

20. Medina, "Discerning the Spirit in Culture," 136.

will override any biblical command to stay silent in church and further develop and deepen their spiritual authority.

In congregations that interpret Pauline texts on women patriarchally, these women are not routinely authorized to take the pulpit in their own right despite their clear gifting. Nevertheless, they engage actively in *la lucha* via the demonstration of their spiritual authority. When asked, "How do you respond to texts that are restrictive of a woman?," one interviewee, Sara, responded, "I fight back with the text."[21] She went on to give examples of women from biblical texts, like Mary and Martha, who participated in Jesus' ministry. Another interviewee, Susanna, went on to say that if the Bible was intended to diminish or restrict women from responding to God, "Why then did Jesus first appear to a group of women, after his resurrection?"[22] When presented with obstacles to their faith and spirituality, Latinas use the same force to combat these views.

This research also suggests that Latinas subvert gendered readings of the text. They reject, for example, the idea that Esther might be the only female example who could appropriately be used as a model for women's spirituality. Instead, these women also draw upon examples of men from the Bible whom they look to as spiritual models; three used David as an example of someone classed as "lesser" yet recorded in the Bible as a man "after God's heart." Within David's example they read the example of a person whose humanity, flaws, and sins did not exclude him from leadership.[23] For these Pentecostal Latinas, authorization of spiritual authority goes beyond the female examples in the biblical text and looks to the broader narrative of the biblical story—examples of both men and women, characterized by their minority or "lesser" status, who participate and play an active role in the narrative of salvation and transformation. Such readings of biblical texts are proactively inclusive and subvert patriarchal readings of Scripture that restrict women's permission to participate in official ecclesial roles of authority.

As the spiritual mentors or mothers of their communities, transnational Latinas also seek to protect the community and its members. This is also seen in the practices of *mujerista* theology, which seeks the total liberation of Latina women in every area of their lives, *lo cotidiano* (everyday life), as outworked in their faith, families, communities, and beyond.[24] When the community's wellbeing or morality come into question, Latinas "fight back

---

21. Author's interview with Sara, recorded May 14, 2019.

22. Author's interview with Susanna, recorded May 27, 2019.

23. Author's interview with Sonya, recorded April 27, 2019.

24. Isasi-Díaz, *En La Lucha*, locs. 1468–71.

with the text."[25] That is, they look to examples of the biblical text that combat views that otherwise restrict or diminish the potential flourishing as well as the participation of any member of their community. In other words, Latinas do not see their gender and the Bible as limitations. Rather their lived spirituality in *lo cotidiano* mitigates the influence of their culture, their socially constructed roles of womanhood, and their status of marginalization. For those who are seen as "lesser," this in fact provides them permission to "do ministry."

Similar to Tia Loli, these Latinas have learned to practice their spirituality outside or beyond traditional positions of power. This is not to suggest they decry this power. However, they have reimaged spiritual authority and reflect Pentecostal liturgical values of vocalization, inclusivity, participation, and spontaneity. In this, women contribute freely, without any fear of conflict or retribution for trespassing into male-dominant spaces. This subverts traditionally defined roles of the pastor and the authority of the pulpit in reimagining authority as accessed by grace in the same way that salvation is accessed by grace. From an unmerited or "lowly" status, transformation takes place. There are two important points of note. First, this spiritual authority combats the images of a dominant, controlling, power-enforcing figure seen in the history of the conquistador and the ages of colonialism and Spanish "evangelization" of the Americas. Second, the Pentecostalism of transnational Latinas allows subversion of ecclesial and cultural norms that hold women as inferior to men in religious and private sectors, and they find creative ways to cherish inclusion and participation.

Tia Loli's story is also quite similar to the stories of these transnational Latinas in other ways. They share the migrant's story of leaving family, country, language, and the security of familiarity in hope of more opportunities and a better life. This move is costly for many reasons, but often it also bears a spiritual weight. It is often described as obedience to "the call" of God, and with that obedience comes spiritual authority. At the same time, the Western cultural context of Canada presents a different context. For some Latinas, moving to Canada provides safety or escape from danger or the political turmoil of their countries of heritage. Canadian society also presents more social equality and support for women. Once living in Canada, they have access to relief agencies and more social support than Latinas living in Latina America. For other Latina Pentecostals such as Tia Loli there were few to no social options to escape a life of pain. While her faith and spirituality provided her with the power to forgive and heal, she lacked access to any external supports if she chose to oppose the different abusive and limiting

25. Author's interview with Sara, recorded May 14, 2019.

structures. In the same way that she learned to subvert her story of pain, she learned to subvert powerlessness and restriction in church. Every one of the transnational Latinas who participated in the research study shared a story of domestic abuse or violence. It was heartbreaking to hear these stories but worse that they were described as common experiences. Many of the women responded, "But that's *machismo*," in a way to explain and, perhaps, empathize with so many other women who share their story and their *lucha*.

For Canadian Latinas in Pentecostal churches, the cultural impact of *machismo* has meant that the male-centered pulpit is inaccessible to their participation. Like Tia Loli, these Latinas have learned to practice their spirituality outside or beyond traditional, culturally defined positions of power. In doing so, they have reimaged spiritual authority in ways that reflect Pentecostal liturgical values. The positions of resistance are various. Some women may not desire formal liturgical authority. Others may fear conflict or retribution for trespassing into male spaces. For most, however, these inaccessible spaces have little potential to add to their opportunity and authority, which is fundamentally spiritually configured. Tia Loli's story and the stories of the Latina Canadians demonstrate *la lucha* in the way that they fight back with the text and subvert machismo and religiously enforced power structures. Their vision of spiritual authority is creating a space of inclusion, welcomed participation, and freedom. If that results in a measure of liturgical authority, they will rise to this, but that is generally not their quest. This subversive spirituality is exemplified by their resilience and obedience to listen and follow what is described as the Spirit's call.

Conclusion

To this day, Pentecostal worship is still vocalized, participatory, inclusive, and spontaneous. However, in the restrictions on the ministries of Tia Loli and transnational Latina women, we can glimpse ways in which these values have been dampened. While Pentecostal worship has achieved much influence globally because of its dynamism and enthusiasm, Tia Loli and transnational Latina women invite us to reconsider how Pentecostal liturgical values interact with male-dominated manifestations of liturgical authority.

Tia Loli's story and the stories of other transnational Latinas reveal that Pentecostal liturgical space is contested space. That contestation expands our awareness of how liturgy is not limited to the sanctuary on Sunday morning. To understand the impact of the faith upon the lived experience of Pentecostal women in practical terms today, we need to appreciate that the liturgy and worship experience does not end at the male-dominated pulpit and extends far beyond what we see on television and hear on the albums of global megachurches. Indeed, *la lucha,* against a culture of machismo and ecclesial structures, encompasses every area of life. This subversive spiritual authority does not come from the pulpit and formal liturgical authority; rather, it is evidenced in coffee shops as well as in choir rooms, in small groups just as on the street, in the church lobby, and in the market hall. Such forms of mission and ministry are ritualized demonstrations of Pentecostal liturgy in operation that implicitly or explicitly critique exclusivity and call us to a more expansive vision and practice of Pentecostal liturgical values.

The spiritual authority of women across Pentecostal churches is significant, diverse, and concrete, and it contests restrictive approaches to liturgical authority. This subversive spiritual authority of transnational Latinas deserves greater acknowledgment and understanding, even though it is suppressed in patriarchal traditions. The many accomplishments and gifts to the church of Tia Loli and these Canadian Latinas, distinctive as they are, are mirrored and paralleled in the lives of Pentecostal women all over the globe who together stand as a powerful testimony to Pentecostalism and wider Christianity of the liturgical capacity of a people struggling for liberation.

Bibliography

Bowler, Kate. *The Preacher's Wife: The Precarious Power of Evangelical Women Celebrities.* Princeton: Princeton University Press, 2019.

Daniels, David Douglas, III. "'Gotta Moan Sometime': A Sonic Exploration of Earwitnesses to Early Pentecostal Sound in North America." *Pneuma* 30.1 (2008) 5–32.

Isasi-Díaz, Ada Maria. *En La Lucha/In the Struggle: Elaborating a Mujerista Theology.* 10th Anniversary Spanish Edition. Minneapolis: Augsburg Fortress, 2003. Kindle.

———. "*Lo Cotidiano*: A Key Element of Mujerista Theology." *Journal of Hispanic/Latino Theology* 10.1 (Aug. 2002) 5–17.

Martell-Otero, Loida I., et al. *Latina Evangélicas: A Theological Survey from the Margins.* Eugene, OR: Cascade, 2013.

Martin, Bernice. "The Pentecostal Gender Paradox: A Cautionary Tale for the Sociology of Religion." In *The Blackwell Companion to the Sociology of Religion*, edited by Richard K. Fenn, 52–66. Oxford: Blackwell, 2001.

Medina, Nestor. "Discerning the Spirit in Culture: Toward Pentecostal Interculturality." *Canadian Journal of Pentecostal-Charismatic Christianity* 2 (2011) 131–65.

Mendez, Dorothy. "'Ser Mujer' (To Be Woman)—Re-imaging Latina Spiritual Authority in Pentecostalism: An Ethnographic Analysis of the 'Lived Religion' of Latina-Canadian Pentecostals in *Lo Cotidiano* (Everday Life)." MTh diss., Hillsong College, 2020.

Nolivos, Virginia, and Eloy H. Nolivos. "Pentecostalism's Theological Reconstruction of the Identity of the Latin American Family." *Pentecostal Power* (January 2011) 205–26.

Payne, Leah. *Gender and Pentecostal Revivalism: Making a Female Ministry in the Early Twentieth Century.* Christianity and Renewal Interdisciplinary Studies. New York: Palgrave Macmillan, 2015.

Qualls, Joy E. A. *God Forgive Us for Being Women: Rhetoric, Theology, and the Pentecostal Tradition.* Eugene, OR: Pickwick, 2018.

Vondey, Wolfgang "The Making of a Black Liturgy: Pentecostal Worship and Spirituality from African Slave Narratives to American Cityscapes." *Black Theology* 10.2 (2012) 147–68.

10

The Power of Shared Sacramental Leadership

Free and Frequent Communion: Worship, Power, and Laity in the Christian Church (Disciples of Christ)

CASEY T. SIGMON

Introduction

SOMETIMES, IT IS ONLY when one encounters another culture that one comes to see one's own culture more clearly.

Such was the case a decade ago when my husband and I first attended worship at Vine Street Christian Church (Disciples of Christ) in 2011. We met at a seminary associated with the Presbyterian Church (USA) in Chicago. I had been in the PC(USA) world long enough to know the magic at an ordination service as an ordinand spoke the words of institution at the table for the very first time with the liturgical authority bestowed by the office. Those words and that place of authorial presence behind the table were not just for anybody to inhabit—only clergy.

Up until communion that Sunday at Vine Street, the liturgy and location for worship seemed an awful lot like a Presbyterian order of worship. The preacher donned robes. Elevated pulpit and centered table. Hymns and special music. A children's message. A moment to recognize mission.

Then came the record-scratch moment.

When it came to be time for the words of institution, I looked down at the bulletin and noticed that the words of Jesus were in bold. Bold, as in church-speak for, "Hey congregant! Now is your turn to speak!" We both hesitated at first, assuming someone made a typo. However, sure enough, as we approached those words that seminarians at our school worked for years to earn the privilege to say to the congregation, words that long signify a change in the elements from ordinary bread and juice to the extraordinary presence of Jesus Christ, the congregation spoke in unison: *Take, eat. This is my body, broken for you . . .*

We at that moment entered the legacy of lay sacramental table leadership of the Christian Church (DOC) as the congregation's voice became Christ's and the ordained minister, head bowed, received that blessing in preparation of the meal.[1] The question for a visitor from a Word and Sacrament clergy tradition might be: Who has liturgical power and authority in the CC (DOC)? And why?

The CC (DOC) is a young denomination. Formally, it was organized in 1968 in the drafting of the Provisional Design, though the movement that birthed this denomination, known as the Stone-Campbell tradition, began amid the Second Great Awakening. The hyphenated tradition refers to three founding fathers, all Presbyterian immigrants to the United States from Scotland: Barton Stone and the father/son duo of Thomas and Alexander Campbell.

The ambiguity around liturgical authority in the CC (DOC) is apparent even in the books attempting to not only define authority but to articulate our identity.[2] One liturgical scholar on the tradition put it this way over three decades ago: the CC (DOC) is simultaneously Catholic, Reformed, and Free.[3] How can one tradition be all these things?

As we will see in this chapter, institutional bishops, priests, and pastors with bestowed authority apart from local community are not the ultimate sources of authority to order and lead proper worship. Instead, the movement articulates the source of power for proper worship as beginning and ending with Jesus, but encountered within a local body, with its own

---

1. Hereafter referred to as CC (DOC).

2. Morgan, *Disciples Eldership*; Cummins, *Disciples*; Friedly, *Search for Identity*.

3. Harrison, "Early Disciples Sacramental Theology," 49–100.

authority to set apart particular leaders within itself to order worship. The interpretation of Jesus as giving directive in the New Testament for table-centered worship is an enduring feature of the tradition as well. For many years, this framework for liturgical power and authority empowered a nonprofessional cadre of frontier leaders in local congregations. While the legacy endures in the accumulation of multivalent worship practices that still emphasize free and frequent communion, empowered nonprofessional leadership is not as pronounced as it once was. As the church looks upon a different sort of frontier, one that includes virtual spaces, the unsustainability of full-time professional clergy, and institutional upheaval born of shifts in technoculture, the tradition stands ready to move with purpose if it remembers its roots and takes up the challenge to empower theological leaders beyond paid clergy.

Any statements in the following chapter that slip into orthodoxy will nonetheless inherently be flawed. Though currently organized as a formal denomination, this tradition remains noncreedal and localized in its polity, practice, and theology. Thus, I join the chorus of many liturgical scholars before and those who follow in my footsteps, saying there is no single systematic or programmatic theology of the CC (DOC). Nonetheless, this chapter attempts to trace the threads of practice that weave the story disciples tell themselves about their origin from the Stone-Campbell Movement as the story begins with the themes of this book: questions of worship and power. As historian Phyllis Tickle, in *The Great Emergence,* notes, "each time of re-formation has the same central question: Where, now is the authority?"[4]

Resourcing Liturgical Authority and Power in the Stone-Campbell Tradition

"A man is the creature of God, but a lay-man is the creature of priests."[5]

Where does one find a definition for liturgical authority and power in a tradition that is traditionally resistant to creeds and extrabiblical directives for church belief and practice? The search for a proposed (certainly not the) definition of liturgical authority can be sourced by turning to practice, including aspects of practice that founders of the Stone-Campbell tradition inherited and resisted from their Presbyterian and Church of Scotland traditions.

4. Tickle, *Great Emergence,* 72.

5. Berean, "On the Rights of Layman," 208–9.

Liturgical Authority in Scottish Presbyterianism

Many features of the Stone-Campbell emergence of the 1800s are deeply rooted in the at-times-radical reformations of the Church of Scotland (roughly 1528–1688). While the tradition is indeed American-born, one need only look at the chalice symbol of the denomination, with its Saint Andrews cross, to suggest roots in Scotland. Among those distinctions was the desire to break from tradition to return the church's worship life to what was perceived to be its early simplicity and purity. How some reformers pursued this order was by a turn to the Bible alone for norming worship, stripping away everything else that accumulated. Traditions of the medieval church, such as images, statues, stained-glass windows, the cult of the saints, even liturgical seasons other than Easter and Sunday, were treated as distortions, idolatry.[6]

John Knox (1513–72) embodied the story of reformation in Scotland as he navigated pressure from the English monarchy and the radical energy of Scottish reformers. Some anticlerical reformers were a bit too radical a leap from clergy-centric structures of the medieval church. An example is a Saint Andrews man who reported to a deacon that "I shall buy a pint of wine and a loaf and I shall have as good a sacrament as the best of them shall have."[7] *The Scots Confession* and *The First Book of Discipline* emerged in 1560 and state clearly that the Kirk of Scotland is known by two markers: the faithful preaching of the word of God and the right administration of sacraments. So, while anticlericalism was popular, the authorities of the Kirk of Scotland quickly affirmed the need for clergy as those with authority and power for the right administration of sacraments.

However, Knox does reform some clergy-centric practices of the medieval church. The first Book of Common Order, commonly known as "Knox's Liturgy," was authorized for use in Scotland in 1564. Knox's Liturgy insisted on frequent celebrations of the Lord's Supper and elevated its importance in worship. The right practice of the Lord's Supper was to be discerned by looking at the practice of Jesus, meaning, at the time, in the Kirk of Scotland, the congregation would receive communion by gathering and sitting around the table. Gone is the posture of kneeling before an altar. Removed are fences and screens that only allow clergy to approach the sacramental elements of bread and wine. Instead, clergy and laity together were enabled to approach the sacrament equidistant from each other. Rather than clergy administering the elements to all, congregants would pass the

---

6. Forrester, "Reformed Tradition in Scotland," 473.

7. Forrester, cited in McMillan, *Worship of the Scots-Reformed Church*, 40.

elements to their neighbors around the table. This practice embodies a royal priesthood.[8]

A final, significant influence of this reformation period in Scotland is the suspicion of nonlocal control, including tension with the English monarchy. Beginning in 1615, Charles I and Archbishop William Laud wanted Scotland to adopt the English prayer book. This news resulted in opposition in Scotland. Then, in 1637, another effort from the crown surfaced, this time to introduce a "substantially altered Scottish prayer book."[9] Riots in Edinburgh and other towns were the result. Nonetheless, the English parliament ordered in 1645 that "the *Westminster Directory [of Public Worship]* be observed throughout England, Ireland, and Scotland."[10] The Church of Scotland continued to navigate the tension between monarchal instructions from England and local customs of worship up until the establishment of Presbyterianism in 1688.

Nearly a century later, Barton Stone and Thomas and Alexander Campbell resisted and reimagined worship through the lens of their cultural inheritance in Scotland. The Scottish Reformers' desire to reorder worship by the simplicity of the early church as revealed in the Bible influenced them. They also were influenced by the desire for local control over proper worship, first in resistance to Romanism, then England and the monarchy's overreach into Scotland. Legacies of the Scottish Kirk remain within the denomination. Even today, most CC (DOC) congregations pass communion trays to one another, echoing Knox's Liturgy some 450 years ago.

Nevertheless, the Stone-Campbell branch of the movement soon to organize in the new republic would also reform certain aspects of Scottish Presbyterianism such as fencing and limiting who could gather at the table as the emphasis on free and frequent communion emerged.

Liturgical Authority Articulated by Alexander Campbell

Alexander Campbell (1788–1866) was not the founder of the movement, per se. Nevertheless, when articulating the movement's aims and practices, Alexander was undoubtedly the most influential leader of the Stone-Campbell Movement. In Alexander's writings you can see the development of what he considered to be right liturgical practice for the emerging movement. As we will see, definitions for "right" practice continue to emerge from the authority of the New Testament as well as the authority of human

8. Forrester, "Reformed Tradition in Scotland," 476.

9. Forrester, "Reformed Tradition in Scotland," 478.

10. Forrester, "Reformed Tradition in Scotland," 478.

reason as it encounters the Scripture. Alexander's authority to articulate his reasoning for believer's baptism, lay empowerment, frequent communion, an unfenced table, and other disciple characteristics were not through ordination to a particular ecclesial office. Instead, it was through establishing and owning two free journals, which he edited over four decades. As W. T. Moore, himself an historian and editor in the movement, observed in 1909, "the chief authority in regard to all important questions has been the Disciple press."[11] Before we turn to his deliberative liturgical theology, let us review critical events in his life pertinent to this chapter.

Alexander's father, Thomas, was a pastor in the Seceder Presbyterian Church in Ireland. In the spring of 1807, Thomas sailed to America via Philadelphia. Alexander stayed behind with his mother and siblings. Initially, the Campbells attempted to join Thomas in the fall of 1808. However, the Hibernia ended up stranded near an island of the Hebrides in a storm. During the storm, a troubled Alexander vowed to follow in his father's steps and become a minister of the gospel. So, instead of Philadelphia, the family settled in Glasgow while they waited to book another passage to America.[12] This storm sets the stage for Alexander's turn to ecumenism and the wariness of fenced denominational tables.

The storm gifted Alexander with a year of study at Glasgow University, where his father Thomas attended school. While there, Campbell studied Greek, literature, French, and philosophy, notably Thomas Paine's *Common Sense*. He also met independent reformers in the Church of Scotland such as John Gas, Robert Sandeman, and James and Robert Haldane. These independents separated from the Church of Scotland (the state church) "mainly over the independence of each congregation and the freedom of private interpretation of Scripture."[13] Both of these ideas were rooted in Alexander and emerged in his reform movement in the new republic.

Greville Ewing, the pastor of a large independent church in Glasgow, was a powerful influence on Alexander. Ewing believed the church should have weekly communion and a structure of local church leadership that included a plurality of lay leaders. Like many Scots reformers, Ewing called for a restoration of primitive Christianity and rejected clerical privilege. Ewing did not extend this call to the practice of immersion at this point, but the Haldanes did. Alexander witnessed these debates and reforms to practice before he joined his father in Pennsylvania.[14]

---

11. Friedly, "Journalism," 434.

12. Garrett, "Alexander Campbell," 117.

13. Garrett, "Alexander Campbell," 118.

14. Garrett, "Alexander Campbell," 118.

These encounters with the so-called enemies of the Seceder church led to an event often spoken of as an origin story in the CC (DOC). Before crossing over the Atlantic, Alexander prepared for semiannual communion in the Presbyterian Church. He arrived to be examined by the elders in order to receive his token. This leaden token granted permission to be seated at the Communion table on Sunday. Legend has it that in the spring of 1809, Alexander waited in line to be seated, yet kept moving himself to the back of the line as he decided what to do about the fencing of this table to fellow Christians like Greville Ewing, whom his elders would deem unworthy to sit at the table for their views and practices. Eventually, Alexander took his seat, allowing the elements to pass without partaking. It was a private protest against church division along the lines of denominations, but an irrevocable shift occurred in his practice and belief.

When Alexander reunited with his father Thomas in Philadelphia, the pair discovered a shared urgency for reform of the church, and plans and principles for the movement began to be articulated and practiced in earnest.[15] They organized the Brush Run Church on May 4, 1811, and Alexander was ordained at Brush Run Church by his father on January 1, 1812. While it may seem odd for an anticlerical and antidenominational leader to accept ordination, we will see that local and communal empowerment of leaders through ordination is not Campbell's concern. Rather, "clericalism," meaning "abusive authority of the ordained" that produced passive laity, was the root of Campbell's disdain for "hireling" ministers.[16]

Another sacramental practice that led to a radical shift from the Seceder church in America and Presbyterian tradition was baptism by immersion of those who could profess their faith in Jesus and willingness to follow his way. This turning point resulted from the birth of Alexander and Margaret's first child. When she was born, Alexander encountered a theological crisis. His studies of the Greek New Testament and scholars defending infant baptism convicted Alexander that infant baptism is not the biblical practice and baptism by immersion was the only valid form of baptism. As a result, they did not baptize their child. Instead, on June 12, 1812, both Alexander and Margaret were baptized by immersion.

Primary colors of the CC (DOC)'s understanding of worship authority and power are now identifying themselves through this brief biography of Alexander Campbell. Alexander Campbell would articulate a liturgical theology and practice in the free journals the *Christian Baptist* and the

15. See for example Campbell, *Declaration and Address*.

16. Kinnamon and Linn, *Disciples*, 96.

Millennial Harbinger as he joined others to organize an anticlerical, nonhierarchical movement.

Organizing a Nonhierarchical Movement (1808–1950s)

The liturgical practice articulated by the CC (DOC) would distinguish itself from these roots in Scotland with one fundamental sacramental reform: believer's baptism. Through this reform, a more horizontal model for liturgical leadership would attempt to take root, resulting in another distinction of the tradition: lay local presiders at table.

While the movement pursued nonhierarchical ways of organizing itself, the power to articulate the distinctive identity, practice, and beliefs of the movement took place for many years in various free journals in the United States. Beginning with Elias Smith (1769–1846) and his journal *Herald of Gospel Liberty* (1808), "as many as 400 journals related to the Stone-Campbell Movement were founded."[17] Turning to these journals, one can observe the articulation of embedded theologies of liturgical power and authority.

One such inquiry to the editor of the journal *The Evangelist* highlights the norm of lay ownership of, and authority to lead, worship and the role of journals and editors in norming worship practice. "Bro. Strong of Kentucky" wrote to editor Walter Scott on the matter of worshiping without clergy. He asked, "Ought a church to meet, and keep the ordinances, though it has no elders and deacons?" Scott replied, "Go on, beloved; be strong, hold forth the Word of Truth, to all around, and the very God of peace be with you . . ."[18] Scott's articulated right practice—that is, celebrating communion every week no matter what ordained person is or is not in the congregation—reinforces directives from Thomas Campbell in 1812. A norm is being established. Essential to Christian worship in the movement is gathering at the Lord's Table. Thus, this ordinance takes precedence over any concern to wait for an institutionally credentialed leader to correctly preside and administer the sacrament.

A crucial piece of Alexander's argument for frequent communion in his compilation of essays on communion is the freedom of the so-called laity to come to the table and offer thanksgiving to God without any human mediator:

---

17. Friedly, "Journalism," 434.

18. Scott, *Evangelist*, 238–39.

> But allow common sense to whisper a word into the ears of priests' "laymen," but Christ's "royal priests." Do you not thank God for the cup while the priest stands by the table; and do you not handle the loaf and cup when they come to you? And would not your thanksgiving have been as acceptable, if the human mediator had not been there, and your participating as well pleasing to God, and as consolatory to yourself, if you had been the first that had handled the loaf or the cup, as when you are the second, or the fifty-second, in order of location? Let reason answer these two questions, and see what comes of the haughty assumptions of your Protestant clergy!"[19]

The two features of the tradition, free and frequent communion, go hand in hand and lead to lay empowerment. For Christians to live out Christ's ordinance to break bread together on the first day of the week, the royal priesthood had to be empowered to approach without any professional clergy.

Alexander did not mince words as he articulated disdain for hierarchy in church governance in his journal, saying, "Nothing is more essentially opposite to the genius and spirit of Christianity" than dividing "the church into the common classes of clergy and laity."[20] Alexander optimistically believed in the capacity for baptized believers to lead the church, including sacramentally. He also believed that local congregations know how best to lead and organize their mission without the oversight of a national or general leadership hierarchy. Campbell viewed the local congregation, not any bishop or clergy council nor individual clergy, as "the highest court of Christ's on earth."[21]

As articulated in Campbell's free journal, all power remains ultimately with Jesus Christ, not through any hired mediators. And this authority is mediated by and through "the body of Christ, under him as its head, animated and led by his Spirit."[22] The body mediates the power, not any one member. To put it in other words, "the community, the church, the multitude of the faithful, are the fountain of official power," thus, the church is "the mother of all the sons and priests of God."[23]

While Campbell argued in his journals that all Christians are ordained to ministry through believer's baptism, Alexander insisted on some ministry organization in the local church. Ever in conversation with culture,

19. Campbell, "Breaking of the Loaf," 65.

20. Campbell, "The Clergy. 1," 18.

21. Campbell, "Essays on Ecclesiastical Characters," 73.

22. Watkins, *Breaking of the Bread*, 60, citing Campbell, *Christian System*, 60.

23. Watkins, *Breaking of the Bread*, 60, citing Campbell, *Christian System*, 60.

Campbell used the analogy of citizenship in the United States, "where all citizens have equal rights, privileges, and immunities, yet are not all legislators, magistrates, judges, or governors."[24] While all baptized believers are in the priesthood, not all have gifts for preaching, teaching, and administering ordinances. This order for ministry laid out by Alexander was distinct from the order established in Scottish Presbyterianism.

From his reading of Scripture, Alexander categorized three distinct ministry roles or offices for maintaining the local church: elders, deacons, and evangelists. Contrary to Stone, the primacy of leadership and church maintenance was on lay leaders. Elders and deacons do not have an eternal title and office of power. They are lay leaders granted authority to lead the local body by members of that local body. For free and frequent communion to occur, nonprofessional elders and deacons are "indispensable" since weekly communion "was essential to the existence of a Christian congregation."[25]

Elders, also called overseers and bishops in the New Testament, were authorized by the congregation "to preside over, to instruct, and to edify the community," according to Alexander.[26] Elders made sure that the congregation was nourished with knowledge and understanding, and they presided at the table where the presence of Jesus Christ nourished souls. With so many responsibilities, and because these elders worked other jobs, Campbell encouraged a "plurality" of elders to care for the congregation. One of the elders would be chosen as president (presbyter). In some cases, this appointed president would be compensated for the full-time governance (a foreshadowing of shifts to come) as the other elders assisted part-time, voluntarily.

Deacons were rooted locally like elders. Like lay elders, a plurality of authorized deacons ministered to the congregation. These laypersons were called upon to lead from particular gifts such as treasurer, greeter, and almoner—that is, one responsible for distributing resources to the poor and the Lord's Supper to the homebound. [27]

Evangelists in Alexander's order were deemed less essential to the existence of a local body of Christians. With a smaller pool of trained preachers, congregations might not have a sermon each week as they waited for an evangelist to come to town.

24. Watkins, *Breaking of the Bread*, 59.

25. Blakemore, "Christian Task and the Church's Ministry," 155.

26. Morgan, "Elders, Eldership," 298.

27. Sandifer, "Deacons, Diaconate," 261.

It is important to stress that these offices were ordained, not given through a hierarchy of apostolic succession, because of specific education qualifications such as seminary, or by a governing regional or general body. Instead, local societies ordained leaders for these vital roles in one time and place. Authority was relational and local, and so power was not inherent, with title apart from community. Thus, if a member moved to another congregation, the ordination did not travel with anyone. Rather, they had to settle in another body and perhaps be called out for elder or deacon by their new local congregation.

With emphasis on local and lay power through the practice of believer's baptism, one might assume that the movement experienced the emergence of radical leadership at this time akin to Quakers or early Pentecostalism. Unfortunately, the democratization of authority in the movement mirrored that of the young nation, with limits placed on women as well as Black, Asian, and Latinx people. The powers of implicit sexism and racism in society stifled the emergence of a wholly egalitarian movement. Cultural hermeneutics masked as common sense, or constitutional ideals of who counts as a "citizen" of the new democracy, or a plain reading of Scripture often limited the liturgical imaginations of local congregations when it came to leadership, ordained and lay, in the movement. Thankfully scholars today are unearthing these stories and articulating the disciples' struggle to embody the sort of first-century church described in the New Testament.[28] Along with this historical attention, the denomination also has lived into missional foci in recent years to be antiracist and proreconciling. These accountability measures seek to right the wrongs of embedded racism and sexism that easily flew under the radar in the first century and a half of the movement.

From Movement to Denomination: Worship, Power, and Laity (1968 to Today)

As early as 1870, Disciples congregations began to shift from ministerial leadership by lay, unpaid elders toward calling ordained ministers from outside the local congregation who were college educated. Ordaining authority also slowly shifted from a local congregation to a council at the level of regional ministry.

By the 1950s, it was becoming more challenging to observe a distinct tradition at worship in just about any North American Protestant tradition.

28. See for example Jha, *Room at the Table*, and Sigmon, "Clara Babcock to again Occupy the Pulpit," 169–79.

So, it was only a matter of time before discussion of restructuring the movement into a denomination picked up momentum. After 160 years of resisting the concept of denomination, in 1968, "the Disciples became the one thing they had most eloquently decried."[29] The movement declared itself a denomination. By 1971, "churchwide policies for ordination were developed" and the power of a local congregation to ordain and select its leadership was limited.[30]

Still, the CC (DOC) did not adopt a sacramental understanding of ordination, even if the roadmap to ordination resembled the path for other Protestant denominations with a sacramental understanding. The decentralized and antihierarchical order for ministry described by the Campbells remained in the DNA of the denomination's structure. Without this sacramental understanding, clergy were ordained "to vocational ministry" to "serve as representatives of the church, not representatives of Christ to the church."[31] Elders are still eligible to preside, and clergy are primarily part of the church body rather than set apart through ordination.

After the restructure of 1968, leaders in the denomination still wrestled to articulate authority within this representative, nonhierarchical framework. In 1980, a consultation developed and spent two years researching and writing about the role of authority in the CC (DOC). The resulting 1983 document "A Word to the Church on Authority" distinguishes between authority—"a gift of the Gospel"—and authoritarianism—abuse of authority and power.[32] The authors of the report caution the young denomination to reflect on authority, warning the community that not doing so may result in the church being "controlled by biblicism, self-seeking individuals, or self-serving institutions."[33] The quality of authority granted to the church by God is based in "covenantal bonds of freedom, responsibility, and accountability."[34] Reflecting the anticoercive power of authoritarianism in its theological stance, the commission also highlights that this gift from God—authority—must be accepted in order to be exercised by the church. Once again, a shared mutual essence of authority and power is articulated as the model for the CC (DOC).

How the lineage of lay, local liturgical authority manifests itself in congregations today is inconsistent. Some tables are still fenced off from the

---

29. Landon, "Ambivalence by Design," 28.

30. Toulouse, "Christian Church (Disciples of Christ)," 180.

31. Cornwall, *Freedom in Covenant*, 59.

32. Crow and Duke, *Church for Disciples of Christ*, 101.

33. Crow and Duke, *Church for Disciples of Christ*, 101.

34. Crow and Duke, *Church for Disciples of Christ*, 105.

hired clergy at the moment of fraction and/or the words of institution. In these congregations, only the lay local elders stand behind to co-celebrate with the One, Jesus Christ, presiding at all tables. The clergy stand to the side. Like the congregation described at the beginning of this chapter, some print Jesus' words of institution in bold, since the congregation speaks these holy words which are reserved for hired and ordained clergy in other denominations. More practices reflect the impact of denominational restructuring and collaborative work in liturgical renewal with the World Council of Churches and other ecumenical efforts, with the clergy behind the table offering the words of institution while an elder prays for the loaf and cup. While free and frequent communion is still stressed in the denomination today, the need for lay leadership is less so. While the general theology of ordination remains nonsacramental for the Disciples tradition today, most congregations still rely upon professional clergy for liturgical leadership rather than lay leaders.

Not all CC (DOC) leaders today place the weekly frequency of communion as a defining feature of a Disciples congregation, including the General Minister and President Rev. Dr. Theresa Hord Owens. Many congregations, particularly those with ties to Baptist traditions, do not practice weekly communion. The reader needs to remember that the tradition is congregationalist and covenantal in its polity, meaning local authority is empowered to direct the church's praxis rather than bishops (or in our tradition, Regional Ministers) or even the General Minister and President. The intentions and aims of a movement's founder do not always make it through the generations. So, while Alexander Campbell and others most certainly argued for the importance of weekly communion in the movement, resulting in a more lay-led sacramental practice, weekly communion cannot be commanded by a nonlocal clerical authority. However, for most congregations in the tradition, the defining feature of communion every Sunday remains. It took a pandemic to remind many disciples of this fact.

Matters of form and procedures at the table are multivalent. Members of the CC (DOC) family are "caught from the beginning in the Enlightenment conflict between spiritual autonomy and institutional authority, between individualism and pragmatism."[35] As a sweep through the history of the Stone-Campbell Movement for its definition and application of liturgical authority draws to a close, it is clear to see what Dennis L. Landon observed in 1987, "The Gordian knot of our ambivalence about authority has been neither untied nor severed."[36]

35. Landon, "Ambivalence by Design," 39.
36. Landon, "Ambivalence by Design," 32.

Open Tables, Closed Buildings: COVID-19 and Free and Frequent Communion

"But all we aim at here is to show that the community under Christ is called 'the house of God.' Paul once calls it a house of God, and once the house of God."[37]

We no longer have editor-bishops in the CC (DOC) to host dialogue and articulate deliberative theology on worship matters. The age of mass media, including free print journals, is being eclipsed by social media. So, it is no surprise that the frontier spirit of disciples led to forums on Facebook (as well as threads on Twitter) for theology and practice to be wrestled with collaboratively in covenant with one another.

In a Facebook group called "Disciples Colosseum," I raised the question of whether Disciples congregations paused from communion when pandemic restrictions closed the doors to worship houses and sent the gathering of believers online. My hunch from local experience is that there was no freeze prohibiting freedom and frequency to come to the table, even in an adaptive way. Moreover, from the responses I received across the country, my hunch was confirmed.[38]

> Eastern NC, not a single question by anyone. We gathered and continue to gather on FB Live together, we encourage people to adapt the elements to whatever they have on hand and we pass the peace! It has been unifying and a moment of community when we otherwise are distanced.

> once a month, when I preside, I say that it's ok to use your coffee and toast as elements (or whatever you have) as long as you have a sincere desire to take part in the Communion ritual, and that we are living stones, building blocks of God's spiritual house (1 Peter 2), wherever we are.

> Our congregation was clear that Communion WILL happen at each worship service. We invite folks to use whatever elements they have to represent the bread and juice/wine. We are clear that the important thing is to commune together.

> I never read or heard of anyone saying communion could not be done by people in a digital format. In fact, it has seemed to be the thing that unites congregations worshiping on zoom, etc. I have heard one or two people say that they have chosen not to have

---

37. Campbell, *Christian System*, 303.

38. Facebook post in "Disciples Colosseum," private Facebook group. March 2, 2021. Responses are anonymous, but these are verbatim replies to my question.

communion because they feel as if the feeling of community is missing on line.

No pushback whatsoever on communion from my context...

The Disciples tradition of recognizing members of the congregation to officiate at the table made the transition to online community very easy for my congregation. No objections voiced at all.

One of the ways we've adapted our table liturgy is asking people to raise to the camera and break their bread with the officiant, and to raise their cup and bless it with the officiant. It's really quite powerful to see this on Zoom.

My congregation would be bothered if we didn't recognize the bread and the cup while worshipping in a Zoom format. We try to do breakout rooms for the sharing of bread to create community.

No problem or arguments in my context. There is even something powerful in not just each elder carefully writing their prayers and speaking their spirituality into the service, but that they each held up a cup or loaf of bread from whatever they had ended up reaffirming the table's extension into our homes in this unusual time. We may keep some sort of hybrid element of this going and allow elders to send in videos of their prayers if they do not feel comfortable returning to in person worship.

These practitioners are not citing Campbell or Stone, *The Christian System*, the General Minister and President, or a book of worship for their practice. Instead, the authority of a tradition of free and frequent communion empowers the church to continue gathering at table, even if the form, location, and mode are novel. Jesus is the host at table, all tables throughout the communion of believers. *Ex opere locus* (by the place of the work) should not go on the list of limitations for performing the sacrament of communion. A building is not an authority. The people gathered (in whatever means) are the house of God, accepting and exercising God's authority to proclaim the good news revealed in Jesus Christ through the sacramental symbols of table. In the house of God, there is always a table where Jesus hosts the community. We turn once more to Alexander Campbell:

> It is scarcely necessary to add, that if it be shown that in the Lord's house there is the Lord's table, as a part of the furniture, it must always be there, unless it can be shown that only some occasions require its presence, and others its absence; or that the Lord is poorer or more churlish at one time than at another;

that he is not always able to keep a table, or too parsimonious to
furnish it for his friends.[39]

Jesus is always able to keep a table for his friends. Jesus could keep it
on the frontier in camp meetings. Jesus could keep it in a hush harbor. Jesus
could even keep it in a Zoom room. Jesus has the power and authority to
do so and offers this power and authority to the church to be exercised and
shared. This interpretation of Jesus' power and authority is important as the
church continues its mission to bring wholeness to a fragmented world in
Jesus' name in an ever-changing environment.

As the church looks upon a different sort of frontier, one that includes
virtual spaces, the unsustainability of full-time professional clergy, and
institutional upheaval born of shifts in technoculture, the tradition stands
ready to move with purpose. As Disciples theologian Bob Cornwall explains, "Disciples continue to be a frontier people" who then "adapt to their
surroundings, making do with what they have at their disposal."[40]

In a postmodern world, not even the institution of Christianity can
assume power to influence culture by asserting sole possession of absolute
truth. Joshua Cooper Ramo, in his book *The Seventh Sense*, proclaims that
we are on the brink of a radical paradigm shift akin to the stirrings that
led to the Enlightenment 300 years ago. According to Ramo, evidence of
these shifts is found in legitimacy collapse, something that happened in the
Reformation and that is happening again now. Ramo argues that respect for,
and trust in, institutions has collapsed, including our political, banking, and
educational institutions. I would add this is also the case for our churches
and any assumed authority within them associated with an individual's title.

The covenantal, relational embodiment of power and authority of the
Disciples was ahead of its time, reflecting the sort of capacities that suit
postmodernism. Yet we have not fully lived into our potential by empowering a cadre of lay, local theologians to take ownership of Christ's mission of
healing and justice as producers rather than consumers of gospel in network
culture. But through a sacramental understanding of baptism and a nonsacramental view of ordination, the body of Christ is empowered to imagine
and enact worship and table fellowship in novel ways. Our essentials are our
strength, for because of them we will not allow situational novelty to prevent
us from gathering at the Lord's table, freely and frequently, to receive suste-
nance for the work of healing a fragmented world in Jesus' name.

---

39. Campbell, *Christian System*, 304.
40. Cornwall, *Freedom in Covenant*, xiv.

The question to answer, as the CC (DOC), but also as a church universal, is: How will we empower the body for this shared responsibility of healing and justice in Jesus' name?

Bibliography

Berean, A. [pseud.]. "On the Rights of Layman." *The Christian Baptist* 3.6 (January 2, 1826) 208–9.

Blakemore, W. B. "The Christian Task and the Church's Ministry." In *The Revival of the Churches*, edited by W. B. Blakemore, 3:150–88. 3 vols. St. Louis: Bethany, 1963.

Campbell, Alexander. "The Breaking of the Loaf." *The Millennial Harbinger-Extra* 2 (December 1830) 61–88.

———. *The Christian System, in Reference to the Union of Christians, and a Restoration of Primitive Christianity, as Plead in the Current Reformation.* 3rd ed. Pittsburgh: Forrester & Campbell, 1840.

———. "The Clergy. 1." *The Christian Baptist* 1.3 (October 6, 1823) 18–23.

———. "Essays on Ecclesiastical Characters, Councils, Creeds, and Sects." *The Christian Baptist* 1.12 (July 5, 1824) 72–75. https://webfiles.acu.edu/departments/Library/HR/restmov_nov11/www.mun.ca/rels/restmov/texts/acampbell/tcb/TCB112.HTM#Essay1.

Campbell, Thomas. *Declaration and Address.* SCM E-print Edition. St. Louis: SCM, 2010.

Cornwall, Robert D. *Freedom in Covenant: Reflections on the Distinctive Values and Practices of the Christian Church (Disciples of Christ).* Eugene, OR: Wipf & Stock, 2015.

Crow, Paul A., Jr., and James O. Duke, eds. *The Church for Disciples of Christ: Seeking to Be Truly Church Today.* St. Louis: Christian Board of Publication, 1998.

Cummins, D. Duane. *The Disciples: A Struggle for Reformation.* St. Louis: Chalice, 2009.

Forrester, Duncan B. "The Reformed Tradition in Scotland." In *The Oxford History of Christian Worship*, edited by Geoffrey Wainwright and Karen B. Westerfield Tucker, 473–83. Oxford: Oxford University Press, 2006.

Friedly, Robert L. "Journalism." In *The Encyclopedia of the Stone Campbell Movement*, edited by Douglas A. Foster et al., 434–38. Grand Rapids: Eerdmans, 2004.

———. *The Search for Identity: Disciples of Christ—The Restructure Years.* St. Louis: Chalice, 1987.

Garrett, Leroy. "Alexander Campbell." In *The Encyclopedia of the Stone Campbell Movement*, edited by Douglas A. Foster et al., 112–34. Grand Rapids: Eerdmans, 2004.

Harrison, Richard L., Jr. "Early Disciples Sacramental Theology: Catholic, Reformed, and Free." In *Classic Themes of Disciples Theology: Rethinking the Traditional Affirmations of the Christian Church (Disciples of Christ)*, edited by Kenneth Lawrence, 49–100. Fort Worth: Texas Christian University Press, 1986.

Jha, Sandhya. *Room at the Table: Struggle for Unity and Equality in Disciples History.* St. Louis: Chalice, 2009.

Kinnamon, Michael, and Jan Linn. *Disciples: Who We Are & What Holds Us Together.* St. Louis: Christian Board of Publication, 2019.

Landon, Dennis L. "Ambivalence by Design: Disciples Structure of Church." In *Interpreting Disciples: Practical Theology in the Disciples of Christ*, edited by L. Dale Richesin and Larry D. Bouchard, 27–48. Fort Worth: Texas Christian University Press, 1987.

Morgan, Peter M. *Disciples Eldership: A Quest for Identity and Ministry*. St. Louis: Chalice, 2003.

———. "Elders, Eldership." In *The Encyclopedia of the Stone Campbell Movement*, edited by Douglas A. Foster et al., 297–99. Grand Rapids: Eerdmans, 2004.

Ramo, Joshua Cooper. *The Seventh Sense: Power, Fortune, and Survival in the Age of Networks*. Boston: Little, Brown, 2016.

Sandifer, J. Stephen. "Deacons, Diaconate." In *The Encyclopedia of the Stone Campbell Movement*, edited by Douglas A. Foster et al., 260–62. Grand Rapids: Eerdmans, 2004.

Scott, Walter. *The Evangelist* 3 (October 1834) 238–39.

Sigmon, Casey. "Clara Babcock to again Occupy the Pulpit: Reclaiming Her Voice as Preacher and Pioneer in Disciples of Christ History." *Restoration Quarterly* 55.3 (2013) 169–79.

Tickle, Phyllis. *The Great Emergence: How Christianity Is Changing and Why*. Grand Rapids: Baker, 2012.

Toulouse, Mark G. "Christian Church (Disciples of Christ)." In *The Encyclopedia of the Stone Campbell Movement*, edited by Douglas A. Foster et al., 177–84. Grand Rapids: Eerdmans, 2004.

Watkins, Keith. *The Breaking of the Bread*. St. Louis: Bethany, 1966.

Watkins, Sharon. *Whole: A Call to Unity in Our Fragmented World*. St. Louis: Chalice, 2014.

Afterword

John D. Witvliet

A GENERATION AGO, THE vast majority of academic works on the history, theology, and practice of Christian public worship and the vast majority of scholars in the North American Academy of Liturgy represented "liturgical traditions" (Roman Catholic, Eastern Orthodox, Anglican, Lutheran and some Presbyterian, Reformed, and Methodist traditions). Over the past thirty years, there has been a rather stunning explosion of academic work on worship practices of Baptist, Mennonite, Pentecostal, charismatic, Holiness, Restorationist, Apostolic, and nondenominational traditions, as well as other Presbyterian, Reformed, and Wesleyan traditions not represented in earlier scholarship. The sheer quantity of this recent work and the stunning pluriformity of practices in evidence not only across these traditions, but also within them offers all of us devoted to the study and renewal of worship both a compelling invitation and a set of vexing challenges.

The invitation is to come and see the remarkable gifts of God offered to us across the spectrum of denominational traditions and cultural contexts, including the scholars embedded in these traditions who help us learn to understand them. In my own Reformed tradition, the Heidelberg Catechism interprets the "communion of saints" as an invitation to see how "believers one and all, as members of this community, share in Christ and in all his treasures and gifts," and also how this compels us to "consider it a duty to use these gifts readily and joyfully for the service and enrichment of the other members."[1] That vision applies not only to a local congregation but to the global church.

These essays, and others by the scholars included in this volume, function like tour guides to introduce the rest of us to unique gifts, practices, and explanatory frameworks from their traditions. Engaging with these—whether or not we agree with them—is profoundly instructive. With more

---

1. *Heidelberg Catechism*, QA55, in *Ecumenical Creeds and Reformed Confessions*, 35.

and more of this work emerging, it will also soon be possible to imagine some fascinating comparisons of liturgical pluriformity not only across Free Church traditions but also between Free Church and liturgical traditions as a whole.[2] At the same time, additional work on Free Church traditions will be essential, acknowledging the many Free Church denominations and cultural contexts not represented in this volume, with attention to the potent political alignments that divide Free Churches from each other, and the dynamics of church size which shape the nature of ecclesial agency and influence.

The challenges in all of this arise out of the profoundly complex interplay of historical circumstances, theological convictions, cultural dynamics, and methodological differences involved in shaping these traditions and their scholars. At times, it can feel as if we are talking about entirely different things using entirely different methods informed by entirely different worlds of discourse and quite different norms and sensibilities about how those norms arise. As a young doctoral student from the Christian Reformed Church in North America, I arrived at the University of Notre Dame and was assigned in a ritual studies class to visit and learn both from and with a charismatic Roman Catholic community on campus. We shared the Bible, the Nicene Creed, the use of the English language, a few common liturgical phrases, as well as a few songs and a common system of musical notation—and also a common cultural ritual on six fall Saturdays involving 85,000 people at Notre Dame stadium. Yet even after many shared conversations and experiences and hundreds of pages of background reading it was very common to be in conversation and realize that we were using a given term in entirely different ways without realizing it. The same experiences can easily happen as we converse with others within and across these Free Church Protestant traditions.

I am deeply grateful for this group of colleagues and the ways they are embracing this invitation and responding to these challenges. One of the best audiences for this work may well be the hundreds of students taught every year by the authors of this volume. To see our teachers interacting in this kind of multidenominational space helps us learn from them and understand them as they hold us accountable for learning (itself an exercise of power!)—even as we hold them accountable to represent the traditions that shape us.

In light of this good work, I am picturing one of my favorite moments in a seminar group at the North American Academy of Liturgy—the moment at the end of each seminar where colleagues customarily ask what

---

2. Fink, "Liturgy and Pluriformity," 97–107.

work should be prioritized for the following year. Rarely, but occasionally, the conversations sputter. But in years with especially generative conversations, the ideas for future work flow abundantly. The generativity of this book sparked for me many promising pathways forward, of which I will prioritize three.

Cruciform Power

First, this volume is an invitation to renewed attention to a cruciform definition, understanding, and practice of power, and to development of a shared methodology for comparing the interplay of speech about divine power and practices of exercising human power in our traditions.

Here, I begin in repentance. My own unconsidered definition of "power" needs to be healed. When I think of what power looks like, I too quickly call to mind images of raw-fisted power, capricious power, corrupted power, a clinging-to-power. Surreptitiously, deep cultural forces have shaped my soul. If I am not vigilant, these deeply formed impulses will come out in my own acts of exercising influence in Christian community, even in the quotidian exercises of choosing a song for my congregation to sing or in shaping the wording of an intercessory prayer or setting an agenda for a conversation. We all need a daily dying to self, a daily purging of distorted visions of power, a daily turning toward a cruciform vision of faithful Christian life—including the Christian scholarly life.

For this essential work, the term "power" is never enough on its own. It needs to be qualified in some way, anchored to a particular telos or set of norms. Notice in this volume Sarah Kathleen Johnson's description of Arendt's concept of power "as communicative and collective *that is anchored in the normative ideal of reciprocity and mutuality*," or the co-editors' description of Foucault's understanding of power as "pervasive, relational, dynamic, and productive rather than assuming it is a form of coercive domination."

Here, Paul's arresting paradoxical words in 1 Corinthians challenge us: "The message of the cross is foolish to those who are headed for destruction! But we who are being saved know it is the very power of God." It is Christ who is the "power of God and the wisdom of God." And the point of it is that "God's foolishness is wiser than human wisdom, and God's weakness is stronger than human strength" (1 Cor 1:18, 24).

As Daniel Migliori reflects:

> God is not the supreme will-to-power over others but the supreme will-to-community in which power and life are shared.
> To speak of God as that ultimate power whose being is in giving,

> receiving, and sharing love, who gives life to others and will to
> live in community, is to turn upside down our understandings
> of both divine and human power. The reign of the triune God is
> the rule of sovereign love rather than the rule of force. A revo-
> lution in our understanding of the true power of God and of
> fruitful human power is thus implied when God is described
> as triune.[3]

And this christological vision is complemented aptly by a pneumatological vision that sees the fruit of living of the power of the Holy Spirit in terms of "love, joy, peace, patience, kindness, generosity, faithfulness, gentleness, and self-control" (Gal 5:22–23).

Divine power that is worthy of praise *both* because of its magnitude *and* the way in which it is deployed, most supremely in Jesus' self-sacrifice— not one without the other. Ecclesial and liturgical expressions of authority and power become noteworthy when they reflect this cruciform vision. My hypothesis is that these are deeply connected: communities with more robust traditions of decluttering the cultural baggage that attaches to the term "power" are places that nurture exemplars of this cruciform.[4] This volume helps us recognize compelling examples of this cruciform vision as well as examples that are sullied by different, more coercive, understandings of power.

Given that most of us who describe worship in our traditions using historical, sociological, or anthropological methods also teach our students to shape, lead, and assess Christian liturgical practices, it is essential that we devote ourselves to renewed efforts to both study and promote cruciform expressions of agency and influence. Our call is to aim for coherence and integrity so that a revolution in understanding power is reflected in 1) our normative theological vision, 2) our typical ways of praising God, 3) our ways of helping students prepare to exercise authority in Christian community, and 4) our descriptive methods for studying worship practices—including our choices of case studies.

Power Distance and Cultural Humility

Second, this volume is an invitation to explore the implicit cultural dynamics and values that shape the expression of power and authority. Over the past generation, cultural anthropologists have helped us see more clearly

---

3. Migliori, *Faith Seeking Understanding*, 63.

4. Gorman, *Cruciformity*; Pickett, "Through the Lens of the Cross"; Purves, *Crucifixion of Ministry*.

astonishing differences across cultures in terms of how the exercise of power shapes relationships and dynamics in community.

One of the most common ways to analyze these differences is in terms of the concept of "power distance": "the extent to which the less powerful members of institutions and organizations within a country expect and accept and expect that power is distributed unequally."[5] A generation of research has explored complex dynamics of baseline assumptions that vary widely from one country to another, even within the same region of the world, as well as differences of cultural values among different organizations (e.g., military vs. small businesses).

These dynamics are readily apparent in families, classrooms, and neighborhoods. In some families, children are treated as autonomous decision-makers early on, while in others independent decision-making is not encouraged until children grow older. Students from a low-power-distance culture casually address a professor by first name, while those from a high-power-distance culture use formal titles. In the same neighborhood, churches with a high-power-distance culture may naturally reserve a parking place for a senior or lead pastor, while other churches recoil at the suggestion of it. In one culture, employees love it when their boss rides a bike to work; in another, employees find it embarrassing.[6] In one culture, people call each other out for showing too much deference to a leader (boss?! pastor?! professor?! bishop?!) while in another they do so for showing too little deference.[7] In one culture, decisions tend to be made by an individual after only modest consultation, while in another widespread consultation is necessary to move anything forward. Sometimes surprises emerge: Japanese culture is both very hierarchical and very consultative.[8] And all of these sensibilities, we are learning to understand, are deeply formed within us by cultural dynamics and communication channels that help program what Geert Hofstede has called "the software of the mind."[9]

These deep cultural sensibilities, in turn, powerfully influence the kinds of examples studied in this volume—and the ways that we make judgments about them. If we are not aware of these cultural dynamics, we can easily slip into a naïve judgmentalism or arrogance about it all. We may laud egalitarian visions of shared power without realizing how judgmental that may be of those formed in a high-power-distance culture. From a

5. Hofstede, *Cultures and Organizations*, 61.

6. Meyer, *Culture Map*, 123–24.

7. Meyer, *Culture Map*, 139–40.

8. Meyer, *Culture Map*, 154.

9. Hofstede, *Cultures and Organizations*.

high-power-distance culture, we may well signal noble deference to a given authority figure in a way that rattles and offends those with low-power-distance sensibilities. Much of this analysis is designed to prompt cultural humility, teaching us to see the good in people who are wired very differently from us—just as, for example, personality tests have taught us to learn to value the gifts of both introverts and extroverts. The tension emerges when we theologize these differences, rendering normative judgments about the best way power is exercised.

Over time, I look forward to more studies of worship practices that reflect on how power and authority are exercised and pay attention to the dynamic interaction of both denominational context and underlying culture values, including power distance. This crucial area of research and reflection is best done in collaboration, with teams of scholars representing both emic and etic (insider and outsider) perspectives. Exemplary cruciform expressions of influence and agency in a Baptist church in Singapore and Mexico City or a Mennonite community in the Netherlands and Mexico will be different. Each cultural context may well be primed to show new charisms or strengths in cruciform practice, just as each may also be challenged by particular weaknesses and temptations.

Church Polity

Third, this volume is an invitation to explore the interface of liturgy and church polity. A large percentage of academic studies of Christian worship practices focus on traditions that are governed by bishops (Roman Catholic, Eastern Orthodox, Anglican, Episcopal, Methodist, Lutheran). Relatively stable, more-or-less-set liturgies are often embedded within an episcopal form of church polity. At the same time, there is wide variation across these traditions in terms of how power is exercised and the relative flexibility congregations have in shaping worship—and relatively little study about the relative merits of different approaches. Ask the question "What kinds of episcopal leadership have best helped worship practices thrive?" and many scholars will have thoughtful answers. Yet we have few comparative, systematic studies to ground and challenge our thinking. At the same time, there is a much smaller percentage of academic studies of Christian worship focused on traditions shaped by Presbyterian or Congregational church polities. Here, too, there is wide variation of practice within these traditions. A denominational worship office or liturgical book or hymnal is embraced in some of these traditions and resisted in others. Some independent or nondenominational churches expect their ministers to be CEOs while others insist that the congregation holds the authority. In the former, key decisions are made unilaterally, while in the latter, many more congregational votes are held to discern direction. Within the broad world of more-or-less Free Church Protestantism, Seventh-Day Adventists and the Salvation Army are more hierarchical than Mennonites or Congregationalists.

The academic discipline of church polity is the principled study of how power in the church should be exercised with mutual accountability.[10] Given the strong anti-institutional tendencies of many Free Church traditions, there is relatively little academic literature on these operative polities, though there is quite a bit more work published with keywords related to church management and leadership. And what is written is typically not in conversation with work in the field of liturgical studies—even though the act of planning for, leading, and then assessing public worship is, as this volume suggests, a prime site for the exercise of pastoral leadership and authority. Perhaps the next Free Church student to attend the University of Notre Dame could be asked not only to attend a charismatic Catholic worshiping community, but also to interview some Catholic canon lawyers.

I suspect that this direction for future work will run into some significant challenges. I will risk this generalization. Writing about church polity—whether from those steeped in classical canon law or Protestant church orders or in contemporary church leadership literature—tends to relish shared principles: wisdom that crosses cultures, centuries, and types of churches. Scholarship about liturgy among Free Church scholars tends to relish heterogeneity and hybridity, unique and unexpected gifts from a given community or time period. Thriving congregations, denominations, and ecumenical learning communities depend upon both contextual adaptation and the sharing of gifts, wisdom, practices, and convictions across contexts. Endless hybridity and autonomy without cross-cultural sharing and mutual accountability can lead to isolation and loss of balance. Unexamined or imposed conformity can stifle growth and silence voices. A fusion of liturgical and polity scholarship offers one promising way forward for both disciplines.

Given the vivid displays of misused authority and coercive power we have learned about in the life of so many churches in the past few years, collaborative, cross-cultural, cruciform work on all of this is urgent. Thanks to the authors of this book for prompting and launching the conversation.

---

10. See, for example: Matthew van Maastricht, *Foundations of Reformed Church Polity*; Frank, *Polity, Practice, and the Mission of the United Methodist Church*; Maring, *Baptist Manual of Polity and Practice*; and many others.

Bibliography

Ecumenical Creeds and Reformed Confessions. Grand Rapids: CRC, 1988.

Fink, Peter E. "Liturgy and Pluriformity." *The Way* (April 1980) 97–107.

Frank, Thomas E. *Polity, Practice, and the Mission of the United Methodist Church.* Nashville: Abingdon, 2006.

Gorman, Michael J. *Cruciformity: Paul's Narrative Spirituality of the* Cross. Grand Rapids: Eerdmans, 2001.

Hofstede, Geert. *Cultures and Organizations: Software of the Mind.* New York: McGraw Hill, 2010.

Maastricht, Matthew van. *Foundations of Reformed Church Polity: The Rhyme and Reason of Order.* Grand Rapids: Reformed Church, 2022.

Maring, Norman. *A Baptist Manual of Polity and Practice.* Valley Forge, PA: Judson, 2012.

Meyer, Erin. *Culture Map.* New York: Public Affairs, 2014.

Migliori, Daniel. *Faith Seeking Understanding: An Introduction to Christian Theology* Grand Rapids: Eerdmans, 1991.

Pickett, Benjamin D. "Through the Lens of the Cross: Cruciformity as a Model for Teaching Ministry." *Discernment: Theology and the Practice of Ministry* 2.1 (2016) 1–16.

Purves, Andrew. *The Crucifixion of Ministry: Surrendering Our Ambitions to the Service of Christ.* Downers Grove, IL: IVP, 2009.

Index